ACT® Mastery Math

Student Workbook

4th Edition

MasteryPrep

ACT® is the registered trademark of ACT Inc. MasteryPrep has no affiliation with ACT Inc., and the ACT® Mastery program is not approved or endorsed by ACT Inc.

© Copyright 2018 MasteryPrep.

All Rights Reserved. No part of this publication may be reproduced, stored in a retrieval system, distributed, or transmitted in any form or by any means, including photocopying, recording, or other electronic or mechanical methods, without the prior written permission of the publisher. For permission requests, write to the publisher, addressed "Attention: Permissions Coordinator," at the address below.

Inquiries concerning this publication should be mailed to:

MasteryPrep
7117 Florida Blvd.
Baton Rouge, LA 70806

MasteryPrep is a trade name and/or trademark of Ring Publications LLC.

This publication, its author, and its publisher are in no way affiliated with or authorized by ACT Inc. ACT® is a copyright and/or trademark of ACT Inc.

10 9 8 7 6 5 4 3 2 1

ISBN-13: 978-1-948846-05-9

Table of Contents

Lesson 1: Linear Equations 7

Lesson 2: Systems of Equations 19

Lesson 3: Solving Equations: Word Problems 35

Lesson 4: Percentages 49

Lesson 5: Percent Change 63

Lesson 6: Fractions 79

Lesson 7: Operations 97

Lesson 8: Substitution 115

Lesson 9: Averages, Median, Mode and Range 129

Lesson 10: Perimeter and Line Segments 143

Lesson 11: Polygon Area 157

Lesson 12: Circle Area and Circumference 169

Lesson 13: Volume 183

Lesson 14: Inequalities 203

Lesson 15: Exponents and Roots 217

Lesson 16: Angle Properties 235

Lesson 17: Angles and Parallel Lines 253

Lesson 18: Pythagorean Theorem 273

Lesson 19: Similar Triangles 293

Lesson 20: Trig Geometry 307

Lesson 21: Slope 327

Lesson 22: Function Graphs: Coordinate Plane 345

Lesson 23: Circles and Parabolas 367

Lesson 24: Factors 383

Lesson 25: Quadratic Equations 397

Lesson 26: Probability 413

Lesson 27: Patterns and Sequences 429

Lesson 28: Counting 447

Lesson 29: Ratios and Proportions 461

Lesson 30: Number Concepts and Properties 477

Lesson 31: Math Strategy 489

Lesson 32: Math Pacing 509

Math Glossary 538

Get ready to master the ACT® test!

You are about to take part in the most effective and broadly used ACT prep program in the nation! With ACT Mastery, you will learn the most frequently tested content on the ACT test and develop the skills and strategies necessary to achieve the score you desire.

With practice in all four subjects, you will be fully prepared.

The ACT Mastery Math workbook is just one part of a larger program that includes four core subject books, each in line with a subtest found on the ACT: English, math, reading, and science. Each book works to build your mastery of the content most frequently tested on the ACT by providing thorough subject reviews and hundreds of ACT practice questions. By completing this book, you will be prepared for the math subtest; the rest of the program will prepare you for the English, reading, and science subtests.

Test prep is a team effort.

Although you may be tempted to jump ahead, this workbook should be used in conjunction with a teacher's instructions and is not intended for self-guided practice. Each lesson is designed so that the majority of the direction and some of the content is delivered by an instructor either verbally or visually by way of slide presentations or whiteboards. Working ahead will limit your understanding of the ACT content and may actually lead to confusion. Follow the teacher's instructions during the lesson and only work on practice as directed. This will maximize your understanding of the material and, ultimately, your score.

The score you want is within your reach!

The ACT test is a rigorous, challenging marathon of an exam. It can be intimidating. Of the more than two million students who take the test each year, many feel that it is uncoachable—that whatever score they earn on the test is the best they can do. The ACT Mastery program has proven this assumption to be *completely false.* Students dedicated to the program routinely see substantial improvement on their test scores. It will take hard work and determination, but with the content and strategies available to you, anything is possible.

You *can* master the ACT test.

The keys to success with ACT preparation are content, practice, and strategy. As your teacher leads you through the lessons, focus on the content. Take notes on all of the definitions and rules, ask questions to clarify any points of confusion, and participate in all of the activities.

Once you begin to master the content, practice the problems in your workbook. Give your best effort on every question no matter how hard or easy it may seem. Complete any homework your teacher assigns and make sure you ask questions if you do not fully understand a concept.

Finally, as you develop content mastery and practice the ACT questions, work on building your test-day strategy. Look for trends in the questions and answer choices, determine your strongest and weakest areas, and decide how you will pace yourself on the day of the test.

Good luck!

Lesson 1

Linear Equations

CAPTION:

ACT® Mastery Math

1.1 Entrance Ticket

Solve the questions below.

1. For what value of x is the equation $-3x + 7 = -17$ true?

   A. -24
   B. -8
   C. $-\dfrac{10}{3}$
   D. $\dfrac{10}{3}$
   E. 8

2. For what value of x is the equation $2(x - 4) + x = 10$ true?

   F. 2
   G. 6
   H. 12
   J. 14
   K. 18

3. What value of x makes the equation $8x - 2(x - 7) = 20$ true?

   A. $\dfrac{13}{3}$
   B. $\dfrac{17}{3}$
   C. $\dfrac{3}{5}$
   D. $\dfrac{17}{5}$
   E. 1

| Entrance Ticket | Learning Target | Distribution | Variable Isolation | ACT Practice | Sum It Up |

Lesson 1 – Linear Equations

1.2 Learning Target

1. Solve equations with one unknown variable

Self-Assessment

Circle the number that corresponds to your confidence level in your knowledge of this subject before beginning the lesson. A score of 1 means you are completely lost, and a score of 4 means you have mastered the skills. After you finish the lesson, return to the bottom of this page and circle your new confidence level to show your improvement.

Before Lesson

1   2   3   4

After Lesson

1   2   3   4

Entrance Ticket   Learning Target   Distribution   Variable Isolation   ACT Practice   Sum It Up

1.3.1 Distribution

Lesson 1 – Linear Equations

1.3.2 Variable Isolation

1. For what value of x is the equation $2(x + 1) - x = 10$ true?

2. What is the value of x when $\dfrac{3x}{2} + 8 = 11$?

3. The equation shown below is true for what value of x ?
$$3(x - 2) + 2(x + 5) = 9x$$

ACT® Mastery Math

1.4.1 Set One

1. For what value of x is the equation $3(x + 2) - 2x = 12$ true?
   A. 6
   B. 10
   C. 12
   D. 14
   E. 18

2. If $5(x - 6) = -8$, then $x = ?$
   F. $-\dfrac{38}{5}$
   G. $-\dfrac{8}{5}$
   H. $-\dfrac{2}{5}$
   J. $\dfrac{2}{5}$
   K. $\dfrac{22}{5}$

3. If $3(x - 7) = -22$, then $x = ?$
   A. $-\dfrac{43}{3}$
   B. -5
   C. $-\dfrac{1}{3}$
   D. $\dfrac{1}{3}$
   E. 5

DO YOUR FIGURING HERE.

END OF SET ONE
STOP! DO NOT GO ON TO THE NEXT PAGE UNTIL TOLD TO DO SO.

Lesson 1 – Linear Equations

1.4.2 Set Two

4. The equation shown below is true for what value of x?

    $$2(x - 3) - 4(x - 6) = 7x$$

    F. $-\dfrac{18}{5}$

    G. -2

    H. 2

    J. $\dfrac{18}{5}$

    K. $\dfrac{11}{2}$

5. What is the solution to the equation $5x - (x + 4) = 2$?

    A. $-\dfrac{1}{2}$

    B. $\dfrac{1}{2}$

    C. 1

    D. $\dfrac{3}{2}$

    E. 3

6. What value of x makes the equation $6x - (5x + 7) = 10$ true?

    F. $\dfrac{4}{11}$

    G. $\dfrac{17}{11}$

    H. 3

    J. 4

    K. 17

DO YOUR FIGURING HERE.

END OF SET TWO
STOP! DO NOT GO ON TO THE NEXT PAGE
UNTIL TOLD TO DO SO.

1.4.3 Set Three

7. What is the value of x when $\frac{2x}{3} + 12 = 8$?
   - F. −6
   - G. −2
   - H. 2
   - J. 6
   - K. 30

8. If $\frac{5x}{2} + 3 = 18$, then $x = ?$
   - F. $\frac{15}{2}$
   - G. $\frac{75}{2}$
   - H. 3
   - J. 6
   - K. 15

9. If $6x + 4 = 20 - 2x$, then $x = ?$
   - A. 2
   - B. 6
   - C. 8
   - D. 16
   - E. 24

DO YOUR FIGURING HERE.

END OF SET THREE
STOP! DO NOT GO ON TO THE NEXT PAGE
UNTIL TOLD TO DO SO.

Lesson 1 – Linear Equations

1.4.4 Set Four

10. If $3x - 1 = 11$, then $2x = ?$

   F. $\dfrac{20}{3}$

   G. 2

   H. 4

   J. 8

   K. 72

DO YOUR FIGURING HERE.

11. If $5x + 2 = 27$, then $3x = ?$
   A. 3
   B. 5
   C. 15
   D. 45
   E. 75

12. If $2x - 18 = -5$, then $2x = ?$

   F. -23

   G. $-\dfrac{23}{2}$

   H. $\dfrac{13}{4}$

   J. $\dfrac{13}{2}$

   K. 13

END OF SET FOUR
STOP! DO NOT GO ON TO THE NEXT PAGE
UNTIL TOLD TO DO SO.

1.4.5 Set Five

13. For what value of x is $11x - 5 = 7x + 19$ true?

A. $\dfrac{7}{9}$

B. $\dfrac{7}{2}$

C. 6

D. 24

E. 96

14. What is the solution of the equation $-4x = -6(8 + x)$?

F. -24

G. $-\dfrac{24}{5}$

H. $\dfrac{24}{5}$

J. $\dfrac{48}{5}$

K. 24

15. If $\dfrac{2x}{3} + \dfrac{x}{2} = \dfrac{1}{6}$, then $x = ?$

A. $\dfrac{1}{30}$

B. $\dfrac{1}{15}$

C. $\dfrac{1}{7}$

D. $\dfrac{1}{5}$

E. $\dfrac{1}{3}$

DO YOUR FIGURING HERE.

END OF SET FIVE
STOP! DO NOT GO ON TO THE NEXT PAGE
UNTIL TOLD TO DO SO.

Lesson 1 – Linear Equations

Sum It Up

Linear Equations

Rules for Isolation
1. Distribute everything possible.
2. Combine like terms on each side of the equation.
3. Move all of the terms with a variable to the left-hand side of the equation.
4. Move all of the terms without a variable to the right-hand side of the equation.
5. Divide both sides by the coefficient of the variable.

Tips and Techniques

Two Wrongs Make a Right: Two negatives are the same as a positive. Look out for negative signs and treat them with extra precaution. Many careless errors are made when negative signs are overlooked.

Spotting Linear Equations: If the question asks for the value of the only variable in the equation and there are no exponents, you know you're dealing with a linear equation question and need to isolate the variable.

Show Your Work: Always show your work when isolating the variable. This will help you make fewer calculation errors. It is especially important to rewrite the entire equation before taking any of the steps for isolation.

Lesson 2

Systems of Equations

CAPTION:

2.1 Entrance Ticket

Consider the statements below and write a paragraph explaining what condition is necessary for all three of the statements to be true.

1. When I study hard, I pass my tests.
2. When I study hard at the last minute, I have to stay up late.
3. When I study hard but don't get enough sleep, I don't always do well on the test the next day.

Lesson 2 – Systems of Equations

2.2 Learning Targets

1. Use substitution or addition of equations to solve systems of equations

2. Manipulate equations into new forms in order to solve systems of equations

Self-Assessment

Circle the number that corresponds to your confidence level in your knowledge of this subject before beginning the lesson. A score of 1 means you are completely lost, and a score of 4 means you have mastered the skills. After you finish the lesson, return to the bottom of this page and circle your new confidence level to show your improvement.

2.3.1 Equation Elimination

Example:

1. $-2x + y = 14$
   $2x + 8y = 4$

2. $2x + y = 14$
   $3x - y + 4 = 15$

Lesson 2 – Systems of Equations

2.3.1 Equation Elimination

3. $9 - 2x = y$
   $3x - y = 16$

4. $x - 2y = -9$
   $x + 3y = 16$

5. $x - 2y = 1$
   $x + y = 7$

23

2.3.1 Equation Elimination

6. $3x - 2y = -9$
   $x + 3y = -3$

Lesson 2 – Systems of Equations

2.3.2 Substitution

1. $4x + y = 14$
   $x - y = 16$

2. $-2x + y = 14$
   $2x + 8y = 4$

Math Tip

Plug In: Remember that the ACT gives you answer choices. If you are stuck on a system of equations or if the system of equations is taking too long to work out, you can try plugging the various answer choices into the equations and see which choice makes the system of equations true.

2.3.3 In Terms Of

Thank you very much = Muchas gracias   English in terms of _____

Thank you very much = Ευχαριστώ πολύ   English in terms of _____

Thank you very much = Merci beaucoup   English in terms of _____

Example:
$y - 2x = x + 1$

1. Given the equations $y = c + 3$ and $d = x + 7$, which of the following is equivalent to $x + y$, written in terms of c and d ?
   A. $d + c - 10$
   B. $d + c - 4$
   C. $d + c + 10$
   D. $21cd$
   E. $3c + 7d$

2. What is the value of b, in terms of c and d, in the solution of the system of equations below?
   $$a - b = c$$
   $$2a + b = -d$$

   F. $\dfrac{-d - 2c}{3}$

   G. $d - c$

   H. $\dfrac{d - c}{3}$

   J. $d + c$

   K. $\dfrac{c - d}{3}$

Lesson 2 – Systems of Equations

2.3.3 In Terms Of

3. If $q = 3t - 7$ and $r = 4 - t$, which of the following expresses r in terms of q ?

   A. $r = \dfrac{5 - q}{3}$

   B. $r = \dfrac{11 - q}{3}$

   C. $r = \dfrac{19 - q}{3}$

   D. $r = 5 - q$

   E. $r = 19 - q$

4. If $a = b - 2$ and $c = a^2 + 4a - 10$, which of the following expresses c in terms of b ?
   F. $c = 5b - 20$
   G. $c = b^2 - 14$
   H. $c = b^2 - 22$
   J. $c = b^2 + 2b - 14$
   K. $c = b^2 + 4b - 14$

Math Tip

Negatives: Beware of negative signs. When manipulating and changing equations, it is easy to lose track of a minus sign and make a careless error. Be very careful about correctly keeping track of negative signs, as it could be the difference between solving a simple question in 45 seconds and accidentally spending 10 minutes on it.

2.4.1 Set One

1. If $p + q = 36$, and $p - q = 20$, then $q = ?$
   - A. −8
   - B. 8
   - C. 16
   - D. 28
   - E. 56

   DO YOUR FIGURING HERE.

2. Which of the following (a,b) pairs is the solution for the system of equations $2a + b = 3$ and $a - 3b = 5$?

   - F. $(-2, 7)$
   - G. $(0, 3)$
   - H. $(\frac{3}{4}, \frac{6}{4})$
   - J. $(2, -1)$
   - K. $(3, -3)$

3. What is the value of y in the solution to the following system of equations?
   $$x - 4y - 8 = 20$$
   $$2x + y = 20$$
   - A. −4
   - B. −1.8
   - C. 8
   - D. 10
   - E. 14

END OF SET ONE
STOP! DO NOT GO ON TO THE NEXT PAGE
UNTIL TOLD TO DO SO.

Lesson 2 – Systems of Equations

2.4.2 Set Two

4. If $a + b = 28$ and $a - b = 10$, then $b = ?$
   - F. -18
   - G. 9
   - H. 18
   - J. 19
   - K. 38

   DO YOUR FIGURING HERE.

5. What is the solution to the following system of equations?
   $$3x + 7y = 34$$
   $$x + 7y = 30$$

	x	y
A.	-1	1
B.	1	-1
C.	2	4
D.	4	2
E.	32	6

6. Let $3a + 4b = 18$ and $5a + 3b = 19$. What is the value of $7a + 2b$?
   - F. -16
   - G. -4
   - H. 8
   - J. 20
   - K. 24

END OF SET TWO
STOP! DO NOT GO ON TO THE NEXT PAGE
UNTIL TOLD TO DO SO.

Entrance Ticket | Learning Targets | Equation Elimination | Substitution | In Terms Of | ACT Practice | Sum It Up

2.4.3 Set Three

7. If $a = 3b + 4$ and $b = 7$, what is the value of a?

   A. 11
   B. 14
   C. 17
   D. 25
   E. 84

DO YOUR FIGURING HERE.

8. If $y = 5x - 2$ and $x = 4b + 3$, then y is equivalent to which of the following?

   F. $b + 1$
   G. $20b + 1$
   H. $20b + 13$
   J. $20bx + 1$
   K. $5x + 4b + 1$

9. For what value of b is $y = 4$ a solution to the equation $y + 2 = by + 8$?

   A. -2
   B. -0.5
   C. 1
   D. 0.5
   E. 2

END OF SET THREE
STOP! DO NOT GO ON TO THE NEXT PAGE
UNTIL TOLD TO DO SO.

Lesson 2 – Systems of Equations

2.4.4 Set Four

10. Given the equations $Q = x + 6$ and $y = R - 3$, which of the following expressions is equivalent to $Q + R$ written in terms of x and y ?

    F. $x + y + 3$
    G. $x + y + 9$
    H. $x - y - 3$
    J. $18xy$
    K. $6x + 3y$

DO YOUR FIGURING HERE.

11. If $x = 7 - p$ and $y = 3p + 4$, which of the following expresses y in terms of x ?

    A. $17 - x$
    B. $25 - x$
    C. $17 - 3x$
    D. $25 - 3x$
    E. $25 + 3x$

12. Given the equations $A = c + 7$ and $d = B - 4$, which of the following expressions is equivalent to $A - B$ written in terms of c and d ?

    F. $c - d + 3$
    G. $c - d + 11$
    H. $c + d + 3$
    J. $c + d + 11$
    K. $7c + 4b$

END OF SET FOUR
STOP! DO NOT GO ON TO THE NEXT PAGE
UNTIL TOLD TO DO SO.

2.4.5 Set Five

13. If the following system has a solution, what is the x-coordinate of the solution?

$$4x + 8y = 60$$
$$x + 8y = 30$$

A. 6
B. 10
C. 18
D. 30
E. The system has no solution.

14. What is the value of y in the solution to the system of equations below?

$$5x - 5y = 25$$
$$x + 4y = -10$$

F. −22
G. −3
H. −1
J. 3
K. 5

15. If $x = 12 - s$ and $y = 5s + 6$, which of the following expresses y in terms of x ?

A. $66 - 5x$
B. $66 - x$
C. $60 + 5x$
D. $66 + x$
E. $66 + 5x$

END OF SET FIVE
STOP! DO NOT GO ON TO THE NEXT PAGE
UNTIL TOLD TO DO SO.

Lesson 2 – Systems of Equations

Sum It Up

Systems of Equations

Equality
The state of being the same or equal; having the same value

Equation
Shows that two expressions are equal

Tips and Techniques

Plug In: Plug in answer choices if you are stuck or running out of time on a system of equations problem.

Negatives: Watch out for negatives. Any time they show up in a problem, be careful about keeping track of them.

Lesson 3

Solving Equations: Word Problems

Two spacecraft start flying simultaneously toward each other. The initial distance between the two is 140 miles. The first craft is going 80 miles per hour, and the second is going 50 miles per hour. How long will it take for the two spacecraft to pass each other?

Houston, we have a word problem.

CAPTION:

ACT® Mastery Math

3.1 Entrance Ticket

Solve the questions below.

1. On a standardized test, the score starts at 100. For each correct answer, the overall score is increased by 5, and for each incorrect answer, it is decreased by 2. If a question is not answered, it is counted as incorrect. Shelly takes the test and finishes all of the questions. The number of questions she answered correctly is equal to 4 times the number of incorrect answers plus 5. Her overall score is 395. How many questions did she get correct?

    A. 15
    B. 18
    C. 65
    D. 85
    E. 145

2. The table below gives the prices for hair perming and coloring services at Hair Today Salon.

Length of Hair	Color	Perm
Short	$30	$50
Long	$50	$80

    Over the course of one week, Celeste, one of the stylists, collected $840 for coloring the hair of 20 different clients (not counting tips). How many of those clients had long hair?

    F. 4
    G. 6
    H. 8
    J. 10
    K. 12

3. Tad's sister, Tina, asks him how old he is. Tad tells her that if she squares his age and subtracts 3 times his age, the result is 40. How old is Tad?

    A. 4
    B. 5
    C. 8
    D. 10
    E. 13

Lesson 3 – Solving Equations: Word Problems

3.2 Learning Targets

1. Translate word problems into mathematical expressions

2. Solve systems of equations word problems

Self-Assessment

Circle the number that corresponds to your confidence level in your knowledge of this subject before beginning the lesson. A score of 1 means you are completely lost, and a score of 4 means you have mastered the skills. After you finish the lesson, return to the bottom of this page and circle your new confidence level to show your improvement.

Before Lesson

1   2   3   4

After Lesson

1   2   3   4

ACT® Mastery Math

3.3.1 Translating Math Statements

1. What math operation do you think words such as *together*, *and*, *combined*, *both* translate to? _____

2. What math operation do you think words such as *minus*, *without*, *less*, *difference*, *change in* translate to? _____

3. What math operation do you think words such as *times*, *each*, *per*, *of* translate to? _____

4. What math operation do you think words such as *divided into*, *split between* or *among*, *doled out*, *divvyed up* translate to? _____

5. What symbol do the words *equal to*, *is*, *is the same as* translate to? _____

6. What do the words *what*, *unknown*, *a number* translate to? _____

---

1. What is the sum of 2 and 5? → _____

2. Together, 2 hamburgers and 1 drink cost $15. → _____

3. What is 15% of 100? → _____

4. The sum of 2 numbers is 20. → _____

5. The difference of 2 numbers is 5. → _____

Lesson 3 – Solving Equations: Word Problems

3.3.1 Translating Math Statements

1. A certain positive number is multiplied by 4, and then the result is subtracted from the original number. The result is 21 less than 0. What is the number?

   Translated Equation:

2. When asked her age, Susan replied, "If you take my age and square it and then subtract 22 times my age, the result is 75." How old is she?

   Translated Equation:

3. Jack got a rough start in science class this year. He got a 68 on his first test and a 72 on his second. After that, he studied very hard and scored a 100 on each remaining test. At the end of the semester, his total test score average was 88, with each test having equal weight. How many tests, in total, did Jack take in science class this semester?

   Translated Equation:

Math Tip

Decoding: If you are given a word problem with lots of math language and no variables in the answer choices, the best strategy is to translate the word problem into an equation and solve.

3.3.2 System of Equations Word Problems

1. The cost of 2 tacos and a drink is $3.07. The cost of 3 tacos and a drink is $3.86. How much does a drink cost?

    Translated Equations:

2. Josh bought 800 plastic whistles to give away to the kids at a street fair. Some of the whistles were small and cost $0.50 each. The larger whistles cost $0.75. In total, he spent $550 on the whistles. How many of the small whistles did he buy?

    Translated Equations:

3. Sherry bought 20 apples at the grocery store. The Braeburn apples were $0.80 each, and the Granny Smith apples were $0.65 each. All together, the apples cost $14.95. How many Granny Smith apples did she buy?

    Translated Equations:

Lesson 3 – Solving Equations: Word Problems

3.3.2 System of Equations Word Problems

1. The cost of 2 tacos and a drink is $3.07. The cost of 3 tacos and a drink is $3.86. How much does a drink cost?
   A. $0.49
   B. $0.79
   C. $1.49
   D. $1.58
   E. $2.49

2. Josh bought 800 plastic whistles to give away to the kids at a street fair. Some of the whistles were small and cost $0.50 each. The larger whistles cost $0.75. In total, he spent $550 on the whistles. How many of the small whistles did he buy?
   F. 200
   G. 600
   H. 640
   J. 720
   K. 760

3. Sherry bought 20 apples at the grocery store. The Braeburn apples were $0.80 each, and the Granny Smith apples were $0.65 each. All together, the apples cost $14.95. How many Granny Smith apples did she buy?
   A. 7
   B. 9
   C. 11
   D. 12
   E. 13

3.3.2 System of Equations Word Problems

1. Kelly bought 4 shirts and 3 skirts for her doll and paid $11.40 total. After she did a doll fashion show for her best friend, Caitlyn wanted to know how much one of the skirts cost. Kelly remembered that each skirt cost $0.30 more than each shirt. How much did one skirt cost?

   Translated Equations:

   A. $1.50
   B. $1.60
   C. $1.65
   D. $1.75
   E. $1.80

2. Bobby opened a bag of candy and counted how many pieces were in the bag. There were 68 pieces of orange, lime, and cherry candies in total. He separated them by flavor and found that there were 2 more orange than lime and 4 more cherry than orange. How many cherry candies were in the bag?

   Translated Equations:

   F. 20
   G. 22
   H. 24
   J. 26
   K. 28

Lesson 3 – Solving Equations: Word Problems

3.4.1 Set One

1. The sum of the real numbers *x* and *y* is 15. Their difference is 3. What is the value of *xy* ?
   A. 3
   B. 6
   C. 9
   D. 15
   E. 54

DO YOUR FIGURING HERE.

2. Lilly and Laura pooled their money to purchase their brother, Liam, a video game for his birthday. The video game cost a total of $45. If Laura was only able to contribute $\frac{2}{3}$ of what Lilly did, how much did Laura put toward the present?
   F. $18
   G. $21
   H. $24
   J. $27
   K. $30

3. A rectangular field is 3 times as long as it is wide, and it has an area of 192 square yards. How many yards long is it?
   A. 8
   B. 24
   C. 48
   D. 72
   E. 96

END OF SET ONE
STOP! DO NOT GO ON TO THE NEXT PAGE
UNTIL TOLD TO DO SO.

3.4.2 Set Two

4. The sum of the real numbers x and y is 25. Their difference is 13. What is the value of xy ?
   F. 19
   G. 100
   H. 104
   J. 114
   K. 124

DO YOUR FIGURING HERE.

5. Theresa decides to donate money to cancer research each year. Her brother, Tony, also decides to contribute. Together, they donate $1,000 per year to cancer research. If Tony is able to donate $1\frac{1}{2}$ times the amount that Theresa is able to donate, what is the amount in dollars that Tony will donate after 5 years, assuming the amount and proportions remain the same each year?
   A. $2,000
   B. $2,100
   C. $2,450
   D. $3,000
   E. $3,600

6. When asked his age, Michael said, "If you square my age, then subtract 12 times my age, the result is 85." How old is he?
   F. 5
   G. 12
   H. 17
   J. 24
   K. 85

END OF SET TWO
STOP! DO NOT GO ON TO THE NEXT PAGE
UNTIL TOLD TO DO SO.

Lesson 3 – Solving Equations: Word Problems

3.4.3 Set Three

7. The sum of the real numbers x and y is 24. Their difference is 12. What is the value of xy ?
   A. 108
   B. 90
   C. 58
   D. 18
   E. 6

DO YOUR FIGURING HERE.

8. A vending machine sells chips for $0.50 and candy bars for $1.00. If Jim spent $5.50 on snacks in the machine over the course of a week, how many candy bars did he buy?
   F. 1
   G. 2
   H. 3
   J. 4
   K. Cannot be determined from the given information

9. A school held a kiddie carnival to raise money for the PTA. Admission for adults was $8, and admission for children was $5. In the end, 87 people attended the carnival, and they raised $468. How many adults attended the carnival?
   A. 6
   B. 11
   C. 23
   D. 64
   E. 76

END OF SET THREE
STOP! DO NOT GO ON TO THE NEXT PAGE
UNTIL TOLD TO DO SO.

3.4.4 Set Four

10. A group of 10 people go to see a movie. The tickets cost $11.95 for adults and $7.50 for children. If the total cost for tickets was $101.70 for the group, how many adults were in the group?

    F. 4
    G. 5
    H. 6
    J. 7
    K. 8

DO YOUR FIGURING HERE.

11. A restaurant sells burgers and fries. If two burgers and one order of fries cost $5.10, and one burger and two orders of fries cost $4.80, how much is one burger and one order of fries?

    A. $3.00
    B. $3.30
    C. $3.60
    D. $4.00
    E. $4.95

12. Mrs. Jones is handing out candy to trick-or-treaters. She gives out candy bars to kids in costume and small packages of gummies to kids without a costume. The candy bars cost $0.80, and the gummies cost $0.25. At the end of the night, 100 children visited Mrs. Jones's home, and she gave out $69.00 in candy. How many children who visited Mrs. Jones's home were wearing a costume?

    F. 20
    G. 50
    H. 69
    J. 80
    K. 92

END OF SET FOUR
STOP! DO NOT GO ON TO THE NEXT PAGE
UNTIL TOLD TO DO SO.

Lesson 3 – Solving Equations: Word Problems

3.4.5 Set Five

13. Marco bought pens and pencils with his company's name and website address to give away to people at a festival. He bought a total of 300 pens and pencils together and spent $62.50. If pencils cost $0.15 each and pens cost $0.25 each, how many pens did Marco buy?

   A. 175
   B. 165
   C. 140
   D. 130
   E. 125

DO YOUR FIGURING HERE.

14. In a game, Theodore received a handful of coins (pennies, nickels, dimes, and quarters) as a prize. When he got home, he found that he had managed to get $2.09 in change. He noticed that he had three times as many pennies as dimes, one more nickel than dimes, and twice as many quarters as dimes. How many quarters did Theodore get in his prize?

   F. 4
   G. 5
   H. 6
   J. 7
   K. 8

15. Nathan has 102 solid-colored disks that are red, blue, and green. He lines them up on the floor and finds that there are 3 more red disks than blue and 6 more blue disks than green. How many red disks are there?

   A. 26
   B. 29
   C. 31
   D. 35
   E. 38

END OF SET FIVE
STOP! DO NOT GO ON TO THE NEXT PAGE
UNTIL TOLD TO DO SO.

ACT® Mastery Math

Sum It Up

Solving Equations: Word Problems

Value
A number of measurement

Expression
A group of numbers, symbols, and operations to indicate a value

Equation
Two mathematical expressions set equal to each other

Coefficient
The number next to a variable

Combining Like Terms
In an equation, the process of simplifying the equation using mathematical operations

Tips and Techniques

Decoding: If you are given a word problem with lots of math language and no variables in the answer choices, your best strategy is to translate the word problem into an equation and solve.

Lesson 4

Percentages

CAPTION:

ACT® Mastery Math

4.1 Entrance Ticket

Solve the questions below.

1. What is 125% of 20 ?
   A. 21.25
   B. 25.00
   C. 26.25
   D. 32.50
   E. 82.50

2. Liam ate at a restaurant, and the final bill was $30.00. If he wants to leave the waitress a 15% tip, how much will the tip be?
   F. $2.00
   G. $3.00
   H. $3.15
   J. $4.50
   K. $6.00

3. Each of the 500 people in a random sample of the 4,000 students who attend a local community college were asked to name the methods they often use to get to school from home. All 500 people answered the question. The answers were tallied, and the percentages of people who walk, drive, ride a bike, and take a bus are shown in the diagram below.

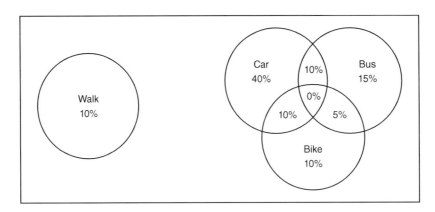

Because this was a random sample, the percentages in the sample are most likely the estimates for the corresponding percentages among all the students in the school. What estimate does this give for the number of people who commonly get to school only by bus?
   A. 75
   B. 150
   C. 600
   D. 800
   E. 1,200

Lesson 4 – Percentages

4.2 Learning Targets

1. Determine the percentage of a number

2. Solve word problems that involve percentages

Self-Assessment

Circle the number that corresponds to your confidence level in your knowledge of this subject before beginning the lesson. A score of 1 means you are completely lost, and a score of 4 means you have mastered the skills. After you finish the lesson, return to the bottom of this page and circle your new confidence level to show your improvement.

Before Lesson

1   2   3   4

After Lesson

1   2   3   4

4.3.1 Percentage of a Number

1. What is 10% of 50 ?

   Answer: _____

2. What is 30% of 100 ?

   Answer: _____

3. What is 85% of 15 ?

   Answer: _____

What: _____
Is: _____
Of: _____
Percent: _____

Lesson 4 – Percentages

4.3.1 Percentage of a Number

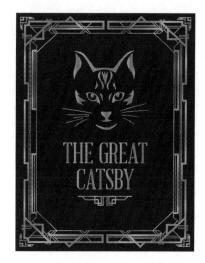

1. What is 38% of $17.99?

Answer: _____

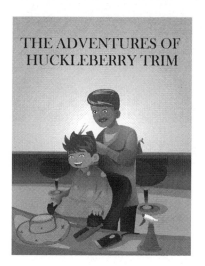

2. What is 45% of $8.99?

Answer: _____

3. What is 4% of $10.65?

Answer: _____

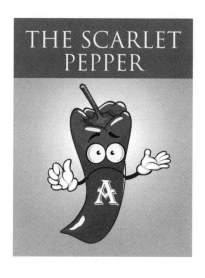

4. What is 47% of $27.99?

Answer: _____

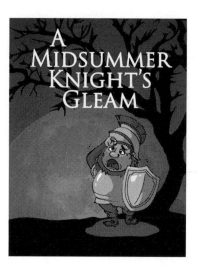

5. What is 40% of $15.00?

Answer: _____

ACT® Mastery Math

4.3.2 Word Problems with Percentages

1. The college sorority Delta Sigma Pi needs to elect a new president. All 80 of the Delta Sigma Pi sisters voted for 1 of the 4 candidates that ran for office. The results are given in the table below.

Candidate	Number of Votes
Buffy	16
Whitney	20
Chelsea	34
Veronica	10

   What percentage of the Delta Sigma Pi sisters voted for the winner, Chelsea?

   A. 12.5%
   B. 20.0%
   C. 25.0%
   D. 34.0%
   E. 42.5%

---

2. Eliza bought a meal that cost $12. She tipped the waiter 25% of that amount. How much was the tip?

   Answer: _____

Math Tip

Start Easy: Many percentage problems can be overwhelming due to all the steps involved. Instead of letting the question overwhelm you, do the first thing you know how to do, and work from there. The problem will probably become much easier as you go.

Lesson 4 – Percentages

4.3.2 Word Problems with Percentages

3. Penny took a poll to find out her classmates' favorite pizza toppings. All 60 of her classmates provided their answers. The results are shown in the table below.

Pizza Toppings	Number of Classmates
Cheese	22
Pepperoni	11
Sausage	19
Peppers	8

What percentage of her classmates chose peppers as their favorite pizza topping?

Answer: _____

4. A florist is told that 40% of the 350 flowers ordered must be red roses. How many red roses must be in the order?

Answer: _____

5. Luis received a discount of $24 on his new phone, which had an original price of $140. By what percentage was the original price discounted?

Answer: _____

Math Tip

Show Your Work: When you encounter a percentage problem, show your work, step by step. If you are over-confident and make mental errors, you will miss out on points. Show your work to prevent yourself from falling into trap answer choices.

4.4.1 Set One

1. What is 15% of 150 ?
   A. 2.25
   B. 3
   C. 10
   D. 15
   E. 22.5

DO YOUR FIGURING HERE.

2. If 120% of a number is 720, what is 50% of that same number?
   F. 300
   G. 360
   H. 432
   J. 600
   K. 1,224

3. What is 4% of 80 ?
   A. 320
   B. 32
   C. 3.2
   D. 0.32
   E. 0.032

END OF SET ONE
STOP! DO NOT GO ON TO THE NEXT PAGE
UNTIL TOLD TO DO SO.

4.4.2 Set Two

4. What is 4% of 50% of 5 ?
   F. 0.01
   G. 0.05
   H. 0.10
   J. 0.50
   K. 1.00

   DO YOUR FIGURING HERE.

5. What is 150% of 264 ?
   A. 132
   B. 176
   C. 296
   D. 396
   E. 3,960

6. What is $\frac{2}{3}$ of 15% of $2,000?
   F. $100
   G. $200
   H. $300
   J. $450
   K. $500

   END OF SET TWO
   STOP! DO NOT GO ON TO THE NEXT PAGE
   UNTIL TOLD TO DO SO.

4.4.3 Set Three

7. The table below shows the distribution of the Cub Scouts throughout Pack 552.

Den	Tigers (6 years old)	Wolves (7 years old)	Bears (8 years old)	Webelos (9 years old)
% of Cub Scouts	19%	36%	17%	28%

What percentage of the Cub Scouts are at least as old as a Bear Scout?

A. 45%
B. 54%
C. 64%
D. 65%
E. 83%

DO YOUR FIGURING HERE.

8. Of the 80 spaces in the XYZ Industries' parking lot, 5% of them are reserved for handicapped parking. Of the non-handicapped spaces, 16 are reserved for company VIPs. How many spaces that are NOT reserved for handicapped parking are available to non-VIP employees?

F. 76
G. 70
H. 64
J. 60
K. 56

9. Patrick and Cheryl dined at a restaurant, and their bill was $42.68. They would like to leave a tip of approximately 16% of their bill. Which of the following is closest to that amount?

A. $6.40
B. $6.83
C. $7.25
D. $8.11
E. $8.96

END OF SET THREE
STOP! DO NOT GO ON TO THE NEXT PAGE
UNTIL TOLD TO DO SO.

4.4.4 Set Four

10. The pie chart below shows how a sports organization makes its profit. Last year the team made $2,000,000 in profit, and this year it increased its profits to $2,500,000. How much money was made on food sales in both years?

Programs: 15%
Tickets: 20%
Food: 40%
Souvenirs: 25%

- F. 1,800,000
- G. 1,000,000
- H.   900,000
- J.   800,000
- K.   500,000

11. Stacie had a meal that cost $36.00. If she tipped the waiter 18% of the total bill for the service, how much was the tip?

- A. $2.00
- B. $3.96
- C. $4.68
- D. $5.76
- E. $6.48

12. While watching television from 8:00–9:00 one morning, Kiera notices that each commercial break is comprised of 3 commercials that are each 40 seconds long, and there are a total of 4 commercial breaks during that time. To the nearest percentage, what percentage of the hour was taken up by commercials?

- F. 7%
- G. 8%
- H. 13%
- J. 15%
- K. 20%

DO YOUR FIGURING HERE.

END OF SET FOUR
STOP! DO NOT GO ON TO THE NEXT PAGE
UNTIL TOLD TO DO SO.

4.4.5 Set Five

13. Brent has a diagram that he needs to place into a report. It is only 3.5" tall × 4" wide, but it needs to be about twice that big to make the impact he wants. Brent has use of a photocopy machine that can enlarge the height and width of an image by 20%. If he repeatedly uses the machine to enlarge each subsequent image, what is the minimum number of times he will have to make a copy to get the image to at least 7" tall?

    A. 1
    B. 2
    C. 3
    D. 4
    E. 5

DO YOUR FIGURING HERE.

14. Kelly needs to get a minimum of 75% on today's 60-point math test in order to pass the class. What is the least number of points that she must score to achieve this goal?

    F. 15
    G. 35
    H. 40
    J. 45
    K. 50

15. 480 is 8% of what number?

    A. 38.4
    B. 60
    C. 488
    D. 3,840
    E. 6,000

END OF SET FIVE
STOP! DO NOT GO ON TO THE NEXT PAGE
UNTIL TOLD TO DO SO.

Lesson 4 – Percentages

Sum It Up

Percentages

Converting Percentages to Decimals
To convert a percentage to a decimal, move the decimal two places to the left and remove the percent sign.
Ex: 42% = 0.42, 5% = 0.05

Converting Decimals to Percentages
To convert a decimal to a percentage, move the decimal two places to the right and add a percent sign.
Ex: 0.33 = 33%, 0.012 = 1.2%

Converting Percentages to Fractions
To convert a percentage to a fraction, set the percentage over 100, remove the percent sign, and simplify.

Ex: $10\% = \dfrac{10}{100} = \dfrac{1}{10}$

Converting Fractions to Percentages
To convert a fraction to a percentage, convert the fraction to a decimal by dividing the numerator by the denominator, and then move the decimal two places to the right and add a percent sign.

Ex: $\dfrac{3}{4} = 0.75 = 75\%$

Percentage
A ratio expressing parts per 100

Tips and Techniques

Start Easy: Don't let the number of calculations overwhelm you. Start with the first thing you can do and work from there.

Show Your Work: Show your work, especially when working a percentage word problem.

Lesson 5

Percent Change

CAPTION:

ACT® Mastery Math

5.1 Entrance Ticket

Solve the questions below.

1. Judy is looking to buy a textbook. The book normally costs $75.82, but it is on sale for 35% below the regular cost. How much will the book cost before taxes if Judy is to buy it while it is on sale? Round to the nearest cent.
   A. $ 26.53
   B. $ 26.54
   C. $ 49.28
   D. $ 56.87
   E. $102.36

2. A pretzel company usually spends $137 per week on salt, but due to a recent salt shortage, the price of salt has increased by 40%. Assuming the company continues to purchase the same volume of salt per week, what is the new weekly cost of salt for the company?
   F. $ 54.80
   G. $ 82.20
   H. $142.48
   J. $191.80
   K. $219.20

3. Kyle is looking to buy a shirt for his girlfriend's birthday that normally costs $85. Lucky for Kyle, the store selling the shirt is having a 30% off sale for all items. After the discount, Kyle must pay 6% sales tax on the shirt. How much does Kyle end up spending on this shirt for his girlfriend?
   A. $ 27.03
   B. $54.57
   C. $59.50
   D. $63.07
   E. $95.02

Lesson 5 – Percent Change

5.2 Learning Targets

1. Solve problems with percent increase

2. Solve problems with percent decrease

3. Solve problems with both percent increase and decrease

Self-Assessment

Circle the number that corresponds to your confidence level in your knowledge of this subject before beginning the lesson. A score of 1 means you are completely lost, and a score of 4 means you have mastered the skills. After you finish the lesson, return to the bottom of this page and circle your new confidence level to show your improvement.

Before Lesson

1   2   3   4

After Lesson

1   2   3   4

ACT® Mastery Math

5.3.1 Percent Increase

You go out to eat, and your bill is $50. You want to tip your waiter 20%. What is the total amount you should pay on this bill?

Answer: _____

Formula for solving *percent increase* problems:

_____

---

1. A car rental service recently purchased all new vehicles. To help cover the cost, rental rates have to increase by 26% from the normal rate of $45.00 per day. What should the new rate be?
    A. $45.26
    B. $47.60
    C. $56.00
    D. $56.70
    E. $71.00

2. Watermelons at a local stand now sell for $5.00 each. To make a profit, the owner marked up the original cost of the watermelons by 25%. What was the original cost of each watermelon?
    F. $3.75
    G. $4.00
    H. $4.75
    J. $5.25
    K. $6.25

Lesson 5 – Percent Change

5.3.1 Percent Increase

3. A computer analyst types at a speed of 80 words per minute. Over the next year, she wants to improve her speed by 20%. How fast does she want to be able to type 1 year from now, in words per minute?
   - A. 64
   - B. 82
   - C. 88
   - D. 96
   - E. 100

4. This summer, Fat Cow Ice Cream Shoppe increased its prices by 10% to try to make more profit. If an ice cream cone used to cost $3.50, how much does it cost now, after the price increase?
   - F. $ 3.15
   - G. $ 3.60
   - H. $ 3.85
   - J. $ 4.20
   - K. $13.50

Math Tip

Process of Elimination: If the question is asking for a percent increase, you can eliminate any answer choices that are smaller than or equal to the original.

5.3.2 Percent Decrease

You are shopping for a new sweatshirt. The sweatshirt you like is $40, and it has a 15% discount on it. What is the price of the sweatshirt after the discount?

Answer: _____

Formula for solving *percent decrease* problems:

_____

1. Josh works on an assembly line at a local factory and makes $400 per week. However, Josh has to pay 23% of his check as taxes. How much money is Josh actually taking home every week?

   A. $ 92.00
   B. $308.00
   C. $318.70
   D. $377.00
   E. $492.00

2. Jeff is paid $9 an hour at the grocery store where he works. He was caught sleeping at work 3 times this past week, so his boss gave him a 15% pay cut. How much does Jeff now earn per hour?

   F. $ 7.65
   G. $ 7.85
   H. $ 8.85
   J. $ 9.15
   K. $10.35

Lesson 5 – Percent Change

5.3.2 Percent Decrease

3. The price of a car was decreased from $13,000 to $11,830. The price decreased by what percentage?
   A. 9%
   B. 11.7%
   C. 83%
   D. 91%
   E. 117%

4. A TV has an original price of $489.99 before taxes. It goes on sale for 35% below the original price. What is the new price (rounded to the nearest cent) of the TV, before taxes?
   F. $171.50
   G. $318.49
   H. $424.99
   J. $454.99
   K. $489.34

Math Tip

Process of Elimination: If one of the answer choices is greater than the original value and the question is asking about a percent decrease, you know that choice can be eliminated.

5.3.3 Percent Increase and Decrease

You are trying to buy a dishwasher, and you see that one is on sale for 20% off. The original price of the dishwasher is $300. What would you pay for the dishwasher if there was a 5% sales tax added to the discounted price?

Answer: _____

When dealing with problems that have both *percent increase* and *percent decrease*:

_____

1. Margaret always makes sure to bring coupons to the store. While shopping for cereal, she finds a box that is discounted by 12% from its normal price of $4.30. Margaret has a coupon that takes an additional 4% off the already discounted price. After a sales tax of 6% on the final price, how much does Margaret spend on the box of cereal?

   A. $3.83
   B. $3.85
   C. $4.00
   D. $4.18
   E. $4.20

2. Alicia went shopping to buy some new clothes. She bought a shirt and a scarf that totaled $41.50, but she had a coupon for 50% off her total purchase before tax. What was the final price Alicia paid for her clothes after the 7% tax was added? Round your answer to the nearest cent.

   F. $19.30
   G. $22.20
   H. $27.75
   J. $35.28
   K. $43.87

Lesson 5 – Percent Change

5.3.3 Percent Increase and Decrease

3. Carl went out to eat with his family for his birthday. The bill was $87.42, but Carl had a 10% off coupon. If Carl gave a 20% tip, what was the final price he paid for the meal?

   A. $78.68
   B. $92.90
   C. $94.41
   D. $96.16
   E. $97.42

Math Tip

Process of Elimination: If you are asked to calculate a percent increase, decrease, or any combination of the two, try to eliminate any answer choices that are too large or too small. Even if you cannot solve the question exactly, you can usually eliminate one or two choices just by looking at the numbers.

5.4.1 Set One

1. Kirk is getting a raise of 5% due to inflation. His normal salary is $56,000 per year. Which of the following calculations gives Kirk's new salary, in dollars?

   A. 56,000 + 5
   B. 56,000 + 56,000(0.05)
   C. 56,000 + 56,000(0.50)
   D. 56,000 + 56,000(5)
   E. 56,000(.05)

2. A bed frame normally weighs 60 pounds. A new, stronger material increases the durability of the frame but makes it weigh 30% more. How many pounds does the new frame weigh?

   F. 63
   G. 66
   H. 78
   J. 90
   K. 102

3. Mifflin Paper Company just upgraded to a heavier cardstock paper for its $42.00 business cards. To compensate for the increase in quality, Mifflin Paper Company is raising its prices by 19%. What is the new price of business cards?

   A. $42.19
   B. $43.90
   C. $47.50
   D. $48.88
   E. $49.98

DO YOUR FIGURING HERE.

END OF SET ONE
STOP! DO NOT GO ON TO THE NEXT PAGE
UNTIL TOLD TO DO SO.

Lesson 5 – Percent Change

5.4.2 Set Two

4. The table below shows average milk prices at the local grocery store for the past 5 years.

Year	Price
2011	$2.36
2012	$2.45
2013	$3.15
2014	$2.50
2015	$3.40

   From 2010 to 2011, the average price of a gallon of milk increased by 14%. What was the average price of a gallon of milk in 2010?
   - F. $2.07
   - G. $2.11
   - H. $2.22
   - J. $2.30
   - K. $2.69

DO YOUR FIGURING HERE.

5. The table below shows the delivery charge per mile for Polly's Pizzeria over the past 3 months.

Month 1	Month 2	Month 3
$0.50	$0.36	$0.45

   By how much did the delivery charge increase from Month 2 to Month 3?
   - A. 9%
   - B. 12%
   - C. 18%
   - D. 25%
   - E. 80%

6. Employees at Anderson Manufacturing receive a raise of 4.5% at the end of each year. An employee with an annual salary of $46,000.00 this year will have what annual salary next year?
   - F. $46,004.50
   - G. $46,045.00
   - H. $48,070.00
   - J. $56,682.00
   - K. $64,722.00

END OF SET TWO
STOP! DO NOT GO ON TO THE NEXT PAGE
UNTIL TOLD TO DO SO.

5.4.3 Set Three

7. Barry bought a new car for $15,000. The value of the car depreciated by 25% after driving off the lot. After a year of driving the car, the value depreciated by an additional 15%. What percentage of the original value is the car now worth? Round your answer to the nearest percentage.

   A. 4%
   B. 10%
   C. 40%
   D. 46%
   E. 64%

DO YOUR FIGURING HERE.

8. The table below gives prices for different services at Quicky Wash.

Wash	Vacuum	Wax	Shine
$12.00	$4.00	$15.00	$10.00

   Albert took his car to Quicky Wash for a wash, wax, and shine. He paid full price for the wash and shine but got 25% off the wax. How much did Albert spend at Quicky Wash?

   F. $11.25
   G. $27.75
   H. $33.25
   J. $34.50
   K. $37.00

9. Shelly wants to tell her friend how large of a sale a local store is having, but she forgets the discount amount. All Shelly knows is that she bought a shirt for $6 that normally costs $10. Shelly can tell her friend that the store has decreased prices by how much?

   A. 4%
   B. 20%
   C. 24%
   D. 35%
   E. 40%

END OF SET THREE
STOP! DO NOT GO ON TO THE NEXT PAGE
UNTIL TOLD TO DO SO.

Lesson 5 – Percent Change

5.4.4 Set Four

10. Polka Dot Boutique is having a sale of 15% off previously marked down items. Gwen finds a pair of jeans originally priced at $45.00 and marked down by 25%. She must pay a 6% sales tax on the final price of the jeans. How much does Gwen spend at Polka Dot Boutique?

    F. $28.62
    G. $30.41
    H. $33.00
    J. $33.99
    K. $51.68

DO YOUR FIGURING HERE.

11. At a gas station, all chips are marked down 10%. A customer brings a bag of chips with a regular price of $2.19 to the register. After the 7% sales tax on the final price, how much does the customer pay for the bag of chips? Round your answer to the nearest cent.

    A. $2.02
    B. $2.09
    C. $2.11
    D. $2.22
    E. $2.24

12. A number is decreased by 50%, and the resulting number is then increased by 300%. The original number is what percentage of the final number?

    F. 20%
    G. 25%
    H. 40%
    J. 50%
    K. 400%

END OF SET FOUR
STOP! DO NOT GO ON TO THE NEXT PAGE
UNTIL TOLD TO DO SO.

Entrance Ticket | Learning Targets | Percent Increase | Percent Decrease | Percent Increase and Decrease | ACT Practice | Sum It Up

5.4.5 Set Five

13. A bakery is having a *buy 4, get 1 free* sale on cakes. This sale is equivalent to what percentage off the regular price of all 5 cakes?

- **A.** 1%
- **B.** 10%
- **C.** 20%
- **D.** 25%
- **E.** 40%

DO YOUR FIGURING HERE.

14. In order for Carlton's Car Dealership to make a profit, it must mark up the dealer price of cars by 14%. After the increase, a new sedan at Carl's Car Dealership is marked to sell for $14,600. What is the dealer price of the sedan?

- **F.** $12,807
- **G.** $12,556
- **H.** $13,114
- **J.** $13,200
- **K.** $14,586

15. The school faculty is having a catered meeting. The catering service charges a $40.00 fee up front. The school buys $33.00 worth of pasta and $45.50 worth of sandwiches. The catering service expects an 18% tip on the food subtotal. How much does the school end up paying for the whole catered meeting?

- **A.** $ 64.37
- **B.** $ 92.63
- **C.** $104.37
- **D.** $132.63
- **E.** $139.83

END OF SET FIVE
STOP! DO NOT GO ON TO THE NEXT PAGE
UNTIL TOLD TO DO SO.

Lesson 5 – Percent Change

Sum It Up

Percent Change

Percent
Parts per 100

Percent Increase
Initial value + (Initial value)(Percent increase) = Value after increase

Percent Decrease
Initial value − (Initial value)(Percent decrease) = Value after decrease

Percent Increase and Decrease
Handle the problem chronologically (do the calculation that comes first, and then do the other)

Tips and Techniques

Process of Elimination: If you get stuck, look at the numbers in the problem and make as many eliminations as you can based on the size of the answer choices.

Lesson 6

Fractions

CAPTION:

ACT® Mastery Math

6.1 Entrance Ticket

Solve the questions below.

1. The largest square shown below is divided into 64 congruent smaller squares. What fraction of the largest square is shaded?

   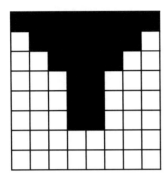

   A. $\dfrac{1}{64}$

   B. $\dfrac{3}{8}$

   C. $\dfrac{1}{2}$

   D. $\dfrac{5}{8}$

   E. $\dfrac{29}{32}$

2. Meghan is making fruit salads and fruit smoothies. The salad recipe calls for $\dfrac{1}{6}$ cup of strawberries, and the smoothie recipe calls for $\dfrac{2}{3}$ cup of strawberries. If Meghan wants to make 2 fruit salads and 2 fruit smoothies, how many cups of strawberries does she need?

   F. $\dfrac{5}{12}$

   G. $\dfrac{5}{6}$

   H. $1\dfrac{1}{6}$

   J. $1\dfrac{2}{3}$

   K. $1\dfrac{5}{6}$

Lesson 6 – Fractions

6.1 Entrance Ticket

3. Of the 482 graduating seniors at Palmdale High School, approximately $\frac{5}{8}$ are going to college, and approximately $\frac{1}{2}$ of those going to college are going to an in-state school. Which of the following is the closest estimate for how many of the graduating seniors are going to an in-state school?

   A. 90
   B. 150
   C. 180
   D. 240
   E. 300

6.2 Learning Targets

1. Add, subtract, multiply and divide fractions and mixed numbers

2. Solve complex problems requiring multiple operations with fractions

Self-Assessment

Circle the number that corresponds to your confidence level in your knowledge of this subject before beginning the lesson. A score of 1 means you are completely lost, and a score of 4 means you have mastered the skills. After you finish the lesson, return to the bottom of this page and circle your new confidence level to show your improvement.

Before Lesson

1   2   3   4

After Lesson

1   2   3   4

Lesson 6 – Fractions

6.3.1 Least Common Multiple

1. _____ and _____. LCM: _____

2. _____ and _____. LCM: _____

3. _____ and _____. LCM: _____

4. _____ and _____. LCM: _____

5. _____, _____, and _____. LCM: _____

6. _____, _____, and _____. LCM: _____

7. _____, _____, and _____. LCM: _____

Entrance Ticket | Learning Targets | Least Common Multiple | Fraction Operations | Ordering Fractions | ACT Practice | Sum It Up

6.3.2 Fraction Operations

1. $\dfrac{3}{8} + \dfrac{6}{7}$

2. $\dfrac{7}{20} - \dfrac{2}{15}$

3. $\dfrac{4}{5} - \dfrac{3}{11} + \dfrac{2}{7}$

4. $\dfrac{12}{13} - \dfrac{2}{3} - \dfrac{2}{39}$

5. $3\dfrac{5}{6} + 1\dfrac{2}{3}$

6. $4\dfrac{1}{4} - 2\dfrac{2}{3} + 7\dfrac{2}{5}$

Math Tip

Process of Elimination: If you are working with a problem that requires lots of work with fractions, you can eliminate the answers that do not have the right denominator, which should be either the least common denominator or a simplified version of it.

Lesson 6 – Fractions

6.3.2 Fraction Operations

1. _____

2. _____

3. _____

---

1. $\dfrac{1}{2} \div \dfrac{3}{4}$

2. $\dfrac{4}{5} \div \dfrac{2}{3}$

3. $\dfrac{7}{11} \div \dfrac{1}{22}$

4. $\dfrac{5}{7} \div \dfrac{6}{13}$

5. $\dfrac{3}{5} \div \dfrac{5}{12}$

6.3.3 Ordering Fractions

1. $\dfrac{1}{3}, \dfrac{5}{12}, \dfrac{1}{5}, \dfrac{3}{7}, \dfrac{4}{13}$

2. $\dfrac{3}{4}, \dfrac{1}{6}, \dfrac{4}{11}, \dfrac{5}{8}, \dfrac{1}{9}$

3. $\dfrac{1}{2}, \dfrac{7}{8}, \dfrac{2}{7}, \dfrac{1}{5}, \dfrac{2}{3}$

4. $\dfrac{4}{9}, -\dfrac{2}{3}, \dfrac{1}{12}, -\dfrac{4}{5}, \dfrac{3}{10}$

5. $\dfrac{7}{10}, -0.5, -\dfrac{1}{3}, \dfrac{5}{12}, 0.45$

Math Tip

Process of Elimination: If an ACT math question asks you to order fractions, begin with the first choice and compare two fractions at a time. As soon as you find one fraction in the wrong sequence, eliminate that answer choice. Don't waste time checking other fractions within that choice. If all of the comparisons work in a choice, you have found the correct answer.

Lesson 6 – Fractions

6.4.1 Set One

1. Lebron played $2\frac{1}{2}$ games of basketball on Friday and $3\frac{1}{3}$ games of basketball on Saturday. What is the total number of games Lebron played during those 2 days?

   A. $5\frac{1}{6}$

   B. $5\frac{1}{5}$

   C. $5\frac{1}{3}$

   D. $5\frac{2}{3}$

   E. $5\frac{5}{6}$

DO YOUR FIGURING HERE.

2. Scotty and Tyler are training for a pizza-eating contest. They are trying to eat 6 pizzas in total. So far, Scotty has eaten $2\frac{3}{4}$ pizzas and Tyler has eaten $1\frac{7}{8}$ pizzas. How much more pizza do they have left to eat?

   F. $\frac{3}{4}$

   G. $1\frac{3}{8}$

   H. $1\frac{3}{4}$

   J. $2\frac{3}{8}$

   K. $4\frac{5}{8}$

GO ON TO THE NEXT PAGE

3. Which of the following fractions is equal to $\dfrac{1}{12^{30}} - \dfrac{1}{12^{31}}$?

A. $\dfrac{1}{12^{31}}$

B. $\dfrac{1}{12^{32}}$

C. $\dfrac{1}{12^{60}}$

D. $\dfrac{11}{12^{31}}$

E. $\dfrac{11}{12^{61}}$

DO YOUR FIGURING HERE.

END OF SET ONE
STOP! DO NOT GO ON TO THE NEXT PAGE
UNTIL TOLD TO DO SO.

Lesson 6 – Fractions

6.4.2 Set Two

DO YOUR FIGURING HERE.

4. $\dfrac{1}{3 + \dfrac{1}{1 + \dfrac{1}{4}}} = ?$

   F. $\dfrac{4}{17}$

   G. $\dfrac{5}{19}$

   H. $\dfrac{5}{12}$

   J. $\dfrac{19}{5}$

   K. $\dfrac{17}{4}$

5. What fraction of $3\dfrac{1}{2}$ is $1\dfrac{1}{6}$?

   A. $\dfrac{1}{2}$

   B. $\dfrac{1}{3}$

   C. $\dfrac{1}{4}$

   D. $\dfrac{1}{8}$

   E. $\dfrac{1}{12}$

6. The expression $\dfrac{4 + \dfrac{1}{8}}{1 + \dfrac{1}{16}}$ is equal to:

   F. 3

   G. $3\dfrac{15}{17}$

   H. $4\dfrac{49}{128}$

   J. $5\dfrac{3}{16}$

   K. 8

END OF SET TWO
STOP! DO NOT GO ON TO THE NEXT PAGE
UNTIL TOLD TO DO SO.

6.4.3 Set Three

7. Which of the following lists orders $\frac{7}{9}$, 0.79, $\frac{2}{3}$, $\frac{7}{10}$, 0.71, and $\frac{3}{4}$ from least to greatest?

    A. $\frac{7}{9}$, 0.79, $\frac{2}{3}$, $\frac{7}{10}$, 0.71, $\frac{3}{4}$

    B. $\frac{7}{10}$, $\frac{2}{3}$, 0.71, $\frac{7}{9}$, $\frac{3}{4}$, 0.79

    C. $\frac{7}{10}$, $\frac{2}{3}$, 0.71, $\frac{3}{4}$, $\frac{7}{9}$, 0.79

    D. $\frac{2}{3}$, $\frac{7}{10}$, 0.71, $\frac{3}{4}$, $\frac{7}{9}$, 0.79

    E. $\frac{2}{3}$, $\frac{3}{4}$, $\frac{7}{9}$, 0.71, $\frac{7}{10}$, 0.79

DO YOUR FIGURING HERE.

8. Madeline is trying to measure the edge of a table with a tape measure. The table is somewhere between $32\frac{1}{4}$ inches and $32\frac{3}{8}$ inches. Which of the following could be the exact measurement of the table?

    F. $32\frac{1}{16}$

    G. $32\frac{3}{16}$

    H. $32\frac{1}{4}$

    J. $32\frac{5}{16}$

    K. $32\frac{7}{16}$

GO ON TO THE NEXT PAGE.

Lesson 6 – Fractions

9. Which of the following inequalities is true for the fractions $\frac{2}{5}$, $\frac{5}{13}$, and $\frac{3}{7}$?

   A. $\frac{5}{13} < \frac{2}{5} < \frac{3}{7}$

   B. $\frac{5}{13} < \frac{3}{7} < \frac{2}{5}$

   C. $\frac{2}{5} < \frac{3}{7} < \frac{5}{13}$

   D. $\frac{2}{5} < \frac{5}{13} < \frac{3}{7}$

   E. $\frac{3}{7} < \frac{2}{5} < \frac{5}{13}$

DO YOUR FIGURING HERE.

END OF SET THREE
STOP! DO NOT GO ON TO THE NEXT PAGE
UNTIL TOLD TO DO SO.

6.4.4 Set Four

10. Of the 627 coins in Jacob's coin jar, approximately $\frac{4}{5}$ are silver, and approximately $\frac{1}{10}$ of those coins that are silver are dimes. Which of the following is the closest estimate for the number of dimes in Jacob's coin jar?

    F. 50
    G. 100
    H. 125
    J. 250
    K. 500

11. When Elton was cleaning his garage, he found 2 bottles of motor oil. According to the labels, the capacity of the larger bottle was three times the capacity of the smaller bottle. He estimated that both the smaller bottle and the larger bottle were about $\frac{3}{4}$ full of motor oil. He poured all the motor oil from the smaller bottle into the larger bottle. Then, about how full was the larger bottle?

    A. $\frac{1}{4}$ full
    B. $\frac{9}{16}$ full
    C. $\frac{7}{8}$ full
    D. Completely full
    E. Overflowing

DO YOUR FIGURING HERE.

GO ON TO THE NEXT PAGE

Lesson 6 – Fractions

12. Pablo works in a factory and has to cut a rectangular metal rod into small cubes. The rod that he needs to cut is $1\frac{1}{4}$ inches by $1\frac{1}{4}$ inches by 8 feet (shown below), and he will cut it so that he will have cubes $1\frac{1}{4}$ inches on a side. He must allow an extra $\frac{1}{2}$ inch for each cut because his saw blade is $\frac{1}{2}$ inch wide. Assuming that the metal rod has no flaws, what is the maximum number of cubes he can make from his 8-foot piece of metal?

DO YOUR FIGURING HERE.

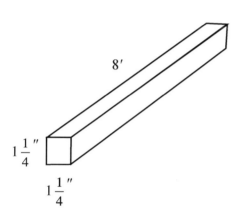

F. 46
G. 55
H. 58
J. 102
K. 118

END OF SET FOUR
STOP! DO NOT GO ON TO THE NEXT PAGE
UNTIL TOLD TO DO SO.

6.4.5 Set Five

13. Zack is taking inventory of loaves of bread at the grocery store where he works. There are 20 loaves in a full case, and Zack has 3 partially filled cases: 1 case is $\frac{1}{2}$ full, 1 case is $\frac{1}{4}$ full, and 1 case is $\frac{2}{5}$ full. How many total loaves of bread are in the 3 partially filled cases?

- A. 11
- B. 16
- C. 19
- D. 23
- E. 30

DO YOUR FIGURING HERE.

14. Which of the following gives the fractions $-\frac{5}{7}$, $-\frac{9}{11}$, and $-\frac{3}{4}$ in order from least to greatest?

- F. $-\frac{5}{7}, -\frac{9}{11}, -\frac{3}{4}$
- G. $-\frac{3}{4}, -\frac{9}{11}, -\frac{5}{7}$
- H. $-\frac{3}{4}, -\frac{5}{7}, -\frac{9}{11}$
- J. $-\frac{9}{11}, -\frac{5}{7}, -\frac{3}{4}$
- K. $-\frac{9}{11}, -\frac{3}{4}, -\frac{5}{7}$

GO ON TO THE NEXT PAGE

15. Savion is eating a pizza for lunch. He eats $\frac{5}{8}$ of it and gives the remaining pizza to his 2 coworkers. What fraction of the whole pizza will each of Savion's coworkers get if they share the remaining pizza equally?

A. $\frac{1}{16}$

B. $\frac{1}{8}$

C. $\frac{3}{16}$

D. $\frac{3}{8}$

E. $\frac{3}{2}$

DO YOUR FIGURING HERE.

END OF SET FIVE
STOP! DO NOT GO ON TO THE NEXT PAGE
UNTIL TOLD TO DO SO.

ACT® Mastery Math

Sum It Up

Fractions

Fraction
A number that represents a part of a whole

Numerator
The top number of a fraction

Denominator
The bottom number of a fraction

Reciprocal
A number that is related to another number so that their product is equal to 1

Least Common Multiple (LCM)
For any two numbers, the lowest number that has both as factors

Least Common Denominator (LCD)
The smallest denominator two fractions can share

Greatest Common Factor (GCF)
For any two numbers, the largest number that is divisible into both

Mixed Number
A number consisting of a whole number and a fraction

Tips and Techniques

Process of Elimination: Eliminate any answers that either have the wrong denominators or break the order asked for in the question.

Lesson 7

Operations

A chef needs to cook 16 potatoes. He has already cooked 7. If each potato takes 5 minutes to cook, how long will it take him to cook the rest?

CAPTION:

ACT® Mastery Math

7.1 Entrance Ticket

Solve the questions below.

1. Calculate the average speed of an airplane, in miles per hour, if it travels 1,000 miles in $2\frac{1}{2}$ hours.
   A. 400
   B. 500
   C. 750
   D. 1,000
   E. 2,500

2. Sandra has a cuckoo clock. At every hour, the cuckoo comes out and chirps: once for 1 o'clock, twice for 2 o'clock, and so on. There is a 3-second pause between consecutive chirps. At 11 o'clock, how many seconds elapse between the first and the last chirp?
   F. 10
   G. 11
   H. 14
   J. 30
   K. 33

3. Leroy invented a new game in which goals are worth 8 points if they are scored in the first 30 minutes of the game. Every goal scored after 30 minutes is worth $2\frac{1}{2}$ times the regular value. How many points does Leroy have if he scores one goal in each minute of a 39-minute game?
   A. 312
   B. 366
   C. 420
   D. 600
   E. 780

Lesson 7 – Operations

7.2 Learning Targets

1. Solve word problems using addition or subtraction

2. Solve word problems using multiplication or division

Self-Assessment

Circle the number that corresponds to your confidence level in your knowledge of this subject before beginning the lesson. A score of 1 means you are completely lost, and a score of 4 means you have mastered the skills. After you finish the lesson, return to the bottom of this page and circle your new confidence level to show your improvement.

Before Lesson

1   2   3   4

After Lesson

1   2   3   4

ACT® Mastery Math

7.3.1 Addition/Subtraction Word Problems

When solving a word problem:

1. _____

2. _____

3. _____

Example:

During a road trip, a car shifts from 25 feet, with respect to sea level, to −15 feet, with respect to sea level. By how many feet has the car descended?

A. 10
B. 15
C. 25
D. 30
E. 40

Operations:

_____

_____

_____

Lesson 7 – Operations

7.3.1 Addition/Subtraction Word Problems

1. When the Jackson family boarded a plane for vacation, the temperature at the airport was 27° Celsius. When they landed at the next airport, the temperature was −12° Celsius. If − denotes a drop in temperature and + denotes a rise in temperature, which of the following best describes the change in temperature from the time the Jackson family left for vacation until they arrived?
   A. +39°C
   B. +15°C
   C. +5°C
   D. −15°C
   E. −39°C

2. Before the Johnson family lit a fire on their camping trip, the temperature at the campsite was 27° Celsius. When the fire was at full blaze, the temperature was −11° Celsius. If − denotes a drop in temperature and + denotes a rise in temperature, which of the following best describes the change in temperature from the time before the Johnson family lit the fire until it was at full blaze?
   F. +38°C
   G. +36°C
   H. +16°C
   J. −16°C
   K. −38°C

3. What is the value of 873 + 155 + 107, rounded to the nearest hundred?
   A. 1,200
   B. 1,100
   C. 1,000
   D. 900
   E. 800

4. What is the value of 322 + 724 + 808, rounded to the nearest hundred?
   F. 1,600
   G. 1,700
   H. 1,800
   J. 1,900
   K. 2,000

ACT® Mastery Math

7.3.1 Addition/Subtraction Word Problems

5. At 11 a.m., the temperature is −10°C. Meteorologists predict that the temperature will decrease 3°C per hour for the next 4 hours. What should be the temperature at 3 p.m. ?
   - A. −22°C
   - B. −13°C
   - C. −7°C
   - D. −6°C
   - E. 2°C

6. At 3 p.m., the temperature in the park is 76°F. For the next 2 hours, the temperature decreases 6°F per hour. What is the temperature at 5 p.m. ?
   - F. 64°F
   - G. 70°F
   - H. 74°F
   - J. 82°F
   - K. 88°F

Math Tip

Show Your Work: Most of the word problems that focus on operations have the easiest math you will find on the test. However, it is easy to make mistakes on these problems if you are not careful. Make sure you show your work, even if you think the question is simple. That way you will avoid needless mistakes.

7.3.2 Multiplication/Division Word Problems

When solving a multiplication word problem:

1. _____

2. _____

Example:

30 miles per hour · 120 minutes = 3,600 miles

Operations:

_____

_____

_____

ACT® Mastery Math

7.3.2 Multiplication/Division Word Problems

1. A snail traveled for exactly 25 seconds at an average speed of 0.80 meters per minute. Which of the following is closest to the total distance, in meters, traveled by the snail?
   A. 1.0
   B. 0.7
   C. 0.4
   D. 0.3
   E. 0.2

2. A taxi driver traveled at an average speed of 35 miles per hour and arrived at her destination in exactly 15 minutes. Which of the following is closest to the total number of miles she traveled?
   F. 5
   G. 7
   H. 9
   J. 15
   K. 18

3. Riding a bike at a constant pace of 30 seconds per third mile, how many minutes would it take to ride 4 miles?
   A. 6.0
   B. 3.6
   C. 2.0
   D. 1.5
   E. 1.2

4. Jogging at a constant pace of 150 seconds per quarter mile, how long would it take to run 3 miles, in minutes?
   F. 30.0
   G. 13.5
   H. 12.0
   J. 7.5
   K. 5.0

Lesson 7 – Operations

7.3.2 Multiplication/Division Word Problems

5. Chet rents a car for a month. It costs a $260 fixed charge to rent the car for one month and $8 for every 100 miles driven in it. Chet drove 3,000 miles in the rental car. What was his total bill for the car?
   A. $ 270
   B. $ 287
   C. $ 500
   D. $2,700
   E. $2,960

6. A small hardware store pays for the electricity it uses. The monthly cost is a fixed charge of $200 plus $12 for every 100 units of electricity used. Last month, the store used 1,200 units of electricity. What was the total cost of electricity for the store last month?
   F. $ 144
   G. $ 214.40
   H. $ 344
   J. $1,440
   K. $1,640

Math Tip

Show Your Work: Many multiplication word problems will try to confuse you with different kinds of units. Be sure to set the problem up by labeling all of the units before you start your calculations.

ACT® Mastery Math

7.3.2 Multiplication/Division Word Problems

1. Bud needs to grow 700 roses for the local farmers market. If Bud knows that the seeds he is planting will yield, on average, 1.25 roses per square foot, Bud needs to plant how many square feet of seeds?
   A. 125
   B. 280
   C. 560
   D. 700
   E. 875

2. A cyclist traveled at an average speed of 18 miles per hour and finished her bike ride in exactly 4 minutes. Which of the following is closest to the number of miles she traveled?
   F. 1
   G. 2
   H. 4
   J. 5
   K. 9

3. A vintage baseball card was purchased 6 years ago for $1,860. The card is currently valued at $2,400. What was the card's average increase in value per year?
   A. $ 90
   B. $270
   C. $310
   D. $350
   E. $400

4. Anna bought her motorcycle 8 years ago for $5,320. It is now worth $2,840. What is the average decrease in value of the motorcycle per year?
   F. $ 310
   G. $ 355
   H. $ 620
   J. $ 665
   K. $1,240

Lesson 7 – Operations

7.3.2 Multiplication/Division Word Problems

5. Cole wants to work enough hours to buy a necklace that costs $370 dollars. He earns $11.25 per hour, and he has already worked 24 hours. What is the minimum number of whole hours that Cole must work in order to afford the necklace?

    A. 7
    B. 8
    C. 9
    D. 16
    E. 33

6. José wants to work enough hours to make at least $93 dollars this week (before taxes are deducted). He has a job that pays $7.25 per hour and has already worked 7 hours. If José can only work in full-hour increments, how many more full hours must he work to meet his weekly goal?

    F. 4
    G. 5
    H. 6
    J. 7
    K. 13

7.4.1 Set One

1. What is the value of 668 + 575 + 453, rounded to the nearest hundred?

   A. 1,100
   B. 1,200
   C. 1,500
   D. 1,600
   E. 1,700

2. An object placed in a super-cooling freezer cools from 33°F to −18°F. By how many degrees Fahrenheit has it cooled?

   F. 18°F
   G. 15°F
   H. 33°F
   J. 51°F
   K. 52°F

3. At 4:00 a.m., the temperature is −17°F. The temperature decreases 3°F per hour. What is the temperature at 6:00 a.m. ?

   A. −23°F
   B. −20°F
   C. −17°F
   D. −14°F
   E. −11°F

DO YOUR FIGURING HERE.

END OF SET ONE
STOP! DO NOT GO ON TO THE NEXT PAGE
UNTIL TOLD TO DO SO.

7.4.2 Set Two

4. When Kaitlyn went to bed, the temperature was 36°F. When she woke up the next morning, the temperature was −9°F. If + represents a rise in temperature and − represents a drop in temperature, which of the following best illustrates the temperature change from the time Kaitlyn went to bed to the time she woke up?

   F. −45°F
   G. −27°F
   H. −12°F
   J. 27°F
   K. 45°F

DO YOUR FIGURING HERE.

5. If boxes of pasta sell at $0.88 per box or 4 boxes for $3.00, how much is saved, to the nearest cent, on each box by buying the boxes 4 at a time?

   A. 12¢
   B. 13¢
   C. 39¢
   D. 52¢
   E. 53¢

6. Hair grows at an average rate of 0.5 inches per month. Courtney refused to cut her hair from the time she was 8 years old until she was 20 years old. If Courtney's hair grew at the average rate, approximately how many inches did her hair grow during the time she refused to cut her hair?

   F. 4
   G. 6
   H. 14
   J. 72
   K. 78

END OF SET TWO
STOP! DO NOT GO ON TO THE NEXT PAGE
UNTIL TOLD TO DO SO.

7.4.3 Set Three

7. Matt purchased a car for $31,400. Four years later, the car is worth $24,700. What was the car's average decrease in value per year?

   A. $1,675
   B. $2,233
   C. $3,350
   D. $3,375
   E. $5,000

DO YOUR FIGURING HERE.

8. Owen purchased 2 boxes of 16-ounce bottles of soap. Each box contained 10 bottles of soap. Owen could have purchased the same amount of soap by purchasing how many 20-ounce bottles?

   F. 8
   G. 10
   H. 16
   J. 20
   K. 24

9. A dog adoption agency is holding a function on the weekend at which families can adopt puppies. On Friday, 3 puppies were adopted; 7 puppies were adopted on Saturday; and 6 were adopted on Sunday. By the end of the weekend, the agency was left with 2 more than a quarter of the puppies they originally had. How many puppies did the adoption agency originally have?

   A. 20
   B. 21
   C. 22
   D. 23
   E. 24

END OF SET THREE
STOP! DO NOT GO ON TO THE NEXT PAGE
UNTIL TOLD TO DO SO.

7.4.4 Set Four

10. Charles ran 30 feet in 4 seconds. At this rate, how many *yards* can Charles run in 3 *minutes*?
    F. 120
    G. 270
    H. 360
    J. 450
    K. 600

11. Joe Watson is a car mechanic who has earned $14,875 doing one car inspection per day since he started working 175 days ago. Joe decides to take off for vacation, and his temporary replacement charges $135 per inspection at one inspection per day. While Joe Watson is on vacation, how many more dollars do the customers spend per day on car inspections?
    A. 40
    B. 50
    C. 60
    D. 75
    E. 85

12. Carlos was accepted to a university that has a tuition cost of $33,000 per year. He took out a loan from the bank for the entire $33,000 and made loan payments of $415 per month for 8 years. After the 8-year period, how much more than the tuition cost did Carlos pay?
    F. $6,840
    G. $4,980
    H. $4,860
    J. $3,320
    K. $3,120

DO YOUR FIGURING HERE.

END OF SET FOUR
STOP! DO NOT GO ON TO THE NEXT PAGE
UNTIL TOLD TO DO SO.

7.4.5 Set Five

13. Jay has 12 classic cars in his garage. He paid $3,500 for each car 5 years ago. The cars are currently worth $4,200 each. How much more must the average value of the cars rise for the combined value of these 12 cars to be exactly $10,800 more than Jay paid for them?

    A. $200.00
    B. $700.00
    C. $800.50
    D. $841.67
    E. $958.33

DO YOUR FIGURING HERE.

14. Trevor and his siblings want to get professional pictures taken for their parents' anniversary. They spend the day finding the location with the best price. They have exactly $150 to spend on the photographs. Snap! Photo Center charges a general fee of $75 and $1.25 per photo proof. Say Gouda Photo Center charges a general fee of $60 and $1.50 per photo proof. Which photo center, if either, allows Trevor and his siblings to get more photo proofs, and how many more proofs?

    F. Snap!, 25
    G. Snap!, 90
    H. Say Gouda, 10
    J. Say Gouda, 15
    K. Trevor and his siblings would get the same maximum number of proofs from each photo center.

15. A train leaves the station traveling at 40 miles per hour. A second train leaves the station traveling at 60 miles per hour. The second train leaves the station 2 hours after the first train leaves. Both trains stop traveling 4 hours after the first train left. Together, the two trains traveled how many miles?

    A. 160
    B. 200
    C. 240
    D. 280
    E. 400

END OF SET FIVE
STOP! DO NOT GO ON TO THE NEXT PAGE
UNTIL TOLD TO DO SO.

Lesson 7 – Operations

Sum It Up

Operations

Indicating Words:

Addition
Sum, combined, plus, added to, total of, more, both, in all, raise, etc.

Subtraction
Difference, drop, decreased by, fewer than, minus, less, left, remaining, take away, etc.

Multiplication
Product, of, multiplied by, times, triple, twice, etc.

Division
Per, divided by, out of, half, etc.

Solving Word Problems:

When solving a word problem:
1. Identify the operation you need to use.
2. Translate the problem into an equation, identifying the value you are solving for.
3. Solve the equation, paying attention to units.

When solving multiplication word problems:
1. Identify the two things that you are multiplying together.
2. Make sure the units are the same.

When solving division word problems:
Set up a proportion if it helps you keep track of units and how different parts relate to one another.

Tips and Techniques

Show Your Work: Be sure to set up all the units and solve the questions carefully. Remember that the easier the question is, the more likely you are to make a simple mistake. Be sure to show your work.

Lesson 8

Substitution

CAPTION:

8.1 Entrance Ticket

Solve the questions below.

1. If $x = -2$, then $x + 4 = $?
   - A. -6
   - B. -2
   - C. 0
   - D. 2
   - E. 6

2. When $x = 3$, what is the value of $x^2 - 4$?
   - F. -1
   - G. 2
   - H. 5
   - J. 9
   - K. 13

3. What is the value of the expression $2x^2 + x$, if x is 3 ?
   - A. 9
   - B. 18
   - C. 21
   - D. 27
   - E. 39

Lesson 8 – Substitution

8.2 Learning Targets

1. Use substitution to find the value of expressions

2. Correctly add, subtract, multiply, and divide negative numbers

3. Correctly use the order of operations

Self-Assessment

Circle the number that corresponds to your confidence level in your knowledge of this subject before beginning the lesson. A score of 1 means you are completely lost, and a score of 4 means you have mastered the skills. After you finish the lesson, return to the bottom of this page and circle your new confidence level to show your improvement.

Before Lesson

1   2   3   4

After Lesson

1   2   3   4

Entrance Ticket   Learning Targets   Order of Operations   Negative Paranoia   ACT Practice   Sum It Up

8.3.1 Order of Operations

P = _____

E = _____

MD = _____ and _____

AS = _____ and _____

Math Tip

Show Your Work: Many answer choices are designed to catch your mistakes and cause you to lose out on points. That is why you must show your work whenever you solve.

Lesson 8 – Substitution

8.3.1 Order of Operations

1. If $x = 6$, what is the value of $2x^2 - 11x$?
   A. −138
   B. −6
   C. 6
   D. 90
   E. 138

2. What is the value of the expression $x(x + 3)^2$, if $x = 2$?
   F. 20
   G. 25
   H. 27
   J. 50
   K. 72

3. If $x = -5$, what is the value of $\dfrac{x^2 + 1}{x^2 - 1}$?

   A. −1
   B. $-\dfrac{9}{11}$
   C. $\dfrac{9}{11}$
   D. $\dfrac{12}{13}$
   E. $\dfrac{13}{12}$

Math Tip

Two Wrongs Make a Right: Remember that multiplying or dividing two negatives will result in a positive value. Also, subtracting a negative number is the same as adding the positive version of that number.

Entrance Ticket   Learning Targets   Order of Operations   Negative Paranoia   ACT Practice   Sum It Up

8.3.2 Negative Paranoia

$6 + (-2) =$

Rule: _____

_____

$6 - (-2) =$

Rule: _____

_____

$6 \cdot (-2) =$

Rule: _____

_____

$\dfrac{6}{-2} =$

Rule: _____

_____

$(-6) \cdot (-2) =$

Rule: _____

_____

$\dfrac{-6}{-2} =$

Rule: _____

_____

$(-2)^2 =$

Rule: _____

_____

$(-2)^3 =$

Rule: _____

_____

Lesson 8 – Substitution

8.3.2 Negative Paranoia

1. If $x = -3$, what is the value of $(x + 2)(x - 4)$?

2. If $x = -1$, what is the value of $(2 - x)(4 - x)$?

3. If $x = -2$, what is the value of $\dfrac{(x-1)^2}{(x+1)^3}$?

8.4.1 Set One

1. If $a = 0.3$ and $b = 0.9$, then $a^2 b^2 = ?$
   A. 0.0729
   B. 0.09
   C. 0.243
   D. 0.27
   E. 0.81

DO YOUR FIGURING HERE.

2. What is the value of the expression $2c(c + 3)^2$ if $c = 2$?
   F. 5
   G. 20
   H. 25
   J. 40
   K. 100

3. Given that $x = \frac{1}{3}$ and $y = \frac{1}{4}$, what is the value of $2\left(\frac{1}{x} - \frac{1}{y}\right)$?

   A. -2
   B. $\frac{1}{6}$
   C. 2
   D. 7
   E. 14

END OF SET ONE
STOP! DO NOT GO ON TO THE NEXT PAGE UNTIL TOLD TO DO SO.

Lesson 8 – Substitution

8.4.2 Set Two

4. What is the value of the expression $(a - b)^3$ when $a = 3$ and $b = 4$?

   F. −3
   G. −1
   H. 1
   J. 3
   K. 27

   DO YOUR FIGURING HERE.

5. If $x = 6$ and $y = 3$, what is the value of the following expression?

   $$\frac{y^2(x+y)^2(y-x)}{y(x-y)}$$

   A. −243
   B. −81
   C. 27
   D. 81
   E. 243

6. If $a = 2$, $b = 5$, and $c = -1$, what is the value of $\dfrac{ab - ac}{c^3}$?

   F. −20
   G. −12
   H. −8
   J. 8
   K. 12

   END OF SET TWO
   STOP! DO NOT GO ON TO THE NEXT PAGE
   UNTIL TOLD TO DO SO.

8.4.3 Set Three

7. What is the value of the expression $(2x + y)(2x - y)$ when $x = 4$ and $y = -5$?

   A. -9
   B. 9
   C. 13
   D. 16
   E. 39

DO YOUR FIGURING HERE.

8. If $x = -3$, what is the value of $\dfrac{x^2 + x}{x^2 - x}$?

   F. -2

   G. -1

   H. $\dfrac{1}{2}$

   J. $\dfrac{3}{4}$

   K. 2

9. What is the value of $50 - 3(x^2 - y^2) + x$ when $x = 6$ and $y = -4$?

   A. -145
   B. -6
   C. -4
   D. 26
   E. 44

END OF SET THREE
STOP! DO NOT GO ON TO THE NEXT PAGE
UNTIL TOLD TO DO SO.

Lesson 8 – Substitution

8.4.4 Set Four

DO YOUR FIGURING HERE.

10. If $y = -4$, what is the value of $\dfrac{y^2 + 2}{y^2 - 2}$?

   F. $-\dfrac{5}{3}$

   G. -1

   H. $\dfrac{7}{9}$

   J. $\dfrac{9}{7}$

   K. $\dfrac{5}{3}$

11. If $x = 15$, $y = -3$, and $z = -2$, what is the value of $\dfrac{x - y}{yz} + x$?

   A. 2
   B. 3
   C. 17
   D. 18
   E. 45

12. If $a = -2$, $b = 3$, and $c = 6$, then $3a^2b^2 - 4ac + c^2 = $?

   F. 36
   G. 48
   H. 96
   J. 192
   K. 228

END OF SET FOUR
STOP! DO NOT GO ON TO THE NEXT PAGE
UNTIL TOLD TO DO SO.

Entrance Ticket   Learning Targets   Order of Operations   Negative Paranoia   ACT Practice   Sum It Up

8.4.5 Set Five

13. If $a = 11$, $b = 3$, and $c = -3$, what does $(a + b - c)(b + c)$ equal?

    A. −17
    B. −11
    C.   0
    D. 17
    E. 102

DO YOUR FIGURING HERE.

14. If $q = -1$, $r = 4$, and $s = 7$, what does $(q + r - s)(r - q)$ equal?

    F. −60
    G. −20
    H. −12
    J. −10
    K. −6

15. If $f = -3$, $g = -5$, and $h = 7$, what does $(f + g + h)(2f + h)$ equal?

    A. −13
    B. −11
    C. −1
    D.   1
    E. 11

END OF SET FIVE
STOP! DO NOT GO ON TO THE NEXT PAGE
UNTIL TOLD TO DO SO.

Lesson 8 – Substitution

Sum It Up

Substitution

Value
A number or measurement

Expression
A group of numbers, symbols, and operations that indicate a value

Tips and Techniques

Show Your Work: Many answer choices are designed to catch your mistakes and cause you to lose out on points. That is why you must show your work whenever you solve.

Two Wrongs Make a Right: Remember that multiplying or dividing two negatives will result in a positive value. Also, subtracting a negative number is the same as adding the positive version of that number.

Lesson 9

Averages, Median, Mode, and Range

CAPTION:

ACT® Mastery Math

9.1 Entrance Ticket

Solve the questions below.

1. The table below gives the price per gallon of whole milk at ShopQuik Grocery Store on January 1 over the last 7 years. What is the mean price per gallon of whole milk, to the nearest cent, on January 1 for the 7 years listed in the table?

Year	Price
2009	$3.58
2010	$3.24
2011	$3.30
2012	$3.58
2013	$3.53
2014	$3.55
2015	$3.76

   A. $3.24
   B. $3.49
   C. $3.51
   D. $3.58
   E. $3.78

2. Fabio's scores on the first 4 tests in his marine biology class were 77, 92, 97, and 84. How many points must Fabio score on the fifth test to average exactly 89 points for these 5 equally weighted tests?
   F. 95
   G. 96
   H. 97
   J. 98
   K. 99

3. The median of a set of data containing 7 items was found. Four data items were added to the set. Of these items, 2 were greater than the original median, and the other 2 items were less than the original median. Which of the following statements must be true about the median of the new data set?
   A. It is less than the original median.
   B. It is the same as the original median.
   C. It is greater than the original median.
   D. It is the average of the 4 new values.
   E. It is the average of the 11 total values in the new data set.

Entrance Ticket | Learning Targets | Using Averages | Using Median, Mode, and Range | ACT Practice | Sum It Up

Lesson 9 – Averages, Median, Mode, and Range

9.2 Learning Targets

1. Solve simple and complex problems involving averages (mean)

2. Recognize the differences between median, mode, and range, and solve related problems

Self-Assessment

Circle the number that corresponds to your confidence level in your knowledge of this subject before beginning the lesson. A score of 1 means you are completely lost, and a score of 4 means you have mastered the skills. After you finish the lesson, return to the bottom of this page and circle your new confidence level to show your improvement.

Before Lesson

1   2   3   4

After Lesson

1   2   3   4

ACT® Mastery Math

9.3.1 Using Averages

Scenario 1 — Science test scores:

_____   _____   _____   _____   _____   _____   _____   _____

Final Answer: _____

Scenario 2 — Pizza parlor profits:

_____   _____   _____   _____   _____

Final Answer: _____

Math Tip

Process of Elimination: When looking for an average on an ACT math question, if an answer choice is outside the middle range or far away from most of the data, it's probably wrong.

Entrance Ticket | Learning Targets | Using Averages | Using Median, Mode, and Range | ACT Practice | Sum It Up

Lesson 9 – Averages, Median, Mode, and Range

9.3.1 Using Averages

Scenario 1 — Number of eggs:

_____ _____ _____ _____ _____ _____ _____

Final Answer: _____

Scenario 2 — Volunteer hours:

_____ _____ _____ _____ _____ _____ _____

Final Answer: _____

Math Tip

Plug In: If you don't know how to set up an average problem, try to plug in the answers. Start with the middle choice and determine whether it is correct. If it is too large, eliminate it and the larger numbers. If it is too small, eliminate it and the smaller numbers. If it is just right, mark it and move on.

Entrance Ticket   Learning Targets   Using Averages   Using Median, Mode, and Range   ACT Practice   Sum It Up

9.3.2 Using Median, Mode, and Range

median: _____

new median: _____

mode = _____

mode: _____

range = _____

range: _____

Lesson 9 – Averages, Median, Mode, and Range

9.4.1 Set One

1. For the first 7 days of January, the daily low temperatures for Burlington were 20°, 14°, 9°, 8°, −8°, −11°, and −4° Fahrenheit. What was the average daily low temperature, in degrees Fahrenheit, for those 7 days?

   A. −1°
   B. 0°
   C. 1°
   D. 4°
   E. 6°

DO YOUR FIGURING HERE.

2. To determine a student's overall homework score for the semester, Mr. Daley drops the 2 lowest homework scores and takes the average of the remaining homework scores. Payton earned the following homework scores in Mr. Daley's class this semester: 85, 56, 67, 90, 95, 86, 0, 83, 100, and 88. What is the overall homework score that Payton earned in Mr. Daley's class this semester? Round your answer to the nearest tenth of a point.

   F. 69.4
   G. 77.1
   H. 86.8
   J. 88.0
   K. 99.1

3. Sydney earned 91, 93, 93, 94, and 96 points on the 5 essays—each out of a total of 100 points—given so far this semester. How many points must she earn on her sixth essay, which is also out of 100 points, to average 90 points for the six essays assigned this semester?

   A. 73
   B. 80
   C. 86
   D. 90
   E. 93

END OF SET ONE
STOP! DO NOT GO ON TO THE NEXT PAGE
UNTIL TOLD TO DO SO.

9.4.2 Set Two

4. What is the mean of the following scores?
   5, 93, 64, 45, 58, 13, 58
   - F. 46
   - G. 48
   - H. 52
   - J. 54
   - K. 58

5. What is the average of 4, 4, and 5 ?
   - A. 4
   - B. $4\frac{1}{3}$
   - C. $4\frac{1}{2}$
   - D. 5
   - E. $5\frac{2}{3}$

6. The stem-and-leaf plot below shows the number of points a basketball player with the New Orleans Krewe scored in each of his 15 games.

Stem	Leaf
0	8
1	0 4 7 7 7 8 9
2	3 5 5 6 8
3	1 2

   (Note: For example, 20 points would have a stem value of 2 and a leaf value of 0.)

   Which of the following is closest to the mean number of points the player scored per game?
   - F. 4.7
   - G. 15.0
   - H. 15.8
   - J. 20.0
   - K. 20.7

DO YOUR FIGURING HERE.

END OF SET TWO
STOP! DO NOT GO ON TO THE NEXT PAGE UNTIL TOLD TO DO SO.

Lesson 9 – Averages, Median, Mode, and Range

9.4.3 Set Three

7. George was absent for the last accounting test. For those who took the test, the mean was 75.8, the median was 74, and the mode was 81. When George took the test later, his score was different from all the other students' scores, and the class mean went up to exactly 76.6. What effect, if any, did George's score have on the class mode?

   A. None, the mode stayed the same.
   B. It decreased the mode exactly 0.8 points.
   C. It increased the mode exactly 0.8 points.
   D. It increased the mode more than 0.8 points.
   E. The effect of George's score on the mode cannot be determined from the given information.

DO YOUR FIGURING HERE.

8. What is the median of the following 9 numbers?
   66, 29, 31, 49, 65, 13, 80, 13, 24

   F. 13
   G. 31
   H. 41.1
   J. 65
   K. 80

9. Julia started exercising August 1 because she wanted to prepare for volleyball season. For 7 days, she recorded the number of pushups she did each day in the table below. What was the range of pushups Julia did during the first 7 days of August?

August	1	2	3	4	5	6	7
Number of pushups	50	75	75	100	130	140	165

   A. 75
   B. 100
   C. 105
   D. 115
   E. 135

END OF SET THREE
STOP! DO NOT GO ON TO THE NEXT PAGE
UNTIL TOLD TO DO SO.

9.4.4 Set Four

10. The table below shows the scoring patterns of 4 different basketball players over the last 5 games. The table gives the number of points each player scored in each game. Which player has the greatest range in points given in the table, and what is that range, in points?

Player A	Player B	Player C	Player D
9	13	15	12
3	22	35	27
7	33	14	22
19	34	24	8
16	23	12	24

F. Player A; 16
G. Player B; 21
H. Player B; 25
J. Player C; 23
K. Player D; 19

DO YOUR FIGURING HERE.

11. The following chart shows the current enrollment for all the youth football teams offered in Arlington.

Division	Team	Enrollment
Cadet	A	35
Junior Peewee	A	32
	B	33
Peewee	A	41
	B	34
	C	36

What is the average number of players enrolled per team in the Peewee division?

A. 34
B. 35
C. 36
D. 37
E. 41

GO ON TO THE NEXT PAGE

Lesson 9 – Averages, Median, Mode, and Range

12. The table below shows information about a car dealership over a 4-year period. The table shows the number of employees on staff, the number of cars sold, and the amount of sales the company made.

Year	Employees	Cars Sold	Sales
2000	39	10	$70,500
2001	40	16	$111,000
2002	44	19	$128,250
2003	51	25	$166,000

To the nearest dollar, what was the average price of a car sold in 2001 ?

F. $2,775
G. $6,640
H. $6,750
J. $6,938
K. $7,050

DO YOUR FIGURING HERE.

END OF SET FOUR
STOP! DO NOT GO ON TO THE NEXT PAGE
UNTIL TOLD TO DO SO.

9.4.5 Set Five

13. Caitlin has earned the following scores on four 100-point tests this year: 94, 81, 87, and 90. What score must Caitlin earn on the fifth and final 100-point test to earn an average score of 90 for the 5 tests?

   A. 90
   B. 92
   C. 96
   D. 98
   E. Caitlin cannot earn an average of 90.

14. A data set contains 6 numbers and has a mean of 6. Five of the numbers are 8, 7, 5, 9, and 4. What is the sixth number in this data set?

   F. 3
   G. 4
   H. 5
   J. 6
   K. 7

15. The table below shows the quarterly sales totals (in thousands of dollars) for a company over a 4-year period. The company's CEO set a sales goal of $140,000 for the quarterly average in 2008. To meet this goal, what must be the minimum fourth-quarter sales in 2008, in thousands of dollars?

Year	Q1	Q2	Q3	Q4
2005	85	89	80	93
2006	100	107	95	115
2007	122	129	125	134
2008	140	143	136	

   A. 138
   B. 139
   C. 140
   D. 141
   E. 142

DO YOUR FIGURING HERE.

END OF SET FIVE
STOP! DO NOT GO ON TO THE NEXT PAGE
UNTIL TOLD TO DO SO.

Lesson 9 – Averages, Median, Mode, and Range

Sum It Up

Averages, Median, Mode, and Range

Data
Pieces of information that can be used for research or analysis

Average (or *mean*)
A calculation of the center of a set of data

$$\frac{\text{sum of all data items in a set}}{\text{total number of data items}}$$

Median
The middle data item in a set

Mode
The number that appears most often in a data set

Range
The difference between the largest number and the smallest number in a data set

Tips and Techniques

Process of Elimination: If an answer choice is outside the middle range or far away from most of the data, it is probably wrong.

Plug In: If you don't know how to set up an average problem, try to plug in the answers. Start with the middle choice and determine whether it is correct. If it is too big, eliminate it and the bigger numbers. If it is too small, eliminate it and the smaller numbers. If it is just right, mark it and move on.

Lesson 10

Perimeter and Line Segments

CAPTION:

10.1 Entrance Ticket

Write a paragraph that answers the following question using complete sentences: What is the perimeter of this room? How did you make your estimate?

Lesson 10 – Perimeter and Line Segments

10.2 Learning Targets

1. Determine the perimeter of shapes

2. Determine the length of line segments

Self-Assessment

Circle the number that corresponds to your confidence level in your knowledge of this subject before beginning the lesson. A score of 1 means you are completely lost, and a score of 4 means you have mastered the skills. After you finish the lesson, return to the bottom of this page and circle your new confidence level to show your improvement.

Before Lesson

1   2   3   4

After Lesson

1   2   3   4

10.3.1 Perimeter

Shelving Cost: _____

Total Cost: _____

Lesson 10 – Perimeter and Line Segments

10.3.1 Perimeter

Perimeter: _____

Perimeter: _____

Perimeter: _____

Length: _____

10.3.1 Perimeter

A triangle $\triangle ABC$ has a perimeter of 22 centimeters with a side that is 7 centimeters long. The lengths of the remaining two sides have a ratio of 2:3. What is the length, in centimeters, of the shortest side of the triangle?

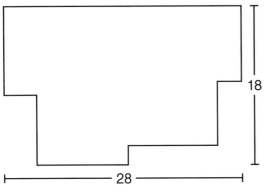

Perimeter: _____

Math Tip

Draw It Out: Most of the perimeter questions can be solved by drawing the shapes and labeling them carefully. If the ACT does not give you the figure or label all of the information, just draw it out.

Lesson 10 – Perimeter and Line Segments

10.3.2 Line Segments

Points X and Y lie on $\overline{WZ}$, as shown below. The length of $\overline{WZ}$ is 12 units, $\overline{WY}$ is 8 units long, and $\overline{XZ}$ is 10 units long. How many units long, if it can be determined, is $\overline{XY}$?

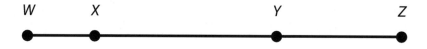

Marie is centering a tapestry on her living room wall. As shown in the figure below, the rectangular wall is 36 feet in length, and the tapestry is 4 feet in height and 8 feet in length. The right edge of the tapestry will be x feet from the right edge of the wall, and the left edge of the tapestry will also be x feet from the left edge of the wall. What is the value of x, in feet?

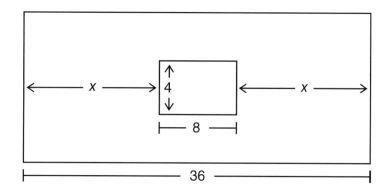

10.4.1 Set One

1. The Summersdale Community Council is planning the renovation of a park in the center of the town. The park will be a rectangular region of 85 feet by 175 feet with an area of 14,875 square feet. There will be a wooden fence along the perimeter of the park. What is the total length of the fence, in feet?

   A. 250
   B. 340
   C. 410
   D. 480
   E. 520

2. The length of a rectangle is 8 inches longer than its width. If the perimeter of the rectangle is 36 inches, what is the width, in inches?

   F. 13
   G. 10
   H. 5
   J. 4
   K. 3

3. The figure below is composed of equilateral triangle $\triangle ABD$ and another equilateral triangle $\triangle BCD$. The length of $\overline{AD}$ is 12 inches. What is the perimeter of figure $ABCD$?

   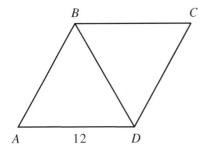

   A. 12
   B. 24
   C. 44
   D. 48
   E. 60

END OF SET ONE
STOP! DO NOT GO ON TO THE NEXT PAGE
UNTIL TOLD TO DO SO.

10.4.2 Set Two

4. A certain square has the same perimeter as a regular pentagon (a 5-sided polygon with all sides and interior angles congruent). If 1 side of the pentagon is 72 millimeters, how many millimeters long is 1 side of this square?

   F. 45
   G. 60
   H. 75
   J. 90
   K. 135

5. The polygon below, whose side lengths are given in meters, has 2 unknown sides. Each angle between adjacent sides measures 90°. What is the polygon's perimeter, in meters?

   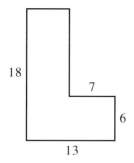

   A. 44
   B. 62
   C. 80
   D. 158
   E. 234

6. Joseph is constructing a rectangular fence for his garden. A diagram of the fence is shown below. Which of the following expressions gives the perimeter of Joseph's fence?

   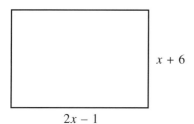

   F. $3x + 5$
   G. $3x + 10$
   H. $6x + 10$
   J. $6x + 20$
   K. $2x^2 + 11x - 6$

DO YOUR FIGURING HERE.

END OF SET TWO
STOP! DO NOT GO ON TO THE NEXT PAGE
UNTIL TOLD TO DO SO.

10.4.3 Set Three

7. Points A, B, C, and D lie on a line in the given order. Point C is the midpoint of $\overline{BD}$, $\overline{AC}$ is 10 mm long, and $\overline{AD}$ is 15 mm long. How many millimeters long is $\overline{BD}$?

   A. 5
   B. 8
   C. 10
   D. 12
   E. 15

8. Justin is centering a mosaic on his bedroom wall. As shown in the figure below, the rectangular wall is 28 feet in length, and the mosaic is 3 feet in height and 6 feet in length. The right edge of the mosaic will be y feet from the right edge of the wall, and the left edge of the mosaic will also be y feet from the left edge of the wall. What is the value of y, in feet?

   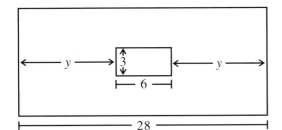

   F. 9
   G. 10
   H. 10.5
   J. 11
   K. 12.5

9. For the line segment below, the ratio of the length of $\overline{XY}$ to the length of $\overline{YZ}$ is 1:6. If it can be determined, what is the ratio of the length of $\overline{XY}$ to the length of $\overline{XZ}$?

   A. 1:5
   B. 1:7
   C. 3:1
   D. 7:1
   E. Cannot be determined from the given information

END OF SET THREE
STOP! DO NOT GO ON TO THE NEXT PAGE
UNTIL TOLD TO DO SO.

10.4.4 Set Four

10. A triangle $\triangle ABC$ has a perimeter of 53 centimeters with a side that is 18 centimeters long. The lengths of the remaining two sides have a ratio of 3:4. What is the length, in centimeters, of the shortest side of the triangle?

    F. 15
    G. 18
    H. 20
    J. 36
    K. 40

11. On the line segment below, the ratio of the length of $\overline{TU}$ to the length of $\overline{UV}$ is 4:7. If it can be determined, what is the ratio of the length of $\overline{TU}$ to the length of $\overline{TV}$?

    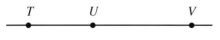

    A. 1:7
    B. 2:11
    C. 4:11
    D. 11:4
    E. Cannot be determined from the given information

12. Points X and Y lie on $\overline{WZ}$ as shown below. The length of $\overline{WZ}$ is 36 inches; $\overline{WY}$ is 16 inches long; and $\overline{XZ}$ is 28 inches long. How many inches long, if it can be determined is $\overline{XY}$?

    F. 4
    G. 8
    H. 12
    J. 16
    K. Cannot be determined from the given information

END OF SET FOUR
STOP! DO NOT GO ON TO THE NEXT PAGE UNTIL TOLD TO DO SO.

10.4.5 Set Five

13. In the figure shown below, each pair of intersecting line segments meets at a right angle, and all lengths are given in millimeters. What is the perimeter, in millimeters, of the given figure?

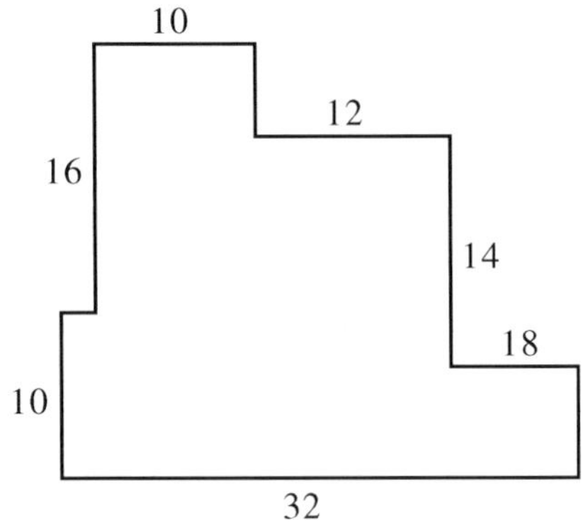

DO YOUR FIGURING HERE.

A. 80
B. 88
C. 96
D. 102
E. 116

GO ON TO THE NEXT PAGE

14. Quadrilateral *WXYZ* shown below is in the standard (x,y) coordinate plane. For this quadrilateral, $WZ = 7$, $YZ = 6$, $XY = \sqrt{53}$, and $WX = 8$, all in coordinate units.

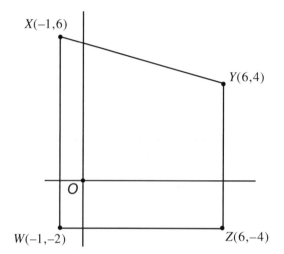

Which of the following is closest to the perimeter of quadrilateral *WXYZ*, in coordinate units?
F. 22.6
G. 25.7
H. 28.3
J. 31.4
K. 35.8

DO YOUR FIGURING HERE.

15. The perimeter of a parallelogram is 76 inches, and the measure of 1 side is 17 inches. What are the lengths of the 3 remaining sides?
A. 17, 17, 17
B. 17, 17, 42
C. 17, 20, 20
D. 17, 21, 21
E. Cannot be determined from the given information

END OF SET FIVE
STOP! DO NOT GO ON TO THE NEXT PAGE
UNTIL TOLD TO DO SO.

ACT® Mastery Math

Sum It Up

Perimeter and Line Segments

Length
The measurement of the side of a figure or shape

Width
The measurement from side to side of a figure or shape

Perimeter
The measurement of the distance around a two-dimensional shape

Tips and Techniques

Draw It Out: Most perimeter questions can be solved by drawing the shapes and labeling them carefully. If the ACT does not give you the figure or label all of the information, just draw it out.

Use Ratios: A ratio can be a useful tool for determining perimeter and dimensions of polygons when there are unknown sides.

Lesson 11

Polygon Area

CAPTION:

ACT® Mastery Math

11.1 Entrance Ticket

Solve the problem below and write about how you found the answer.

Five congruent squares are put together without gaps or overlap to form a figure shaped like a plus sign. The perimeter of the figure is 72 cm. Find the area of the figure, in cm².

Lesson 11 – Polygon Area

11.2 Learning Targets

1. Calculate the area of geometric shapes

2. Find dimensions of geometric shapes when given the area

Self-Assessment

Circle the number that corresponds to your confidence level in your knowledge of this subject before beginning the lesson. A score of 1 means you are completely lost, and a score of 4 means you have mastered the skills. After you finish the lesson, return to the bottom of this page and circle your new confidence level to show your improvement.

Before Lesson

1   2   3   4

After Lesson

1   2   3   4

Entrance Ticket   Learning Targets   Understanding Area   ACT Practice   Sum It Up

ACT® Mastery Math

11.3.1 Understanding Area

Information needed to find total cost: _____

_____

Total cost: _____

Math Tip

Draw It Out: On the ACT, everyone is an artist! Visualizing the problem will help you figure out which math operations to use.

11.3.1 Understanding Area

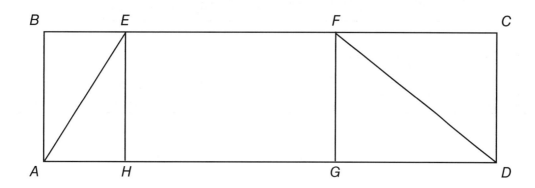

Total area of composite shape: _____

11.4.1 Set One

1. A flyer has a surface area of 88 square inches. If the length of the paper is 11 inches, what is the width, in inches?

    A. 4
    B. 8
    C. 22
    D. 77
    E. 968

2. The dimensions of a right triangle are shown below in feet. What is the area of the triangle, in square feet?

    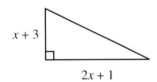

    F. $x^2 + 3$

    G. $x^2 + 9$

    H. $x^2 + \frac{7}{2}x + \frac{3}{2}$

    J. $2x^2 + 7x + 3$

    K. $6x^2$

3. In rhombus $XYZQ$ below, $\overline{XZ}$ is 10 centimeters long, and $\overline{YQ}$ is 4 centimeters long. What is the area of $XYZQ$, in square centimeters?

    A. 8
    B. 10
    C. 20
    D. 40
    E. 100

    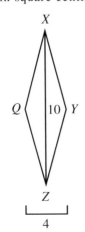

DO YOUR FIGURING HERE.

END OF SET ONE
STOP! DO NOT GO ON TO THE NEXT PAGE
UNTIL TOLD TO DO SO.

Lesson 11 – Polygon Area

11.4.2 Set Two

4. The area of $\triangle ABC$ below is 36 square centimeters. If height $\overline{BD}$ is 9 centimeters, how long is the base of $\overline{AC}$, in centimeters?

   F. 2
   G. 4
   H. 6
   J. 8
   K. 10

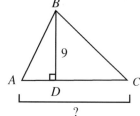

DO YOUR FIGURING HERE.

5. A farmer wants to double the area of his rectangular 6-meter-by-10-meter garden. The 10-meter length will be increased by 2 meters. By how many meters must the width increase?

   A. 2
   B. 4
   C. 6
   D. 10
   E. 12

6. On the standard (x,y) plane below, 1 side of the rectangle is on the axis, and the vertices of the opposite side are on the graph of the parabola given by $y = 7 - x^2$. Let z represent any value of x, such that $0 \le z \le \sqrt{7}$. Which of the following expressions, in terms of z, represents the area of any such rectangle?

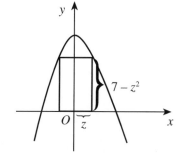

   F. $-z^3 + 7z$
   G. $-z^2 + 7z$
   H. $-z^2 + 7z + 2$
   J. $-2z^3 - 14z$
   K. $-2z^3 + 14z$

END OF SET TWO
STOP! DO NOT GO ON TO THE NEXT PAGE
UNTIL TOLD TO DO SO.

11.4.3 Set Three

7. In a certain rectangle, the ratio of the lengths of 2 adjacent sides is 4 to 3. If the area of the rectangle is 192 square centimeters, what is the length, in centimeters, of the longer side?

   A. 6
   B. 12
   C. 16
   D. 32
   E. 36

8. The length of a rectangle is 4 times the length of a smaller rectangle. The 2 rectangles have the same width. The area of the smaller rectangle is X square units. The area of the larger rectangle is yX square units. Which of the following is the value of y?

   F. $\frac{1}{16}$

   G. $\frac{1}{4}$

   H. 1

   J. 4

   K. 16

9. For trapezoid $ABCD$ shown below, $\overline{AB}$ is 7 inches, $\overline{CD}$ is 4 inches, and the perimeter is 43 inches. What is the area of the trapezoid, in square inches?

   A. 28
   B. 32
   C. 36
   D. 64
   E. 128

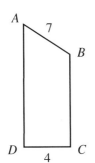

DO YOUR FIGURING HERE.

END OF SET THREE
STOP! DO NOT GO ON TO THE NEXT PAGE
UNTIL TOLD TO DO SO.

Lesson 11 – Polygon Area

11.4.4 Set Four

10. The area of the trapezoid below is 24 square meters, the altitude is 4 meters, and the length of one base is 2 meters. What is the length, x, of the other base, in meters?

    F. 3
    G. 4
    H. 8
    J. 10
    K. 12

    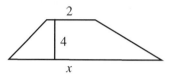

    DO YOUR FIGURING HERE.

11. In the standard (x,y) coordinate plane, if a triangle has vertices at $A(-1,3)$, $B(2,3)$, and $C(2,-4)$, then what is its area, in square coordinate units?

    A. 3
    B. 7
    C. 8
    D. 10
    E. $10\frac{1}{2}$

    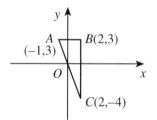

12. In the figure below, the area of the larger square is 100 square inches, and the area of the smaller square is 64 square inches. What is x, in inches?

    F. 2
    G. 8
    H. 10
    J. 18
    K. 36

    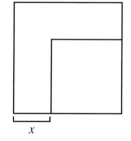

END OF SET FOUR
STOP! DO NOT GO ON TO THE NEXT PAGE
UNTIL TOLD TO DO SO.

11.4.5 Set Five

13. In the figure below, A, E, F, and B are collinear, and the measurements are in inches. The area of rectangle $ABCD$ is 52 square inches. What is the area of trapezoid $CDEF$, in square inches?

A. 26
B. 30
C. 34
D. 40
E. 80

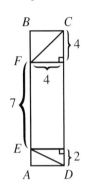

DO YOUR FIGURING HERE.

14. In the figure below, B and C are on $\overline{AD}$, and E and F are on $\overline{DG}$. The measurements are given in meters. Both $ABFG$ and $BCEF$ are trapezoids. The area A of a trapezoid is given by $A = \frac{1}{2}(b_1 + b_2)h$, where h is the height, and b_1 and b_2 are the lengths of the parallel sides.

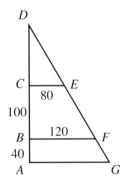

What is the area of $BCEF$, in square meters?
F. 5,600
G. 8,400
H. 10,000
J. 14,000
K. 20,000

GO ON TO THE NEXT PAGE.

Lesson 11 – Polygon Area

15. Each of the 4 sides of a dog dish has the shape of a trapezoid, as shown below.

The length of the bottom of each side is 15 cm, and the length of the top of each side is $12\frac{1}{2}$ cm. What is the length of the median of each trapezoid, in centimeters?

A. 12
B. $12\frac{1}{2}$
C. 13
D. $13\frac{1}{4}$
E. $13\frac{3}{4}$

DO YOUR FIGURING HERE.

END OF SET FIVE
STOP! DO NOT GO ON TO THE NEXT PAGE
UNTIL TOLD TO DO SO.

ACT® Mastery Math

Sum It Up

Polygon Area

Ratios
An expression that measures how two numbers compare to each other

Area Formulas

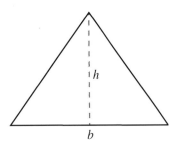

Area = $\dfrac{\text{base} \cdot \text{height}}{2}$

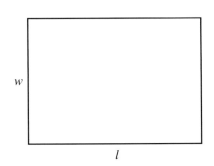

Area = length · width

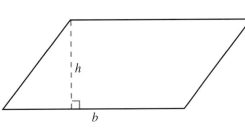

Area = base · height

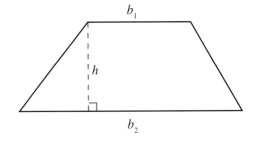

Area = $\dfrac{\text{base}_1 + \text{base}_2}{2}$ · height

Tips and Techniques

Draw It Out: On the ACT, everyone is an artist! Visualizing the problem will help you figure out which math operations to use.

Objects in Mirror are Exactly as They Appear: Questions on the ACT about area often provide pictures, which are almost always drawn to scale. This means that if one side of a figure looks equal to another, it probably is.

Lesson 12

Circle Area and Circumference

CAPTION:

ACT® Mastery Math

12.1 Entrance Ticket

Read the question below, solve, and briefly explain in a paragraph how you arrived at your solution.

A number of children are standing in a circle. They are evenly spaced, and the 7th child is directly opposite the 18th child. How many children are there altogether?

Show Your Work	Write an Explanation

Entrance Ticket   Learning Targets   Circumference   Area   ACT Practice   Sum It Up

Lesson 12 – Circle Area and Circumference

12.2 Learning Targets

1. Calculate circumference and area of circles

2. Work backwards to find dimensions of circles

Self-Assessment

Circle the number that corresponds to your confidence level in your knowledge of this subject before beginning the lesson. A score of 1 means you are completely lost, and a score of 4 means you have mastered the skills. After you finish the lesson, return to the bottom of this page and circle your new confidence level to show your improvement.

Before Lesson

1   2   3   4

After Lesson

1   2   3   4

12.3.1 Circumference

The Circonian Martians travel the outermost ring of Saturn three times before realizing they are going in circles. How far out of their way have they traveled before they get back on the route toward their destination?

Lesson 12 – Circle Area and Circumference

12.3.1 Circumference

1. What is the circumference of Circle A?

2. What is the circumference of Circle B?

3. What is the radius of Circle C?

Math Tip

Math Mirror: Items on both sides of the equal sign are part of the formula. This means that in the formula **area** = πr^2, *area* is part of the formula. It is one of the variables. If you are given the area but not the radius or diameter, you can plug the area into the formula and solve for the unknown.

ACT® Mastery Math

12.3.2 Area

The Circonians leave behind cryptic messages in the form of crop circles all over the fields of this planet called Earth. Solve for the area of each circle to decipher the message that explains what the aliens demand from the citizens of Earth.

Lesson 12 – Circle Area and Circumference

12.3.2 Area

What do the Circonians demand from the humans?

_____ _____ _____ _____ _____ _____
Circle 1   Circle 2   Circle 3   Circle 4   Circle 5   Circle 6

Code Key			
A	19	N	50
B	31	O	28
C	6	P	99
D	113	Q	314
E	2	R	8
F	44	S	79
G	201	T	1,256
H	378	U	707
I	21	V	100
J	1	W	15
K	47	X	0
L	92	Y	571
M	9	Z	10

12.4.1 Set One

1. What is the circumference, in inches, of a circle with a radius of 8 inches?

   A. 4π
   B. 8π
   C. 12π
   D. 16π
   E. 64π

2. The circle shown below has a diameter of 14 inches. What is the circumference of the circle, in inches?

   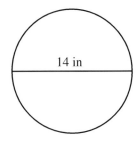

   F. 7π
   G. 14π
   H. 28π
   J. 49π
   K. 196π

3. The perimeter of a circular field is 500 feet. Which of the following is closest to the radius of the field, in feet? (Note: $\pi \approx 3.14$)

   A. 10
   B. 50
   C. 80
   D. 160
   E. 250

DO YOUR FIGURING HERE.

END OF SET ONE
STOP! DO NOT GO ON TO THE NEXT PAGE UNTIL TOLD TO DO SO.

12.4.2 Set Two

4. Circles A, B, and C have radii with measures of x centimeters, $3x$ centimeters, and $6x$ centimeters, respectively. What is the ratio of the radius of Circle B to the diameter of Circle C?

   F. 1:2
   G. 1:4
   H. 1:12
   J. 2:1
   K. 4:1

5. The circle shown in the figure below has a diameter of 12 meters. What is the area of the circle, in square meters?

   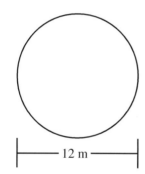

   A. 6π
   B. 12π
   C. 24π
   D. 36π
   E. 144π

6. If a circle has a circumference of 108π inches, how many inches long is its radius?

   F. $\sqrt{108}$
   G. 27
   H. 54
   J. 108
   K. 216

END OF SET TWO
STOP! DO NOT GO ON TO THE NEXT PAGE
UNTIL TOLD TO DO SO.

12.4.3 Set Three

7. If a circle has a circumference of $\frac{6}{5}\pi$ centimeters, how long is its radius, in centimeters?

    A. $\frac{3}{5}$
    B. $\frac{5}{6}$
    C. $\frac{6}{5}$
    D. $\frac{5}{3}$
    E. $\sqrt{\frac{6}{5}}$

8. A circle that lies on the standard (x,y) coordinate plane has its center at $(8,-6)$ and passes through the origin. What is the area of this circle, in square coordinate units?

    F. 14π
    G. 20π
    H. 36π
    J. 64π
    K. 100π

9. Richard brought his dog to the park and tied his leash to a flagpole while he had a picnic. The dog could reach 12 feet from the flagpole in any direction. What is the approximate area of the ground, in square feet, that the dog could reach from the flagpole? (Note: $\pi \approx 3.14$)

    A. 19
    B. 38
    C. 75
    D. 113
    E. 452

DO YOUR FIGURING HERE.

END OF SET THREE
STOP! DO NOT GO ON TO THE NEXT PAGE
UNTIL TOLD TO DO SO.

12.4.4 Set Four

10. The figure below shows four congruent semicircles that touch only at the corners of a square. The path from point X, along the diameters of the semicircles, back to point X is 96 inches long. How long is the path from point X, along the arcs of the semicircles, back to point X, in inches?

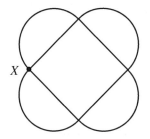

- F. 24π
- G. 48π
- H. 96π
- J. 144π
- K. 288π

DO YOUR FIGURING HERE.

11. The figure below shows a small circle with a diameter $\overline{AC}$ and a large circle with a diameter $\overline{AB}$ that is 32 inches long. Point C is the center of the large circle. What is the area, in square inches, of the small circle?

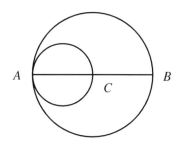

- A. 8π
- B. 16π
- C. 32π
- D. 40π
- E. 64π

12. The square in the figure below has a perimeter of 40 inches. The circle is inscribed in the square and is tangent to the square at the midpoints of its sides. What is the area of the circle, in square inches?

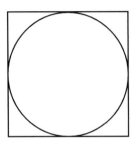

F. 4π
G. 10π
H. 16π
J. 25π
K. 100π

Lesson 12 – Circle Area and Circumference

12.4.5 Set Five

13. The figure below shows a circular well that has a diameter of 7 feet. What is the circumference of the well, in feet?

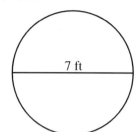

A. $\dfrac{7}{2}\pi$

B. 7π

C. $\dfrac{49}{4}\pi$

D. 14π

E. 49π

DO YOUR FIGURING HERE.

14. Rectangle *ABCD*, shown below, has side lengths of 8 inches and 10 inches. What is the area, in square inches, of the largest circle that can fit within rectangle *ABCD* ?

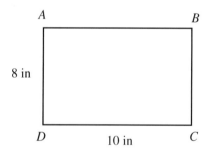

F. 8π
G. 16π
H. 20π
J. 64π
K. 100π

15. If the diameter of a circle is doubled, the area of the resulting circle is how many times the area of the original circle?

A. 2
B. 4
C. 6
D. 8
E. 10

END OF SET FIVE
STOP! DO NOT GO ON TO THE NEXT PAGE
UNTIL TOLD TO DO SO.

ACT® Mastery Math

Sum It Up

Circle Area and Circumference

Circumference of a Circle = $2\pi r$
Remember this formula by saying "Circle circumference is 2-pi-rrrimeter."

Area of a Circle = πr^2
Remember this formula by saying "Circle area is pi-r-sq'area."

Tips and Techniques

Draw It Out: It does not have to be pretty. On the ACT, everyone is an artist.

Drawn to Scale: It is usually safe to assume that figures in ACT math problems are drawn to scale. If it looks like a midpoint, it probably is! If two angles look the same size, they probably are!

Math Mirror: Items on both sides of the equal sign are part of the formula. This means that in the formula *area* = πr^2, *area* is part of the formula. It is one of the variables. If you are given the area but not a radius or diameter, you can plug the area into the formula and solve for the unknown.

Lesson 13

Volume

CAPTION:

ACT® Mastery Math

13.1 Entrance Ticket

Read the question below, solve, and briefly explain in a paragraph how you came to your solution.

If you have a 3-gallon bucket, a 4-gallon bucket, and a water source, how can you measure out exactly 2 gallons?

Show Your Work	Write an Explanation

Lesson 13 – Volume

13.2 Learning Targets

1. Calculate volume of three-dimensional figures

2. Work backwards to find dimensions of three-dimensional figures

Self-Assessment

Circle the number that corresponds to your confidence level in your knowledge of this subject before beginning the lesson. A score of 1 means you are completely lost, and a score of 4 means you have mastered the skills. After you finish the lesson, return to the bottom of this page and circle your new confidence level to show your improvement.

Before Lesson

1   2   3   4

After Lesson

1   2   3   4

Entrance Ticket | Learning Targets | Basic Volume | Advanced Volume | ACT Practice | Sum It Up

ACT® Mastery Math

13.3.1 Basic Volume

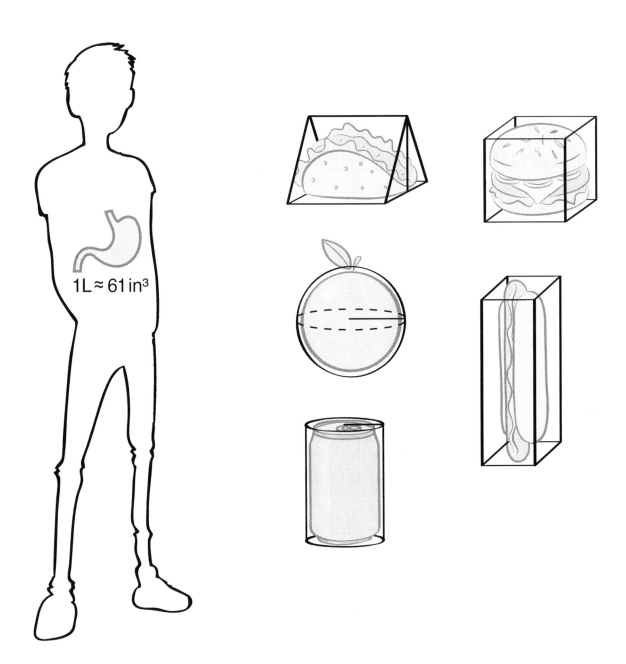

13.3.1 Basic Volume

ACT® Mastery Math

13.3.2 Advanced Volume

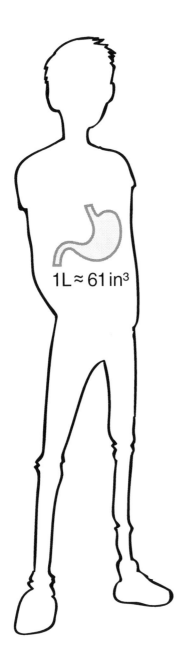

$1L \approx 61 \text{ in}^3$

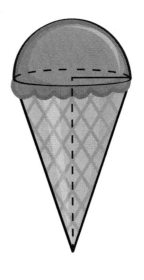

13.3.2 Advanced Volume

ACT® Mastery Math

13.3.2 Advanced Volume

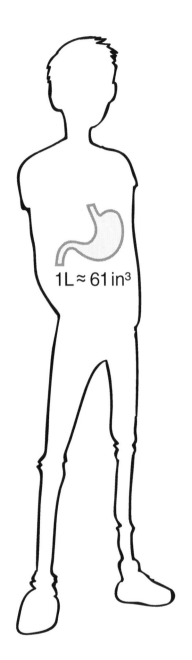

$1L \approx 61 \text{ in}^3$

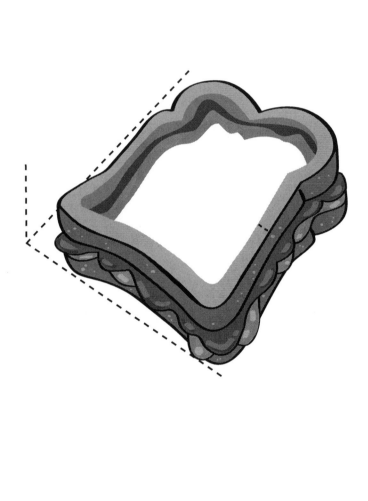

Lesson 13 – Volume

13.3.2 Advanced Volume

ACT® Mastery Math

13.3.2 Advanced Volume

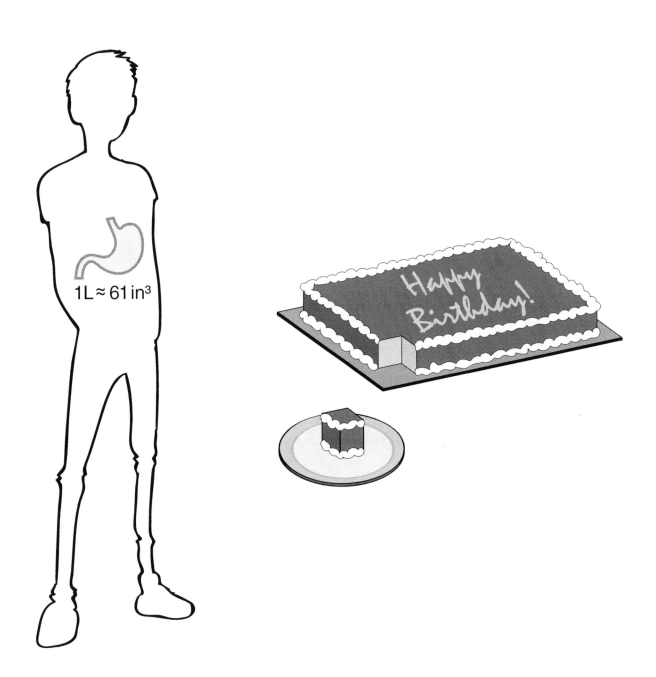

Lesson 13 – Volume

13.3.2 Advanced Volume

13.4.1 Set One

1. A rectangular solid is 5 inches wide, 8 inches long, and 3 inches tall. What is the volume of this rectangular solid, in cubic inches?

   A. 16
   B. 43
   C. 64
   D. 65
   E. 120

2. Eliza's parents are installing an above-ground swimming pool in their backyard. The pool is a right circular cylinder with a diameter of 18 feet and a height of 7 feet, as shown in the figure below.

   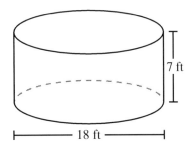

   Once her parents fill the pool, it will have a depth of 6 feet. What is the volume of water, to the nearest cubic foot, that will be in the pool once it is filled?

   (Note: The volume, V, of a right circular cylinder with radius r and height h is given by the formula $V = \pi r^2 h$.)

   F. 170
   G. 1,527
   H. 1,781
   J. 2,375
   K. 6,107

3. What is the height, in centimeters, of a rectangular prism that is 80 centimeters wide, 40 centimeters long, and has a volume of 160,000 centimeters?

   A. 5
   B. 20
   C. 39
   D. 40
   E. 50

DO YOUR FIGURING HERE.

END OF SET ONE
STOP! DO NOT GO ON TO THE NEXT PAGE
UNTIL TOLD TO DO SO.

Lesson 13 – Volume

13.4.2 Set Two

4. Cube A has side lengths that are 3 times as long as Cube B. How many times larger is the volume of Cube A compared to the volume of Cube B?

   F. 2
   G. 3
   H. 6
   J. 9
   K. 27

DO YOUR FIGURING HERE.

5. A large cube has edges that are twice as long as those of a small cube. If the edges of the small cube are 6 inches, how many more cubic inches is the volume of the large cube than the small cube?

   A. 8
   B. 216
   C. 432
   D. 1,512
   E. 1,728

6. There are two right circular cylinders. The large cylinder has a height 2 times the size of the height of the small cylinder and a radius 3 times the size of the small cylinder. How many times larger is the volume of the large cylinder compared to the volume of the small cylinder?

   (Note: The volume, V, of a right circular cylinder with radius r and height h is given by the formula $V = \pi r^2 h$.)

   F. 2
   G. 3
   H. 5
   J. 6
   K. 18

END OF SET TWO
STOP! DO NOT GO ON TO THE NEXT PAGE
UNTIL TOLD TO DO SO.

13.4.3 Set Three

7. A rectangular solid is 13 inches wide, 10 inches long, and 5 inches tall. What is the volume of this rectangular solid, in cubic inches?

   A. 28
   B. 63
   C. 135
   D. 195
   E. 650

8. While baking a cake, Kevin used 82.5 cubic inches of frosting to cover the top. If this frosting were spread in an even layer over the top of the rectangular cake shown below, about how many inches deep would the layer of frosting be? Round your answer to the nearest hundredth of an inch.

   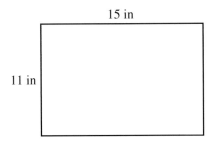

   F. 0.25
   G. 0.50
   H. 0.75
   J. 1.00
   K. 1.25

9. There are two spheres of different sizes. The large sphere has a radius 3 times the size of the small sphere. How many times larger is the volume of the large sphere compared to the volume of the small sphere?

   (Note: The volume of a sphere is $\frac{4}{3}\pi r^3$, where r represents the length of the radius of the sphere.)

   A. 81
   B. 27
   C. 9
   D. 6
   E. 3

DO YOUR FIGURING HERE.

END OF SET THREE
STOP! DO NOT GO ON TO THE NEXT PAGE
UNTIL TOLD TO DO SO.

13.4.4 Set Four

10. Martha's parents are building a concrete basketball court in her backyard so she can practice all the time. The basketball court has a length of 47 feet and a width of 50 feet, as shown below. If the court is 6 inches thick, how much concrete will they need to pour, in cubic feet?

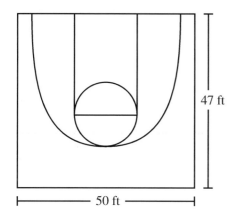

F. 1,175
G. 2,350
H. 4,700
J. 14,100
K. 84,600

DO YOUR FIGURING HERE.

11. Tyler filled up his hot tub, which is a right rectangular prism, with 480 cubic feet of water. The hot tub is 12 feet long and 10 feet wide. What is the depth of the water in the hot tub? Round your answer to the nearest foot.

A. 2
B. 4
C. 22
D. 40
E. 48

GO ON TO THE NEXT PAGE

12. The length of the rectangular prism shown below is three times the width. The height and the width are the same. If the volume of the prism is 81 cubic centimeters, what is the length of the prism, in centimeters?

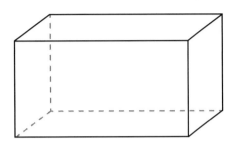

F. 3
G. 9
H. 18
J. 27
K. 49

DO YOUR FIGURING HERE.

13.4.5 Set Five

13. Your dog, Cujo, has a water bowl, shown below, that is in the shape of a right circular cylinder with a diameter of 8 inches. The bowl is filled with water to a uniform depth of 4 inches. What is the volume of the water in the water bowl, in cubic inches?

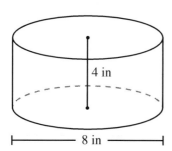

(Note: The volume, V, of a right circular cylinder with radius r and height h is given by the formula $V = \pi r^2 h$.)

A. 12π
B. 16π
C. 32π
D. 64π
E. 256π

DO YOUR FIGURING HERE.

14. Cylinders Q and P are both right circular cylinders. The height of Cylinder Q is 3 times the height of Cylinder P, and the radius of Cylinder Q is 2 times the radius of Cylinder P. The volume of Cylinder Q is how many times the volume of Cylinder P?

(Note: The volume, V, of a right circular cylinder with radius r and height h is given by the formula $V = \pi r^2 h$.)

F. 3
G. 4
H. 5
J. 7
K. 12

GO ON TO THE NEXT PAGE

15. Right triangle △ABC, shown below, has a vertical leg 6 inches long and a hypotenuse 10 inches long. If the triangle was rotated 360° around the vertical leg to form a right circular cone, what would be the volume of this cone, in cubic inches?

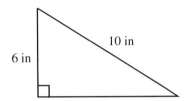

(Note: The volume, V, of a right circular cone with radius r and height h is given by the formula $V = \frac{1}{3}\pi r^2 h$.)

A. 32π
B. 96π
C. 128π
D. 288π
E. 384π

Lesson 13 – Volume

Sum It Up

Volume

Radius
The length of a line segment from a circle's center to its perimeter

Diameter
Any straight line segment that passes through the center of a circle and whose endpoints lie on the circle

Length
The measurement of a side of a figure or shape

Width
The measurement from side to side of a figure or shape

Height
The measurement from top to bottom of a figure or shape

Depth
The measurement of how deep something is (how far down or back it goes)

Lesson 14

Inequalities

CAPTION:

ACT® Mastery Math

14.1 Entrance Ticket

Solve the questions below.

1. Which of the following inequalities correctly matches the number line graph below?

   A. $-3 \leq x$ and $2 \leq x$
   B. $-3 \leq x$ and $2 \geq x$
   C. $-3 \leq x$ or $2 \leq x$
   D. $-3 \geq x$ or $2 \leq x$
   E. $-3 \geq x$ or $2 \geq x$

2. Which of the following is a possible value for b if $|4b - 6| = 14$?

   F. -2
   G. -1
   H. 0
   J. 1
   K. 2

3. A certain lizard species can only survive in temperatures that fall in the range $77° \leq F \leq 95°$. Given that $C = \frac{5}{9}(F - 32)$, where C represents the temperature in degrees Celsius and F represents the temperature in degrees Fahrenheit, what is the corresponding range in degrees Celsius at which this lizard species can survive?

   A. $-5° \leq C \leq 5°$
   B. $5° \leq C \leq 15°$
   C. $15° \leq C \leq 25°$
   D. $25° \leq C \leq 35°$
   E. $35° \leq C \leq 45°$

Lesson 14 – Inequalities

Learning Targets

1. Solve inequalities involving variables

2. Use number lines to visualize and graph inequalities

3. Solve absolute values equations and simple absolute value inequalities

Self-Assessment

Circle the number that corresponds to your confidence level in your knowledge of this subject before beginning the lesson. A score of 1 means you are completely lost, and a score of 4 means you have mastered the skills. After you finish the lesson, return to the bottom of this page and circle your new confidence level to show your improvement.

Before Lesson

1   2   3   4

After Lesson

1   2   3   4

Entrance Ticket | Learning Targets | Inequalities like Equations | Inequalities on Number Line | Absolute Value Inequalities | ACT Practice | Sum It Up

14.3.1 Solving Inequalities like Equations

1. 3 __ 2

2. 70 + 9 __ 80 − 2

3. 2,237 __ 2,732

4. 3 · 5 − 7 __ 2 · 6 ÷ 3

5. 2^3 __ $4 + 2^2$

6. x + 1 __ x + 2

7. All positive even integers __ 1

8. $\dfrac{5}{12}$ __ $\dfrac{1}{3}$

9. Number of boys in the class __ Number of girls in the class

14.3.1 Solving Inequalities like Equations

ACT® Mastery Math

14.3.2 Inequalities on a Number Line

1. _____

2. _____

3. _____

4. _____

Lesson 14 – Inequalities

14.3.3 Absolute Value Inequalities

Rule for solving absolute value inequalities:

x < 12 or x > –6	
x > –22 or x < 8	
x < 47 or x > –17	

14.4.1 Set One

1. Which of the following is equivalent to the inequality $-8 + 6p \leq 4 - 3p$?

   A. $p \leq \dfrac{1}{3}$

   B. $p \leq \dfrac{4}{3}$

   C. $p \geq \dfrac{3}{4}$

   D. $p \geq 3$

   E. $p \leq 12$

2. Given numbers r and q, where $0 < r < q$, which of the following inequalities must be true for all values of r and q ?

   F. $r + 2 > q + 2$

   G. $\dfrac{r}{q} > 1$

   H. $\dfrac{1}{q} > \dfrac{1}{r}$

   J. $r^3 > q^3$

   K. $-r > -q$

3. At a grocery store, muffins sell for $4.00 per package, and cookies sell for $6.25 per package. These bakery items are only sold in packages. Dwayne wants to buy at least one package of muffins and one package of cookies for a party, and he must spend exactly $58.00. What is the maximum number of packages of cookies that he can buy?

   A. 4
   B. 5
   C. 7
   D. 8
   E. 9

END OF SET ONE
STOP! DO NOT GO ON TO THE NEXT PAGE UNTIL TOLD TO DO SO.

14.4.2 Set Two

4. The inequality $-\dfrac{3x}{5} + 2 > 8$ is equivalent to which of the following inequalities?

   F. $x < -\dfrac{18}{5}$

   G. $x < -\dfrac{10}{3}$

   H. $x < -10$

   J. $x > -10$

   K. $x > 10$

DO YOUR FIGURING HERE.

5. To win the school art competition, the finalists must receive over 50% of the votes cast by their peers. If 330 students vote and x represents the minimum number of votes a finalist needs to win the competition, which of the following expressions is true?

   A. $x < 165$
   B. $x = 165$
   C. $x > 165$
   D. $x < 166$
   E. $x > 166$

6. For the system of inequalities given below, which of the following defines the solution set?

   $x \leq 8$
   $6 + 3x \geq 0$

   F. $x \geq -2$
   G. $x \leq 8$
   H. $-18 \leq x \leq 8$
   J. $-2 \leq x \leq 8$
   K. $2 \leq x \leq 8$

END OF SET TWO
STOP! DO NOT GO ON TO THE NEXT PAGE
UNTIL TOLD TO DO SO.

14.4.3 Set Three

7. The real number line graph, shown below, is represented by which of the following inequalities?

A. $-3 \leq x \leq 3$
B. $-3 \leq x < 4$
C. $0 \leq x < 4$
D. $3 \leq x \leq 4$
E. $4 < x \leq -3$

8. The number line graph pictured below is represented by which of the following inequalities?

F. $-2 \leq x$ and $5 \leq x$
G. $-2 \leq x$ and $5 \geq x$
H. $-2 \leq x$ or $5 \leq x$
J. $-2 \geq x$ or $5 \geq x$
K. $-2 \geq x$ or $5 \leq x$

9. The solution set for the inequality $2x - 7 \geq 3$ is represented by which of the following graphs?

A.
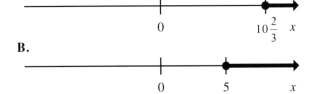

B.

C.
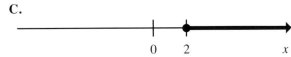

D.
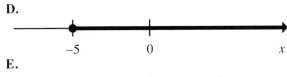

E.
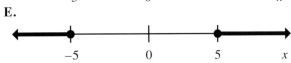

DO YOUR FIGURING HERE.

END OF SET THREE
STOP! DO NOT GO ON TO THE NEXT PAGE UNTIL TOLD TO DO SO.

14.4.4 Set Four

10. Which of the following is a possible value for y if $|3y - 3| = 6$?

    F. -2
    G. -1
    H. 0
    J. 1
    K. 2

DO YOUR FIGURING HERE.

11. What is the smallest positive integer y such that $|3 - y| > 6$?

    A. 2
    B. 6
    C. 7
    D. 9
    E. 10

12. Which of the following is the solution set for $|a - 5| > 2$?

    F. $a < -2$ or $a > 2$
    G. $a < 3$ or $a > 7$
    H. $a > 3$ and $a < 7$
    J. $a > -2$ and $a < 2$
    K. $a > -5$ and $a < 5$

END OF SET FOUR
STOP! DO NOT GO ON TO THE NEXT PAGE
UNTIL TOLD TO DO SO.

14.4.5 Set Five

13. Mr. Sanders produced a progress report for each of the students in his history class. It included the student's scores on homework, quizzes, tests, and projects, as well as class averages on each of these assignments. The progress report for Sara Ortiz is given below.

Student: Ortiz, Sara

Assignment	Possible Points	Student Score	Class Average
Homework #1	100	100	90
Homework #2	100	92	91
Homework #3	100	98	95
Homework #4	100		
Quiz #1	100	97	89
Quiz #2	100	89	83
Quiz #3	100	93	85
Test #1	100	90	82
Test #2	100	96	92
Project #1	100	100	90
Project #2	100		

If Sara wants an average of at least 95 on her homework, the solution to which of the following inequalities will tell her the score, represented by x, she must achieve on homework #4 ?

A. $\dfrac{100+92+98+x}{4} \geq 95$

B. $\dfrac{x-(100+92+98)}{4} \geq 95$

C. $\dfrac{100+92+98+x}{3} \geq 95$

D. $\dfrac{100+92+98+x}{2} \geq 95$

E. $\dfrac{\dfrac{100+92+98}{3}+x}{2} \geq 95$

DO YOUR FIGURING HERE.

GO ON TO THE NEXT PAGE

14. Which of the following represents the greatest integer m that satisfies the inequality $8 > \frac{m}{4} + 3$?

F. 19
G. 20
H. 21
J. 22
K. 24

DO YOUR FIGURING HERE.

15. The solution set for the system of inequalities represented below is illustrated by which of the following graphs?

$2x - 3 > 2$
$-3x > -12$

A.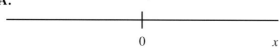

B.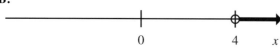

C.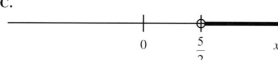

D.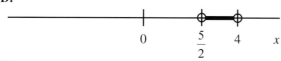

E.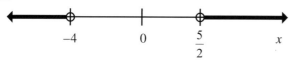

END OF SET FIVE
STOP! DO NOT GO ON TO THE NEXT PAGE
UNTIL TOLD TO DO SO.

ACT® Mastery Math

Sum It Up

Inequalities
<   less than
>   greater than
≤   less than or equal to
≥   greater than or equal to
=   equal to
Closed (filled-in) Circle   Inequality that includes the circled number; use the ≤ or ≥ sign
Open Circle   Inequality that does not include the circled number; use the < or > sign

Lesson 15

Exponents and Roots

CAPTION:

ACT® Mastery Math

15.1 Entrance Ticket

Solve the questions below.

1. What does $(3x^2y)^2 (4x^3y^2)^2$ equal?
   A. $12x^4y^6$
   B. $12x^{48}y^8$
   C. $48x^{10}y^6$
   D. $124x^{48}y^8$
   E. $144x^{10}y^6$

2. What does $(4a^2b^3)(5a^3b^4)$ equal?
   F. $9a^5b^7$
   G. $9a^6b^{12}$
   H. $20a^5b^7$
   J. $20a^6b^7$
   K. $20a^6b^{12}$

3. $\sqrt[3]{8q^9} = ?$
   A. $2q^3$
   B. $2q^6$
   C. $4q^3$
   D. $4q^6$
   E. $64q^3$

Lesson 15 – Exponents and Roots

15.2 Learning Targets

1. Recognize and utilize exponents to calculate solutions to equations

2. Use exponents in conjunction with variables to simplify expressions through multiplication and division

3. Recognize and use common square and cube roots to solve problems

Self-Assessment

Circle the number that corresponds to your confidence level in your knowledge of this subject before beginning the lesson. A score of 1 means you are completely lost, and a score of 4 means you have mastered the skills. After you finish the lesson, return to the bottom of this page and circle your new confidence level to show your improvement.

Before Lesson

1   2   3   4

After Lesson

1   2   3   4

Entrance Ticket | Learning Targets | Multiplying with Exponents | Dividing with Exponents | Square and Cube Roots | ACT Practice | Sum It Up

ACT® Mastery Math

15.3.1 Multiplying with Exponents

$$(2^5)(2^3)$$

$$(2^{5+3})$$

When multiplying terms with exponents that share a common base,

Lesson 15 – Exponents and Roots

15.3.1 Multiplying with Exponents

1. $2^4 5^2 \cdot 2^2 5^3$

2. $(xy^7) \cdot (x^3 y)$

3. $(d^2 f^8 g^3) \cdot (dg^2)$

15.3.1 Multiplying with Exponents

$$(a^3)^3$$

When an expression with exponents is inside parentheses and there is an exponent outside the parentheses, the exponents

15.3.1 Multiplying with Exponents

1. $(2^4 5^2)^2$

2. $(xy^7)^4$

3. $(d^2 f^8 g^3)^3$

Math Tip

Process of Elimination: It is essential to eliminate wrong answers after each step of the problem-solving process. The ACT almost always includes a few answers that will be too small or too large once you have completed a few steps. If you don't have to complete every step of the process to get the right answer choice, you will save valuable time.

15.3.2 Dividing with Exponents and Negative Exponents

$$\frac{x^5 y^6}{x^3 y^3}$$

$$\frac{x^3}{x^7}$$

When dividing two terms with the exponents that share a base,

Negative exponents can also be written as

15.3.2 Dividing with Exponents and Negative Exponents

1. $2^4 5^2 \div 2^2 5^3$

2. $(xy^7) \div (x^3 y)$

3. $(d^2 f^8 g^3) \div (d g^2)$

4. $\dfrac{x^{10}}{x^4} \div \dfrac{y^4}{y}$

5. $6x^3 y z^2 \div 3 x y^2 z$

15.3.3 Square and Cube Roots

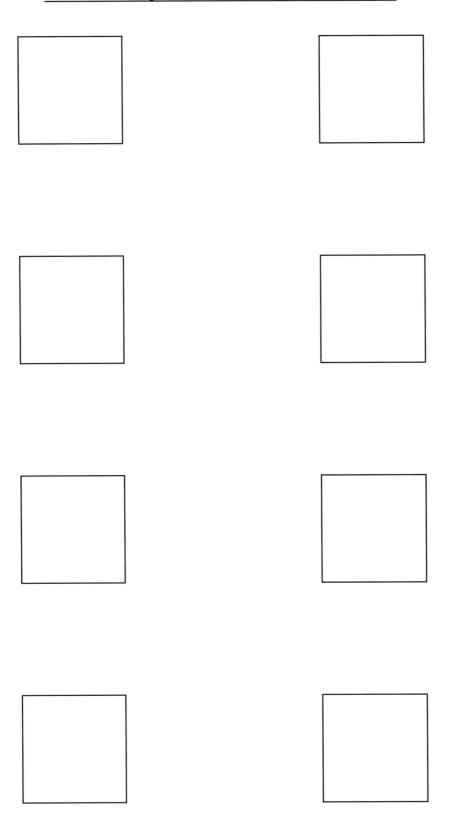

15.3.3 Square and Cube Roots

Can $\sqrt{54}$ be factored?

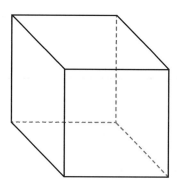

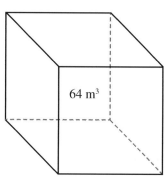

64 m³

Math Tip

Perfect Squares: The square root of **any** real number can be determined by using a calculator, but you will move more quickly on the test if you memorize the squares of the numbers from 1 to 12.

15.4.1 Set One

1. Which of the following expressions is equivalent to $-5a^3(9a^2 - 3a^4)$?

    A. $-45a^6 - 15a^{12}$
    B. $-45a^6 + 15a^{12}$
    C. $-45a^5 - 15a^7$
    D. $-45a^5 + 15a^7$
    E. $-30a$

DO YOUR FIGURING HERE.

2. The expression $(5xy^3)(2x^2y)$ is equivalent to:

    F. $7x^2y^4$
    G. $7x^3y^3$
    H. $10x^2y^3$
    J. $10x^2y^4$
    K. $10x^3y^4$

3. The expression $(x^8)^{16}$ is equivalent to:

    A. x^{-8}
    B. x^2
    C. x^8
    D. x^{24}
    E. x^{128}

END OF SET ONE
STOP! DO NOT GO ON TO THE NEXT PAGE
UNTIL TOLD TO DO SO.

15.4.2 Set Two

4. What is $4x^3 \cdot 6x^5$?
   - F. $10x^2$
   - G. $10x^8$
   - H. $10x^{15}$
   - J. $24x^8$
   - K. $24x^{15}$

5. The expression $(7m^2n)(6mn^3)$ is equivalent to:
   - A. $13m^2n^3$
   - B. $13m^3n^4$
   - C. $42mn$
   - D. $42m^2n^3$
   - E. $42m^3n^4$

6. The expression $3a^2b^3 \cdot 5a^3b^2 \cdot 4b^2$ is equal to:
   - F. $12a^5b^7$
   - G. $12a^6b^{12}$
   - H. $60a^5b^7$
   - J. $60a^6b^{12}$
   - K. $60a^6b^7$

DO YOUR FIGURING HERE.

END OF SET TWO
STOP! DO NOT GO ON TO THE NEXT PAGE
UNTIL TOLD TO DO SO.

ACT® Mastery Math

15.4.3 Set Three

DO YOUR FIGURING HERE.

7. If $x \neq 0$, then $\dfrac{x^9}{x^3}$ equals:
   A. 1
   B. 3
   C. x^2
   D. x^3
   E. x^6

8. What does $3a^3 \cdot 6a^5$ equal?
   F. $9a^2$
   G. $9a^8$
   H. $9a^{15}$
   J. $18a^8$
   K. $18a^{15}$

9. Calculate $\dfrac{3^2 - 1^3}{4^2 - 1^3}$.
   A. $\dfrac{1}{2}$
   B. $\dfrac{8}{15}$
   C. $\dfrac{9}{16}$
   D. $\dfrac{10}{17}$
   E. $\dfrac{2}{3}$

END OF SET THREE
STOP! DO NOT GO ON TO THE NEXT PAGE
UNTIL TOLD TO DO SO.

Entrance Ticket | Learning Targets | Multiplying with Exponents | Dividing with Exponents | Square and Cube Roots | ACT Practice | Sum It Up

15.4.4 Set Four

10. Simplify $\sqrt{24} - \sqrt{54}$.

F. $-\sqrt{6}$
G. -6
H. 6
J. $6\sqrt{6}$
K. $\sqrt{78}$

DO YOUR FIGURING HERE.

11. Given $\dfrac{2\sqrt{11}}{11} = \dfrac{2\sqrt{11}}{p\sqrt{11}}$, what is the value p?

F. 1
G. $\sqrt{11}$
H. 11
J. 22
K. 121

12. If x is a real number, what is $\sqrt[3]{x^{27}}$ equivalent to?

F. x^{-9}
G. $x^{\frac{1}{9}}$
H. $|x^9|$
J. x^9
K. x^{24}

END OF SET FOUR
STOP! DO NOT GO ON TO THE NEXT PAGE
UNTIL TOLD TO DO SO.

15.4.5 Set Five

DO YOUR FIGURING HERE.

13. Find y in terms of x for $\sqrt{y} - \sqrt{x} = 8\sqrt{x}$, where both y and x are positive real numbers.

   A. $81x$
   B. $64x$
   C. $9x$
   D. $8x$
   E. $3x$

14. If $a \neq 0$, then $(a^{-4})^3 = ?$

   F. $\dfrac{1}{a^{12}}$
   G. $\dfrac{1}{a}$
   H. a^7
   J. a^{12}
   K. a^{64}

15. If a and b both $\neq 0$, then $\left(\dfrac{a^{-3}}{b}\right)(a^3 b^3)$ is equivalent to:

   A. $a^{-9}b^3$
   B. $a^{-9}b^2$
   C. $a^{-9}b^{-2}$
   D. b^3
   E. b^2

END OF SET FIVE
STOP! DO NOT GO ON TO THE NEXT PAGE
UNTIL TOLD TO DO SO.

Lesson 15 – Exponents and Roots

Sum It Up

Exponents and Roots

Exponent
The power to which a number or term is raised
Ex: 3 in the expression x^3

Base
The number or variable at the "bottom" of an exponent, which is multiplied by itself the number of times indicated by the exponent
Ex: x in the expression x^3

Coefficient
The number before the base and exponent
Ex: 7 in the expression $7x^3$

Squared
A term that is raised to the second power
Ex: "five squared" is written 5^2 and "x squared" is written x^2

Cubed
A term that is raised to the third power
Ex: "five cubed" is written 5^3 and "x cubed" is written x^3

Negative Exponent
An expression with an exponent that is negative
Ex: 5^{-3} and x^{-3}

Rules for Operations with Exponents

When **multiplying** terms with exponents that have the same base, **add** the exponents.
Ex: $3x^3 \cdot 2x^4 = 6x^{3+4} = 6x^7$

When **raising an expression** with exponents to another power, **multiply** the exponents.
Ex: $(y^3)^5 = y^{3 \cdot 5} = y^{15}$

When **dividing** terms with exponents that have the same base, **subtract** the exponents.
Ex: $\dfrac{a^9}{a^4} = a^{9-4} = a^5$

Lesson 16

Angle Properties

CAPTION:

ACT® Mastery Math

16.1 Entrance Ticket

Solve the questions below.

1. Which of the following is the defining characteristic of a kite?
   A. A kite has 1 pair of parallel sides.
   B. A kite has perpendicular diagonals.
   C. A kite has congruent diagonals.
   D. A kite has 4 congruent sides.
   E. A kite has 4 congruent angles.

2. In the figure below, ∠DBA measures 55°, ∠DCB measures 25°, and ∠ADB measures 90°. What is the measure of ∠ADC ?

   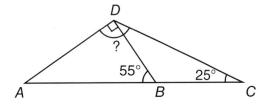

   F. 100°
   G. 120°
   H. 125°
   J. 135°
   K. 155°

3. In the figure below, A, B, D, and E are collinear. $\overline{BD}$, $\overline{CD}$, and $\overline{DE}$ are all the same length, and the angle measure of ∠DCE is as shown. What is the degree of measure of ∠ABC ?

   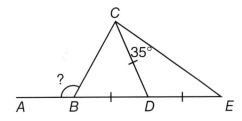

   A. 70°
   B. 110°
   C. 115°
   D. 125°
   E. 145°

Lesson 16 – Angle Properties

16.2 Learning Targets

1. Understand and utilize the angle properties of triangles to solve related problems

2. Understand and utilize the properties of various shapes and their interor and exterior angles to solve related problems

Self-Assessment

Circle the number that corresponds to your confidence level in your knowledge of this subject before beginning the lesson. A score of 1 means you are completely lost, and a score of 4 means you have mastered the skills. After you finish the lesson, return to the bottom of this page and circle your new confidence level to show your improvement.

Before Lesson

1 2 3 4

After Lesson

1 2 3 4

Entrance Ticket | Learning Targets | Angle Properties of Triangles | Angle Properties of Other Polygons | ACT Practice | Sum It Up

ACT® Mastery Math

16.3.1 Angle Properties of Triangles

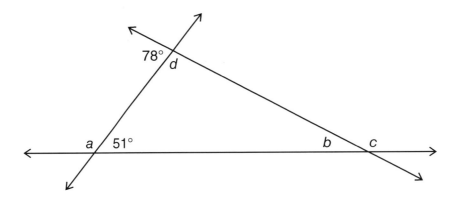

In a triangle, each exterior angle is equal to:

Lesson 16 – Angle Properties

16.3.1 Angle Properties of Triangles

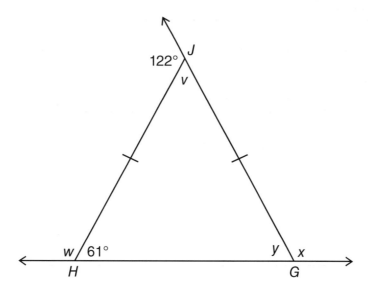

The two interior angles opposite the congruent sides of an isosceles triangle:

_____

ACT® Mastery Math

16.3.2 Angle Properties of Other Polygons

Name: _____

Sum of Interior Angles: _____

Name: _____

Sum of Interior Angles: _____

Name: _____

Sum of Interior Angles: _____

Name: _____

Sum of Interior Angles: _____

Name: _____

Sum of Interior Angles: _____

Rule for interior angles of a quadrilateral:

_____

16.3.2 Angle Properties of Other Polygons

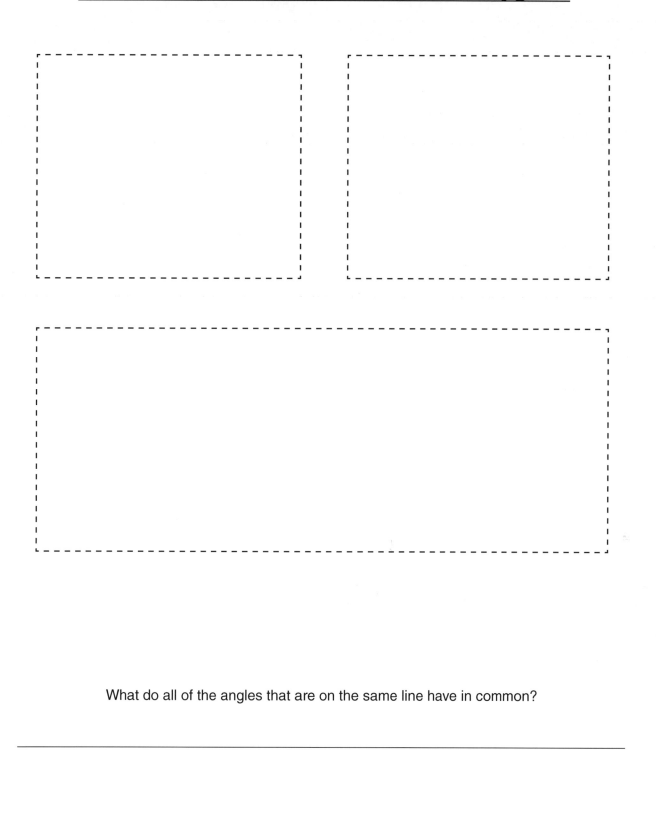

What do all of the angles that are on the same line have in common?

16.3.2 Angle Properties of Other Polygons

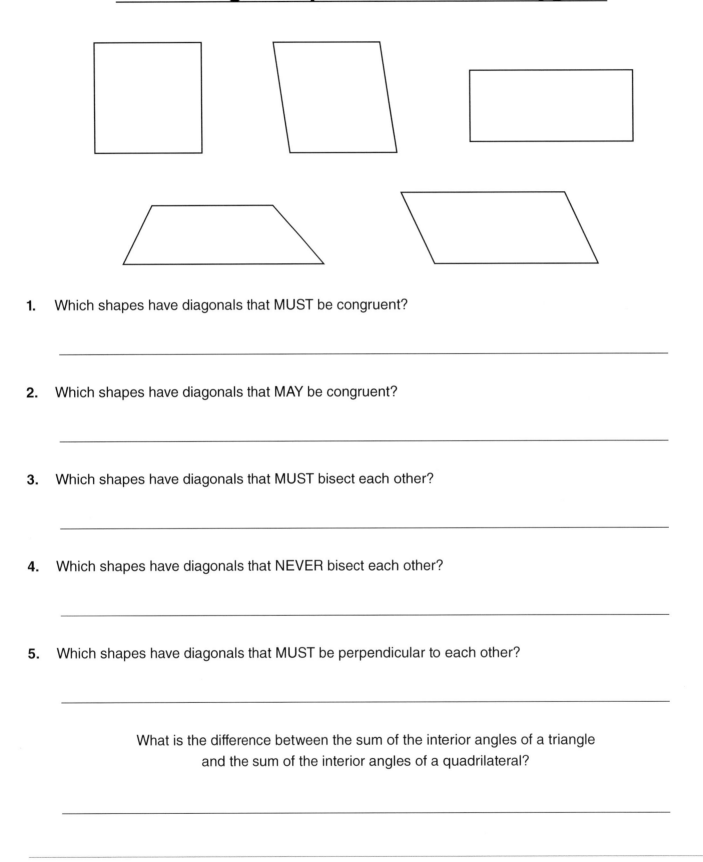

1. Which shapes have diagonals that MUST be congruent?

2. Which shapes have diagonals that MAY be congruent?

3. Which shapes have diagonals that MUST bisect each other?

4. Which shapes have diagonals that NEVER bisect each other?

5. Which shapes have diagonals that MUST be perpendicular to each other?

What is the difference between the sum of the interior angles of a triangle and the sum of the interior angles of a quadrilateral?

Lesson 16 – Angle Properties

16.3.2 Angle Properties of Other Polygons

Rule for the sum of interior angles of a polygon:

_____

1. The sum of the interior angles of a six-sided figure, or hexagon, is _____

2. The interior angles of an equilateral triangle are each _____

3. The interior angles of a square are each _____

4. The interior angles of an equilateral pentagon are each _____

5. The interior angles of an equilateral hexagon are each _____

Math Tip

Objects in the Mirror Are Exactly as They Appear: If the ACT asks you to calculate a lot of angles and you are either stuck or running out of time, you can use your judgement to guess. Trust that if an angle looks small, it is almost always less than 90°, and if an angle looks big, it is almost always more than 90°. Eliminate, mark, and move.

16.4.1 Set One

1. In △QRS, shown below, $\overline{SQ} \cong \overline{SR}$, and the measure of ∠S is 136°. What is the measure of ∠Q ?

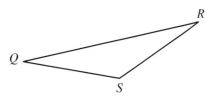

   A. 11°
   B. 22°
   C. 44°
   D. 54°
   E. 68°

2. In the figure below, $\overline{AB}$ is congruent to $\overline{BC}$, and $\overline{AD}$ intersects $\overline{BE}$ at C. What is the measure of ∠B ?

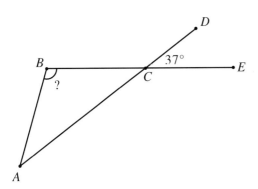

   F. 23°
   G. 37°
   H. 74°
   J. 106°
   K. 143°

3. In △QRS, ∠R and ∠S are congruent, and the measure of ∠Q is 128°. What is the measure of ∠S ?

   A. 21°
   B. 26°
   C. 52°
   D. 64°
   E. 128°

END OF SET ONE
STOP! DO NOT GO ON TO THE NEXT PAGE
UNTIL TOLD TO DO SO.

16.4.2 Set Two

4. For △ABC below, points D and E are on the sides of the triangle. If $\overline{AB}$ is parallel to $\overline{ED}$, what is the measure of ∠EDB ?

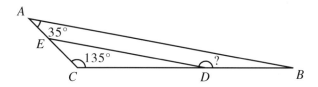

- F. 85°
- G. 100°
- H. 135°
- J. 145°
- K. 170°

DO YOUR FIGURING HERE.

5. Shown below are the triangle △BCD and the collinear points A, B, and D. The measure of ∠C is 73°, the measure of ∠ABC is $(12z)°$, and the measure of ∠DBC is $(6z)°$. What is the measure of ∠D ?

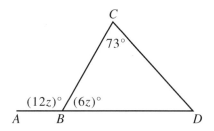

- A. 21°
- B. 47°
- C. 60°
- D. 120°
- E. 133°

6. In △ABC, ∠A measures exactly 88°, and ∠B measures greater than 51°. Which of the following best describes the measure of ∠C ?

- F. Less than 41°
- G. Greater than 41°
- H. Equal to 37°
- J. Equal to 139°
- K. Equal to 41°

END OF SET TWO
STOP! DO NOT GO ON TO THE NEXT PAGE
UNTIL TOLD TO DO SO.

16.4.3 Set Three

7. The blueprint of Jonathan's rectangular farm divided into 6 triangular sections is shown below. The 2 triangles that do not share an edge with the rectangle are congruent (△ABE ≅ △CBD) and will hold a different crop than the other 4 triangles. The blueprint includes the measures of ∠ABE, ∠CBD, and ∠BCD. What is the measure of ∠AEB ?

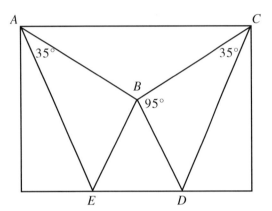

A. 35°
B. 50°
C. 95°
D. 130°
E. 145°

DO YOUR FIGURING HERE.

8. The figure below is made from a trapezoid, ABCD, with congruent sides, $\overline{AB}$ and $\overline{DC}$, and an equilateral triangle, △CDE. What is the the measure of ∠ADE ?

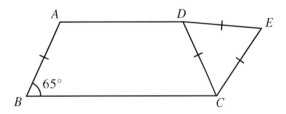

F. 235°
G. 185°
H. 175°
J. 125°
K. 115°

Lesson 16 – Angle Properties

9. In the figure below, the measures of 5 angles of hexagon ABCDE are given. What is the measure of ∠E ?

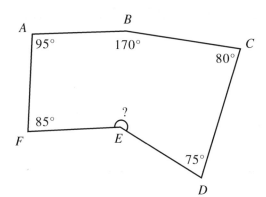

DO YOUR FIGURING HERE.

A. 95°
B. 170°
C. 180°
D. 215°
E. 235°

END OF SET THREE
STOP! DO NOT GO ON TO THE NEXT PAGE
UNTIL TOLD TO DO SO.

16.4.4 Set Four

Shown below is the right triangle $\triangle ABC$ within the rectangle $ABCD$ with the given dimensions.

DO YOUR FIGURING HERE.

10. Which of the following statements is true regarding the measures of the interior angles of $ABCD$?

    (Note: $m\angle ABC$ represents the degree measure of $\angle ABC$.)

    F. $m\angle ACB = m\angle ABC$
    G. $m\angle ACB = m\angle ACD$
    H. $m\angle ACD + m\angle BAC = 90°$
    J. $m\angle ACB + m\angle BAC + m\angle ABC = 360°$
    K. $m\angle ACB + m\angle BAC + m\angle ACD + m\angle DAC = 180°$

11. Pictured below are trapezoids $ABCD$ and $EFGH$ with $\angle A \cong \angle E$, $\angle B \cong \angle F$, $\angle C \cong \angle G$, and $ABCD \cong EFGH$, with $\overline{AB} \parallel \overline{CD}$ and $\overline{EF} \parallel \overline{GH}$. The measure of $\angle B$ is 95°. The measure of $\angle E$ is 65°. What is the measure of $\angle H$?

    A. 95°
    B. 115°
    C. 130°
    D. 150°
    E. The answer cannot be determined from the given information.

GO ON TO THE NEXT PAGE

12. In the parallelogram ABCD below, the measure of ∠DAB is 72°, and the measure of ∠BDC is 28°. What is the measure of ∠ADB?

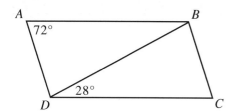

F. 28°
G. 70°
H. 72°
J. 80°
K. 90°

16.4.5 Set Five

13. In △QRT below, $\overline{RT}$ is perpendicular to $\overline{QT}$, points R, S, and T are collinear, and $\overline{QS}$ bisects ∠TQR. If the measure of ∠SRQ is 30°, what is the measure of ∠RSQ ?

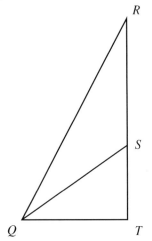

A. 60°
B. 115°
C. 120°
D. 135°
E. 150°

DO YOUR FIGURING HERE.

14. In △ABC, ∠B measures exactly 101° and ∠C measures less than 34°. Which of the following best describes the measure of ∠A ?

F. Less than 45°
G. Greater than 45°
H. Equal to 34°
J. Equal to 45°
K. Equal to 135°

GO ON TO THE NEXT PAGE

15. In the figure below, 2 nonadjacent sides of a regular hexagon (6 congruent sides and 6 congruent angles) are extended until they meet at a point Z. What is the measure of ∠Z ?

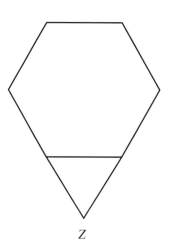

Z

A. 15°
B. 30°
C. 60°
D. 120°
E. Cannot be determined from the given information

DO YOUR FIGURING HERE.

END OF SET FIVE
STOP! DO NOT GO ON TO THE NEXT PAGE UNTIL TOLD TO DO SO.

ACT® Mastery Math

Sum It Up

Angle Properties

Angle
A figure formed by two rays that connect at the vertex

Degrees
The measurement of an angle, denoted by the ° symbol

Parallel Lines
Two lines in a plane that never intersect or touch

Perpendicular Lines
Two lines in a plane that intersect at a 90° angle

Transversal Line
A line that passes through two lines in a plane

Obtuse Angle
An angle greater than 90° but less than 180°

Acute Angle
An angle that is less than 90°

Supplementary Angles
Two angles whose measures add up to 180°

Complementary Angles
Two angles whose measures add up to 90°

Vertical/Opposite Angles
The angles opposite one another when two lines in a plane cross; they are always equal

Corresponding Angles
Angles in the same position when a transversal cuts across parallel lines; they are always equal

Congruency
Equal in length or measure
Congruent angles have the same measure, and congruent lines have the same length. Congruent polygons have congruent angles and lines.

Tips and Techniques

Objects in Mirror Are Exactly as They Appear: Use the picture to help you arrive at your answer, especially if you are stuck.

Entrance Ticket   Learning Targets   Angle Properties of Triangles   Angle Properties of Other Polygons   ACT Practice   Sum It Up

Lesson 17

Angles and Parallel Lines

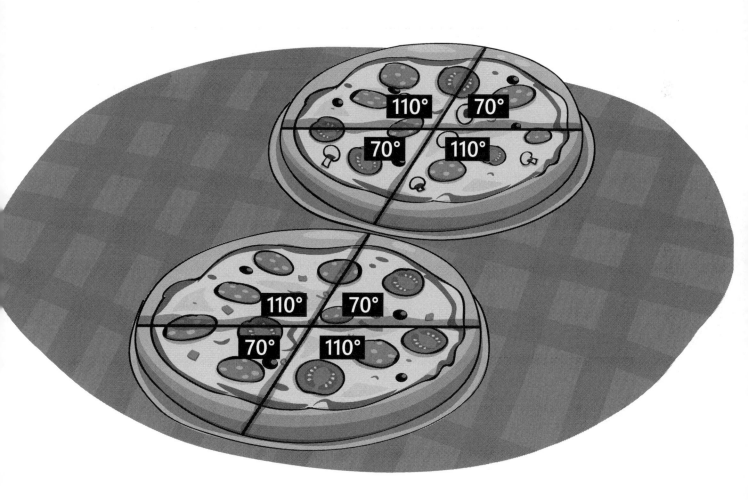

CAPTION:

ACT® Mastery Math

17.1 Entrance Ticket

Solve the questions below.

1. In the diagram below, lines a and b are NOT parallel and are cut by transversal c. Which of the following statements *must* be true?

   A. ∠3 ≅ ∠6
   B. ∠3 ≅ ∠7
   C. ∠5 ≅ ∠6
   D. ∠5 ≅ ∠7
   E. ∠5 ≅ ∠8

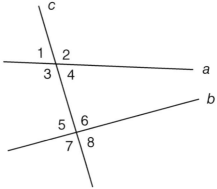

2. Parallel lines *l* and *k* intersect parallel lines *m* and *n* in the figure below. If it can be determined, what is the sum of the degree measures of ∠1 and ∠2 ?

   F. 200°
   G. 180°
   H. 160°
   J. 120°
   K. Cannot be determined

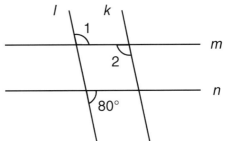

3. In the figure below, lines a and b are parallel, and transversals c and d intersect to form an angle of measure Z°. Given the 2 angle measurements below, what is the value of ∠Z ?

   A. 20°
   B. 30°
   C. 45°
   D. 65°
   E. 70°

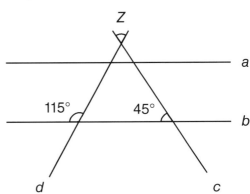

Lesson 17 – Angles and Parallel Lines

17.2 Learning Targets

1. Understand and utilize the concept of complimentary and supplementary angles to solve related problems

2. Understand and utilize the properties of angles created by the intersection of one or more lines with two parallel lines to solve related problems

Self-Assessment

Circle the number that corresponds to your confidence level in your knowledge of this subject before beginning the lesson. A score of 1 means you are completely lost, and a score of 4 means you have mastered the skills. After you finish the lesson, return to the bottom of this page and circle your new confidence level to show your improvement.

Before Lesson

1   2   3   4

After Lesson

1   2   3   4

17.3.1 Calculating Angles

1.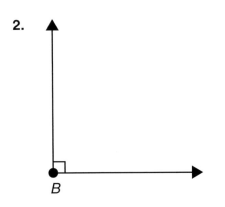

   Answer: _____

2.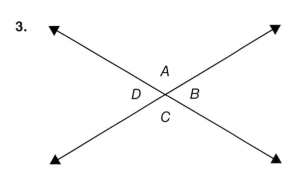

   Answer: _____

3.

   Answer: _____

Lesson 17 – Angles and Parallel Lines

17.3.1 Calculating Angles

When calculating supplementary angles,

_____

When calculating complementary angles,

_____

When calculating opposite/vertical angles,

_____

17.3.1 Calculating Angles

1. ∠B and ∠F are complementary angles, and ∠F measures 49°. ∠B measures _____.

2. ∠k and ∠d are supplementary angles, and ∠k measures 49°. ∠d measures _____.

3. ∠J and ∠L are complementary angles, and ∠L measures 34°. ∠J measures _____.

4. ∠h and ∠r are supplementary angles, and ∠h measures 113°. ∠r measures _____.

5. What are the angle measurements of ∠A, ∠B, and ∠D in the following figure if ∠C = 106°?

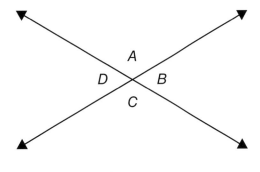

Answer: _____

Lesson 17 – Angles and Parallel Lines

17.3.2 Angles Created by Parallel Lines

1. Instead of slicing the pizza into four quarters, as usual, the new worker accidentally cuts all the pizza into these four slices. The pizza parlor is too busy to correct the mistake and decides to price the larger slices at $3 and the smaller slices at $2.

   A customer wants to buy the two smaller slices, but he wants to know if they are the same size. What do you tell him?

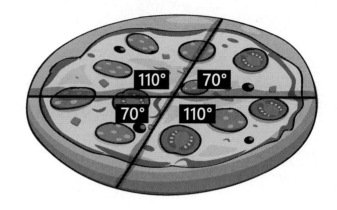

2. In this display case, are the horizontal cuts in the two pizzas parallel? How do you know?

3. Are the corresponding angles equal?

4. How many sets of supplementary angles are there?

5. How many sets of vertical angles are there?

17.3.2 Angles Created by Parallel Lines

1. Angle r = _____

2. Angle s = _____

3. Angle t = _____

4. Angle u = _____

5. Angle w = _____

6. Angle x = _____

7. Angle y = _____

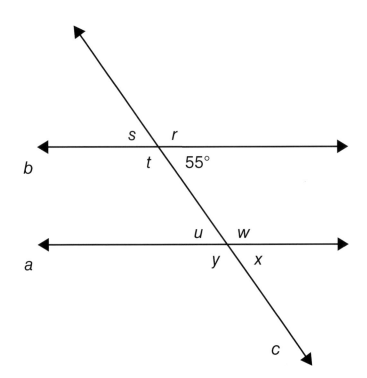

Math Tip
Objects in Mirror are Exactly as They Appear: Questions on the ACT about angles usually provide pictures, which are almost always drawn to scale. This means that if one angle looks smaller than another, it probably is. If one angle looks the same size as another, it probably is.

17.4.1 Set One

1. In the figure below, line *m* and line *n* are parallel. The 2 transversals intersect on a point on line *m*. Which of the following pairs of angles is not necessarily congruent?

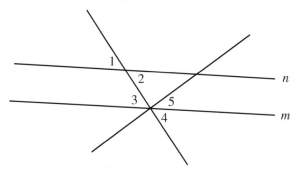

- A. ∠1 and ∠2
- B. ∠2 and ∠3
- C. ∠2 and ∠4
- D. ∠3 and ∠4
- E. ∠3 and ∠5

2. In the diagram below, lines *l* and *k* are cut by transversal *r*. Lines *l* and *k* are NOT parallel. Which of the following *must* be true?

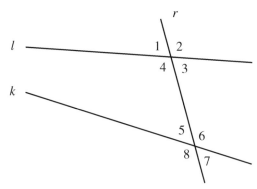

- F. ∠1 ≅ ∠5
- G. ∠2 ≅ ∠8
- H. ∠5 ≅ ∠6
- J. ∠5 ≅ ∠7
- K. ∠7 ≅ ∠3

3. The sum of ∠B and ∠C is 90°, and ∠A ≅ ∠C. What must be true about the measures of ∠A and ∠B?

- A. m∠A + m∠B = 90°
- B. m∠A + m∠B = 180°
- C. m∠B > m∠A
- D. m∠B < m∠A
- E. m∠B = m∠A

DO YOUR FIGURING HERE.

END OF SET ONE
STOP! DO NOT GO ON TO THE NEXT PAGE UNTIL TOLD TO DO SO.

17.4.2 Set Two

4. The points X, Y, and Z are collinear, Y is between X and Z, and Q is not on the same line as X, Y and Z. Which of the following statements about the measure of the angles must be true? (Note: The figure is only 1 possible arrangement of these points.)

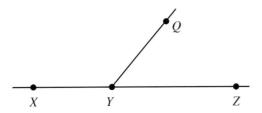

F. $m\angle XYQ > m\angle ZYQ$
G. $m\angle ZYQ > m\angle XYQ$
H. The difference of $m\angle XYQ$ and $m\angle ZYQ$ is 45°
J. The sum of $m\angle XYQ$ and $m\angle ZYQ$ is 180°
K. The sum of $m\angle XYQ$ and $m\angle ZYQ$ is 360°

5. In the figure below, lines a and b are parallel, and line c is a transversal that intersects a and b at D and E. Which of the following must be true?

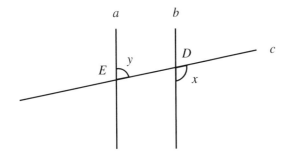

A. $y = x$
B. $y = 2x$
C. $x - y = 90°$
D. $x + y = 180°$
E. $x + y = 270°$

6. The figure below shows 2 sets of parallel lines: $a \parallel b$ and $c \parallel d$. The acute angle that d intersects a is 65°. What is the measure of the acute angle that c intersects b?

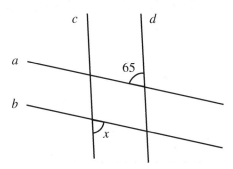

F. 15°
G. 25°
H. 65°
J. 75°
K. 85°

17.4.3 Set Three

7. A metal beam is lifted by a forklift, as shown in the figure below. The beam creates an 83° angle with the inside of one of the tongs of the forklift. What angle is made between the beam and the other parallel tong, as indicated below?

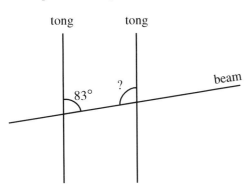

A. 83°
B. 87°
C. 91°
D. 95°
E. 97°

8. In the figure below, lines a and b are cut by transversal line c. The 8 angles at the intersections are labeled. When true, which of the following statements cannot always be used to prove that a and b are parallel?

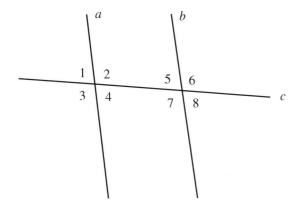

F. $\angle 1 \cong \angle 5$
G. $\angle 2 \cong \angle 6$
H. $\angle 2 \cong \angle 7$
J. $\angle 3 \cong \angle 5$
K. $\angle 4 \cong \angle 5$

DO YOUR FIGURING HERE.

9. In the figure below, $a \parallel b$, and transversals c and d intersect a at point X and intersect b at points Y and Z, respectively. Point Q is on b, the measure of $\angle XZQ$ is 120°, and the measure of $\angle ZXY$ is 60°. How many of the angles formed by a, b, c, and d have a measure of 60° ?

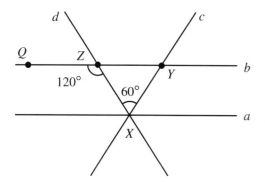

A. 4
B. 6
C. 8
D. 10
E. 12

17.4.4 Set Four

10. In the figure below, lines a and b are parallel, line c is a transversal, and 3 angle measures are given in degrees. What is the value of $m - n$?

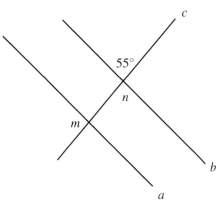

- F. -70
- G. 55
- H. 70
- J. 125
- K. 180

11. In the figure below, Z is on x, and $x \parallel y$. Which of the following angle congruencies must hold?

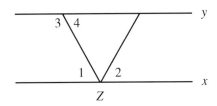

- A. $\angle 1 \cong \angle 2$
- B. $\angle 1 \cong \angle 4$
- C. $\angle 2 \cong \angle 3$
- D. $\angle 2 \cong \angle 4$
- E. $\angle 3 \cong \angle 4$

DO YOUR FIGURING HERE.

GO ON TO THE NEXT PAGE.

Lesson 17 – Angles and Parallel Lines

12. Lines k, l, m, and n are shown below, and m and n are parallel. Which of the following is the set of angles that must be supplementary to angle x ?

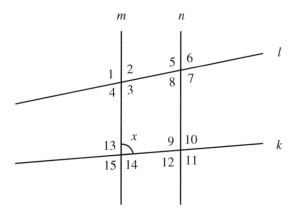

DO YOUR FIGURING HERE.

F. {13, 14}
G. {1, 3, 13, 14}
H. {9, 11, 13, 14}
J. {1, 3, 9, 11, 13, 14}
K. {1, 3, 5, 7, 9, 11, 13, 14}

END OF SET FOUR
STOP! DO NOT GO ON TO THE NEXT PAGE
UNTIL TOLD TO DO SO.

17.4.5 Set Five

13. In the figure below, transversal c crosses both a and b, and $x°$ and $y°$ are measures of the indicated angles, both between $0°$ and $180°$. Lines a and b will cross somewhere to the right of the transversal c. Which of the following statements best expresses a true relationship between x and y for all possible positions of transversal c ?

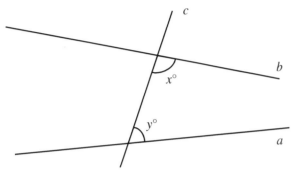

A. $x < y$
B. $y < x$
C. $y = x$
D. $x + y > 180$
E. $x + y < 180$

DO YOUR FIGURING HERE.

14. In the figure below, parallel lines a_1, a_2, and a_3 intersect transversal b. What is the value of $x + y + z + q$?

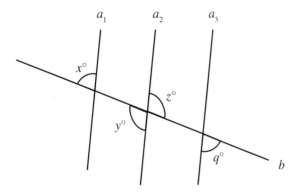

F. 90
G. 180
H. 270
J. 360
K. 450

GO ON TO THE NEXT PAGE.

Lesson 17 – Angles and Parallel Lines

15. In the figure below, segment $\overline{AB}$, $\overline{CD}$, and $\overline{EF}$ all intersect at point X, with angle measures as marked. What is the measure of $\angle CXE$?

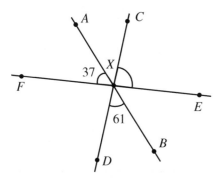

A. 53°
B. 82°
C. 98°
D. 119°
E. 143°

DO YOUR FIGURING HERE.

END OF SET FIVE
STOP! DO NOT GO ON TO THE NEXT PAGE
UNTIL TOLD TO DO SO.

ACT® Mastery Math

Sum It Up

Angles and Parallel Lines

Triangle
A figure with three sides and three angles. The sum of the interior angles of ANY triangle always equals 180°.

Isosceles Triangle
A triangle with two sides of equal length. The angles opposite the equal sides are also equal.

Right Triangle
A triangle containing one right (90°) angle

Equilateral Triangle
A triangle with three equal sides. The angles of an equilateral triangle each measure 60°.

Interior Angle
An angle inside a shape's perimeter

Exterior Angle
An angle outside a shape's perimeter

Congruency (Angles and Sides)
Identical in size, measure, or length

Quadrilateral
A four-sided polygon with four angles. Types include trapezoids, parallelograms, rectangles, squares, rhombuses, etc.

Trapezoid
A quadrilateral with only one pair of parallel sides

Isosceles Trapezoid
A special case of a trapezoid in which the base angles and two sides are equal

Parallelogram
A quadrilateral that has parallel opposite sides

Lesson 17 – Angles and Parallel Lines

Sum It Up

Rhombus
A parallelogram with equal sides

Diagonal
A line joining two opposite corners of a quadrilateral

Pentagon
A figure with five sides and five angles

Hexagon
A figure with six sides and six angles

Tips and Techniques

Objects in the Mirror are Exactly as They Appear: If the ACT asks you to calculate lots of angles and you are either stuck or running out of time, you can use your judgement to guess. Trust that if an angle looks small, it is almost always less than 90°, and if an angle looks big, it is almost always more than 90°. Eliminate, mark, and move.

Lesson 18

Pythagorean Theorem

CAPTION:

ACT® Mastery Math

18.1 Entrance Ticket

Solve the question below.

A scalene triangle has integer lengths of unknown value.

What is the least possible integer perimeter of this triangle? _____

Lesson 18 – Pythagorean Theorem

18.2 Learning Targets

1. Use the Pythagorean Theorem to determine unknown lengths

2. Recognize Pythagorean Triples to avoid time-consuming calculations

Self-Assessment

Circle the number that corresponds to your confidence level in your knowledge of this subject before beginning the lesson. A score of 1 means you are completely lost, and a score of 4 means you have mastered the skills. After you finish the lesson, return to the bottom of this page and circle your new confidence level to show your improvement.

Before Lesson

1   2   3   4

After Lesson

1   2   3   4

Entrance Ticket | Learning Targets | Pythagorean Theorem Calculations | Hidden Triangles | ACT Practice | Sum It Up

18.3.1 Pythagorean Theorem Calculations

TV #1

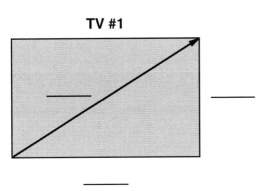

TV #2

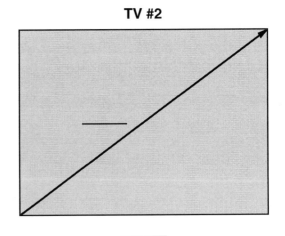

TV #1:	TV #2:

Was the claim true or false? _____

Lesson 18 – Pythagorean Theorem

18.3.2 Hidden Triangles

1.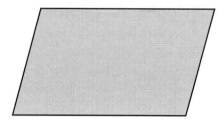

2.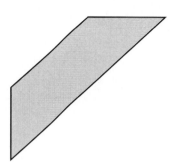

3.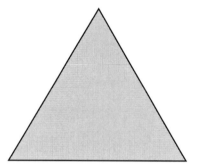

4.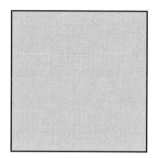

Math Tip

Draw It Out: Most Pythagorean Theorem questions tend to hide the triangles inside other shapes. Make sure you draw out the triangle and label everything. Once the problem is fully set up, write down your formula and start solving.

18.3.2 Hidden Triangles

1. Jason is mowing a flat, rectangular lawn that is 20 feet wide and 36 feet long. About how many feet long is a diagonal of the lawn? Round your answer to the nearest foot.
   - A. 28
   - B. 30
   - C. 41
   - D. 56
   - E. 1,696

2. A train leaves a station heading east. After traveling 33 miles east, the train travels 56 miles south. How far is the train from the station?
   - F. 33
   - G. 56
   - H. 65
   - J. 72
   - K. 89

3. The slide below is 10 feet long and covers a distance of 8 feet across the ground. How many feet high is the slide at its highest point?

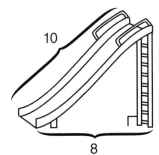

Answer: _____

18.3.2 Hidden Triangles

4. In the right triangle below, how many feet long is $\overline{BC}$?

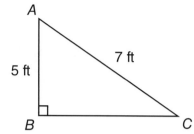

Answer: _____

5. Rhombus $ABCD$ is shown in the figure below. If $\overline{AB} = 41$ inches and $\overline{AC} = 18$ inches, then what is the length of $\overline{BD}$, in inches?

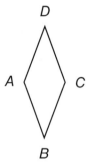

A. 18
B. 20
C. 40
D. 80
E. 82

6. The parallel sides of the isosceles trapezoid shown below are 20 feet long and 10 feet long, respectively. What is the distance between the 2 sides, in feet?

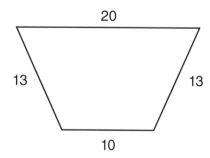

F. 5
G. 10
H. 12
J. 13
K. 20

18.3.2 Hidden Triangles

7. The shape below was a square with 25-inch sides before a triangle was removed. What is the perimeter of the new shape, in inches?

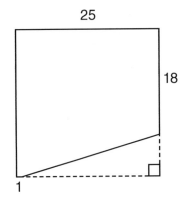

- A. 69
- B. 76
- C. 93
- D. 94
- E. 100

8. In the figure below, the diagonal of a smaller square is a side of a larger square. The area of the smaller square is 16 square inches. What is the area of the larger square, in square inches?

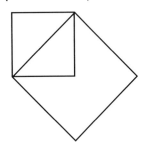

- F. 32
- G. 40
- H. 56
- J. 64
- K. 72

18.4.1 Set One

1. The dimensions of the right triangle shown below are given in feet. What is the length of the hypotenuse of the triangle, in feet?

   A. $\sqrt{11}$
   B. 7
   C. $\sqrt{65}$
   D. 11
   E. 65

   DO YOUR FIGURING HERE.

2. In the right triangle $\triangle EFG$ shown below, H is halfway between point E and point G. To the nearest tenth, how long is $\overline{EH}$?

   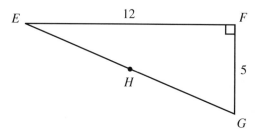

   F. 6.5
   G. 7.5
   H. 13
   J. 84.5
   K. 169

   GO ON TO THE NEXT PAGE.

3. In the triangle below, which of the following is an expression for b in terms of a ?

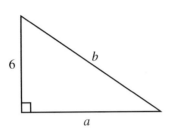

A. $6 + a$
B. $\sqrt{a^2 + 6}$
C. $\sqrt{a^2 + 12}$
D. $\sqrt{a^2 - 36}$
E. $\sqrt{a^2 + 36}$

DO YOUR FIGURING HERE.

END OF SET ONE
STOP! DO NOT GO ON TO THE NEXT PAGE
UNTIL TOLD TO DO SO.

Lesson 18 – Pythagorean Theorem

18.4.2 Set Two

4. The legs of a right triangle measure 10 feet and 24 feet. What is the length of the hypotenuse, in feet?

    F. 27
    G. 26
    H. 34
    J. $\sqrt{1,644}$
    K. 48

DO YOUR FIGURING HERE.

5. A bicycle ramp, shown below, measures 25 feet long and is 7 feet off the ground at its highest point. How many feet long is the base of the ramp?

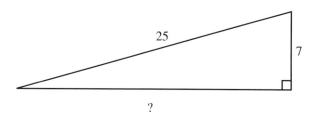

A. 18
B. 24
C. 48
D. $\sqrt{18}$
E. $\sqrt{674}$

GO ON TO THE NEXT PAGE.

6. What is the length of $\overline{AC}$ in inches?

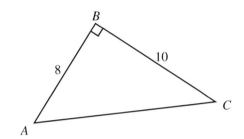

- F. 10
- G. 18
- H. $\sqrt{18}$
- J. $\sqrt{36}$
- K. $\sqrt{164}$

END OF SET TWO
STOP! DO NOT GO ON TO THE NEXT PAGE
UNTIL TOLD TO DO SO.

18.4.3 Set Three

7. Jason is making an arrow for his archery tournament. The base of the arrowhead, $\overline{BC}$, is 16 cm long. The sides of the arrowhead, $\overline{AB}$ and $\overline{AC}$, are both 17 cm long. The shaft of the arrow, $\overline{DE}$, is 18 cm in length. How long is the length of the total arrow, $\overline{AD}$, in cm?

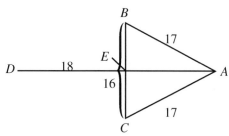

- A. 15
- B. 33
- C. 35
- D. $\sqrt{545}$
- E. $\sqrt{613}$

DO YOUR FIGURING HERE.

8. A right triangle has legs with lengths of 6 feet and 9 feet. The hypotenuse of the triangle, in feet, is between:
- F. 4 and 5
- G. 6 and 9
- H. 9 and 10
- J. 10 and 11
- K. 11 and 13

GO ON TO THE NEXT PAGE.

9. The figure below shows James's house, Kyle's house, and a grocery as the 3 vertices of a right triangle. James and his sister are on their way to a party at Kyle's house. James goes straight to Kyle's house, but his sister stops to pick up snacks at the grocery store and then goes to Kyle's house. How much further does James's sister drive than James, in miles?

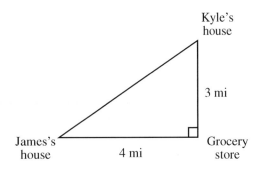

A. 1
B. 2
C. 3
D. 4
E. 5

18.4.4 Set Four

10. The dimensions of the triangle below are given in feet. If the legs of the triangle doubled in length to become legs of a new triangle, what would the length of the longest side of the new triangle be?

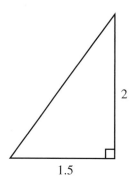

F. 3
G. 4
H. 4.5
J. 5
K. 7

DO YOUR FIGURING HERE.

11. Rod is building a ramp for a stunt. The length and height of the ramp are given in meters and are shown in the figure below. To the nearest meter, what is the perimeter of Rod's ramp?

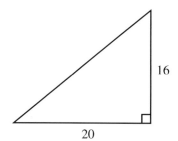

A. 25
B. 36
C. 45
D. 62
E. 70

GO ON TO THE NEXT PAGE.

12. In the figure below, *EFGH* is a square with a side length of 8 feet. *A*, *B*, *C*, and *D* are midpoints of each side. What is the perimeter of *ABCD* in feet?

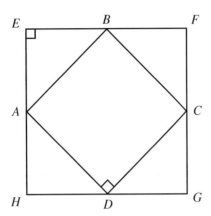

F. 12
G. $12\sqrt{2}$
H. $16\sqrt{2}$
J. $20\sqrt{2}$
K. 32

18.4.5 Set Five

13. The diagonal $\overline{BD}$ cuts the quadrilateral ABCD into a right triangle, $\triangle ABD$, and an equilateral triangle, $\triangle BCD$. The dimensions are given in inches. How many inches long is $\overline{DC}$?

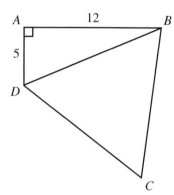

- A. $\sqrt{10}$
- B. 10
- C. 13
- D. 17
- E. 34

DO YOUR FIGURING HERE.

14. The polygon below was a square with 20-meter sides before a triangle was removed. What is the new perimeter of the polygon, in meters?

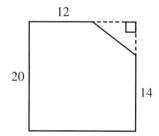

- F. 66
- G. 70
- H. 76
- J. 78
- K. 80

GO ON TO THE NEXT PAGE.

15. When Brad threw the winning touchdown pass, he was 15 yards behind the 50-yard line and 17 yards from the sideline, as shown in the figure below. How far was Brad from the center of the end zone when he threw the pass? Round your answer to the nearest yard.

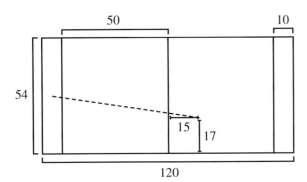

A. 66
B. 71
C. 76
D. 79
E. 84

Lesson 18 – Pythagorean Theorem

Sum It Up

Pythagorean Theorem

Right Angle
90° angle

Right Triangle
A triangle that has a 90° angle

Hypotenuse
The side opposite the right angle in a right triangle; the longest side of a right triangle

Leg
A side of the right triangle that is not the longest side

Pythagorean Theorem
In a right triangle, the square of the hypotenuse is equal to the sum of the squares of the legs.

$$c = \sqrt{a^2 + b^2}$$

Tips and Techniques

Draw It Out: Draw any shapes the word problem describes, label necessary information, write down the relevant equation, and then start plugging in the values to solve.

Lesson 19

Similar Triangles

CAPTION:

ACT® Mastery Math

19.1 Entrance Ticket

Write a paragraph (5-7 sentences) describing someone who is similar to you. What things do you have in common? What is different about you?

Lesson 19 – Similar Triangles

19.2 Learning Targets

1. Determine the value for side lengths of similar triangles using ratios

2. Determine side length of similar triangles with shared components

Self-Assessment

Circle the number that corresponds to your confidence level in your knowledge of this subject before beginning the lesson. A score of 1 means you are completely lost, and a score of 4 means you have mastered the skills. After you finish the lesson, return to the bottom of this page and circle your new confidence level to show your improvement.

Before Lesson

1   2   3   4

After Lesson

1   2   3   4

Entrance Ticket | Learning Targets | Scaling Up | Scaling Down | ACT Practice | Sum It Up

19.3.1 Scaling Up

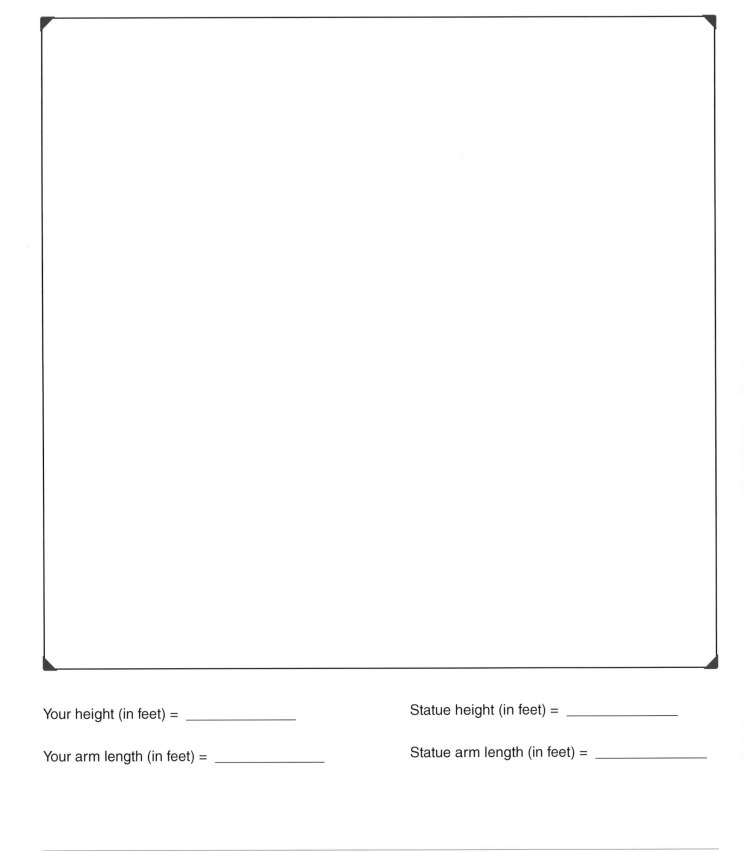

Your height (in feet) = _____

Your arm length (in feet) = _____

Statue height (in feet) = _____

Statue arm length (in feet) = _____

19.3.1 Scaling Up

Statue height (in feet) = _____

Statue arm length (in feet) = _____

Statue height (in feet) = _____

Statue arm length (in feet) = _____

ACT® Mastery Math

19.3.2 Scaling Down

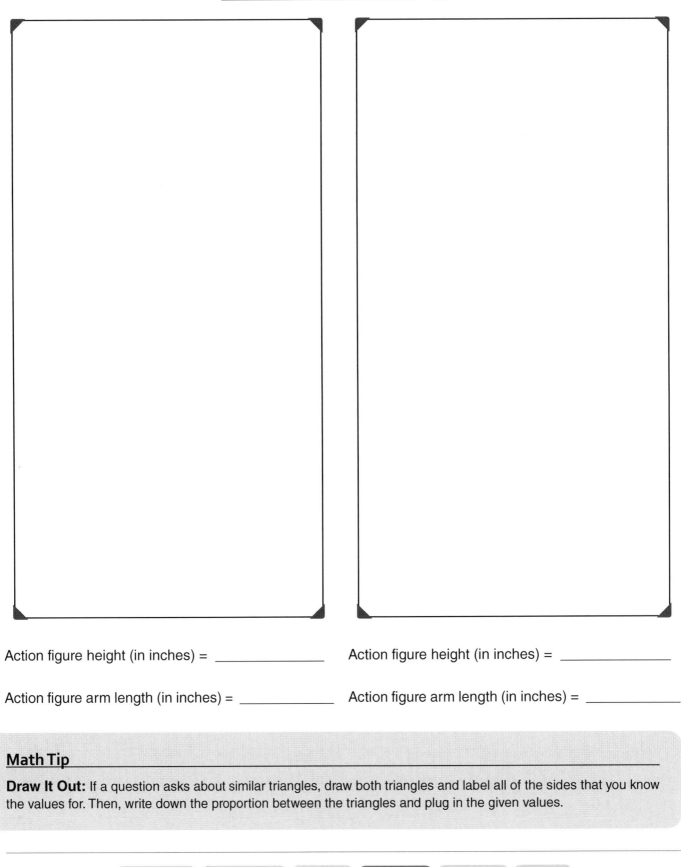

Action figure height (in inches) = _____

Action figure arm length (in inches) = _____

Action figure height (in inches) = _____

Action figure arm length (in inches) = _____

Math Tip

Draw It Out: If a question asks about similar triangles, draw both triangles and label all of the sides that you know the values for. Then, write down the proportion between the triangles and plug in the given values.

19.4.1 Set One

1. The two triangles in the figure below are similar, $\triangle JKL \sim \triangle J'K'L'$. In these similar triangles, $j = 6$, $k = 15$, $l = 18$, and $k' = 25$, where all lengths are given in inches. What is the value of j'?

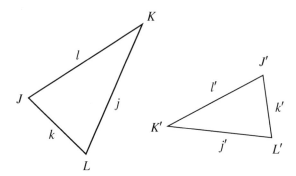

- A. 10
- B. 15
- C. 25
- D. 30
- E. 35

2. In the image below, $\triangle HJI$ and $\triangle NMO$ are similar triangles with the given side lengths in inches. What is the perimeter, in inches, of $\triangle HJI$?

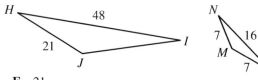

- F. 21
- G. 42
- H. 48
- J. 69
- K. 90

3. The lengths of corresponding sides of 2 similar triangles are in the ratio of 4:6. If one of the sides of the smaller triangle is 3 inches long, how many inches long is the corresponding side of the larger triangle?

- A. 1.5
- B. 4
- C. 4.5
- D. 10
- E. 24

DO YOUR FIGURING HERE.

END OF SET ONE
STOP! DO NOT GO ON TO THE NEXT PAGE
UNTIL TOLD TO DO SO.

19.4.2 Set Two

4. City planners want to determine the distance between two buildings, represented by $\overline{MN}$ in the figure below. They place stakes at points M, N, O, P, and Q so that O is the intersection of $\overline{MQ}$ and $\overline{NP}$ and so that $\overline{MN}$ is parallel to $\overline{PQ}$. The distances between certain stakes are shown in the figure below, in feet. What is the distance between the buildings, in feet?

F. 12
G. 16
H. 22
J. 24
K. 26

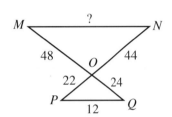

DO YOUR FIGURING HERE.

5. In the right triangle $\triangle MON$ below, $\overline{PQ}$ is parallel to $\overline{MN}$, and $\overline{PQ}$ is perpendicular to $\overline{NO}$ at Q. The length of $\overline{MO}$ is 25 meters, the length of $\overline{PQ}$ is 4 meters, and the length of $\overline{QO}$ is 3 meters. What is the length, in meters, of $\overline{NM}$?

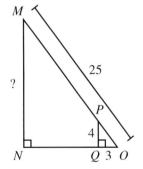

A. 10
B. 15
C. 20
D. 25
E. 30

GO ON TO THE NEXT PAGE

6. On a map, the distances between three small islands that form a triangle are 3, 7, and 9 inches. The longest side has an actual length of 1,000 meters. Which of the following is closest to the actual length, in meters, of the shortest side?

F. 300
G. 333
H. 556
J. 600
K. 1667

DO YOUR FIGURING HERE.

END OF SET TWO
STOP! DO NOT GO ON TO THE NEXT PAGE
UNTIL TOLD TO DO SO.

19.4.3 Set Three

7. On level ground, a vertical flagpole 32 feet tall casts a shadow 14 feet long, and at the same time, a nearby 16-foot vertical tree also casts a shadow. What is the length of the tree's shadow?

   A. 4
   B. 7
   C. 14
   D. 16
   E. 21

8. Shown below are similar triangles $\triangle JKL$ and $\triangle MNO$ with $\angle K \cong \angle O$ and $\angle L \cong \angle N$. The given lengths are in centimeters. What is the length, in centimeters, of $\overline{JL}$?

   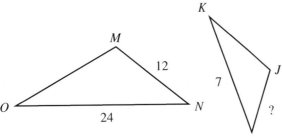

   F. 2
   G. $3\frac{1}{2}$
   H. $4\frac{1}{6}$
   J. $4\frac{5}{7}$
   K. 19

9. Brandon is building a right triangular clock stand based on a scale blueprint he found online. One of the legs of the scale blueprint is 3 inches long and the other leg is 6 inches long. If Brandon wants the longer leg of his clock stand to be 27 centimeters long, how many centimeters long should the other leg be?

   A. 1.5
   B. 4.5
   C. 9
   D. 13.5
   E. 56

DO YOUR FIGURING HERE.

END OF SET THREE
STOP! DO NOT GO ON TO THE NEXT PAGE
UNTIL TOLD TO DO SO.

19.4.4 Set Four

10. In the figure below, where △EFG ~ △LMN, lengths are given in inches. What is the perimeter, in inches, of △LMN ?

(Note: the symbol ~ means "is similar to.")

F. 40
G. 48
H. 68
J. 78
K. 88

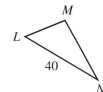

DO YOUR FIGURING HERE.

11. For the triangles in the figure below, which of the following ratios of side lengths is equivalent to the ratio of the perimeter of △MNO to that of △QMO ?

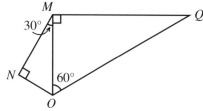

A. MN:NO
B. MN:OQ
C. MO:OQ
D. NO:QM
E. NO:OQ

12. What is the measure of ∠RPQ in the figure below?

F. 15°
G. 30°
H. 45°
J. 60°
K. 75°

END OF SET FOUR
STOP! DO NOT GO ON TO THE NEXT PAGE
UNTIL TOLD TO DO SO.

19.4.5 Set Five

13. △MNO and △PQR are similar triangles with a scale factor of △MNO to △PQR of $\frac{3}{5}$. The perimeter of △PQR is 50 centimeters. What is the perimeter of △MNO, in centimeters?
    A. 15
    B. 20
    C. 25
    D. 30
    E. 35

DO YOUR FIGURING HERE.

14. The figure below shows the triangle △PNM. The segment $\overline{QO}$ is parallel to $\overline{PN}$, and the lengths given are in inches. Given that PN denotes the length, in inches, of $\overline{PN}$, which of the following proportions involving PN *must* be true?

    F. $\dfrac{PN}{5} = \dfrac{20}{4}$

    G. $\dfrac{PN}{4} = \dfrac{20}{5}$

    H. $\dfrac{PN}{5} = \dfrac{4}{20}$

    J. $\dfrac{PN}{4} = \dfrac{5}{20}$

    K. $\dfrac{PN}{16} = \dfrac{5}{4}$

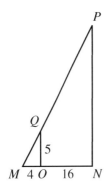

GO ON TO THE NEXT PAGE

15. A rope is attached to the top of a vertical tree, as shown in the figure below. The rope makes an angle of 60° with the tree at a point such that 64 feet of rope is needed to anchor the rope to the ground. Approximately how many feet away from the base of the tree is the rope anchored?

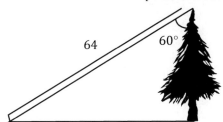

A. 32
B. 55
C. 64
D. 111
E. 128

Sum It Up

Similar Triangles

Congruent Triangles
Triangles that are exactly identical to each other; they have the same three angle measurements and the same three sides lengths, even though one triangle may be flipped around or in a different orientation

Similar Triangles
Triangles that have identical angles; their sides are proportional to each other, but one triangle can be larger than the other or presented in a different orientation

Tips and Techniques

Draw It Out: If a question asks about similar triangles, draw both triangles and label all of the sides that you know the values for. Then, write down the proportion between the triangles and plug in the given values.

Lesson 20

Trig Geometry

CAPTION:

ACT® Mastery Math

20.1 Entrance Ticket

Solve the questions below.

1. In the right triangle below, the side lengths are given in meters. Which of the following statements is true about $\angle F$?

   A. $\sin F = \dfrac{4}{5}$

   B. $\cos F = \dfrac{4}{5}$

   C. $\tan F = \dfrac{4}{5}$

   D. $\sin F = \dfrac{5}{4}$

   E. $\cos F = \dfrac{5}{4}$

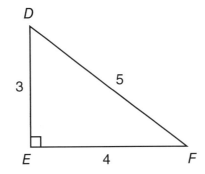

2. When Jason is standing on his stilts, he casts a shadow 24 feet long, and the angle of elevation from the tip of Jason's shadow to the top of his head has a sine of $\dfrac{5}{13}$. How tall is Jason on his stilts? Give the answer in feet.

   F. 8.7
   G. 9.2
   H. 9.6
   J. 10.0
   K. 10.1

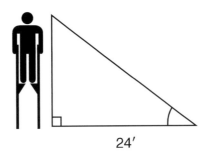

Entrance Ticket | Learning Targets | Finding an Angle | Trigonometry Word Problems | ACT Practice | Sum It Up

Lesson 20 – Trig Geometry

20.1 Entrance Ticket

3. The side lengths in the right triangle below are given in centimeters. Which of the following expressions equals the sine of $\angle B$?

A. $\dfrac{y}{x}$

B. $\dfrac{x}{y}$

C. $\dfrac{z}{x}$

D. $\dfrac{x}{z}$

E. $\dfrac{z}{y}$

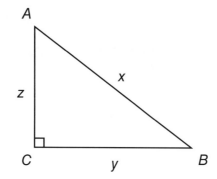

ACT® Mastery Math

20.2 Learning Targets

1. Understand and recognize trigonometric functions with right triangles

2. Apply trigonometric functions with right triangles to find the measures of sides of right triangles and solve other related problems

Self-Assessment

Circle the number that corresponds to your confidence level in your knowledge of this subject before beginning the lesson. A score of 1 means you are completely lost, and a score of 4 means you have mastered the skills. After you finish the lesson, return to the bottom of this page and circle your new confidence level to show your improvement.

Before Lesson

1   2   3   4

After Lesson

1   2   3   4

Entrance Ticket | Learning Targets | Finding an Angle | Trigonometry Word Problems | ACT Practice | Sum It Up

Lesson 20 – Trig Geometry

20.3.1 Finding an Angle

S: _____   C: _____

O: _____   A: _____

H: _____   H: _____

T: _____

O: _____

A: _____

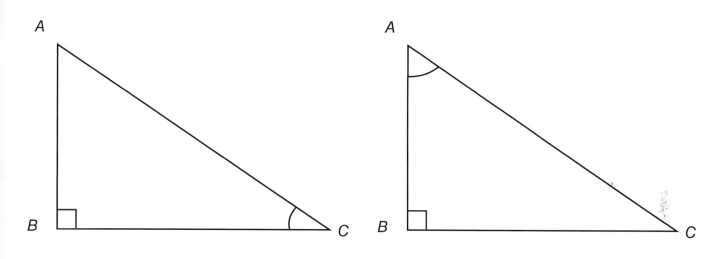

SOH: _____

CAH: _____

TOA: _____

ACT® Mastery Math

20.3.1 Finding an Angle

1. In right △GHD, sin ∠D = _____

2. In right △GHD, tan ∠D = _____

3. In right △GHD, cos ∠D = _____

4. In right △GHD, cos ∠G = _____

5. In right △GHD, tan ∠G = _____

6. In right △GHD, sin ∠G = _____

7. In right △QRS, the tangent of the smallest angle = _____

8. In right △QRS, the cosine of the 2nd largest angle = _____

9. In right △QRS, the sine of the smallest angle = _____

10. In right △QRS, the tangent of the 2nd largest angle = _____

Math Tip

Process of Elimination: Start eliminating answer choices as soon as you figure out one side. For example, if a question asks for the sine of a certain angle where the hypotenuse of the triangle is $\sqrt{85}$, eliminate all answer choices without $\sqrt{85}$ in the denominator.

20.3.2 Trigonometry Word Problems

A group of friends boarded a tour boat for a 3-hour tour. They hit a storm and were washed ashore on an island exactly 100 miles northeast of port. The Coast Guard station that is sending a rescue boat is located due east of port and due south of the island. The sine of the angle created by the lines from port to the island and from port to the Coast Guard station is $\frac{4}{5}$. How far does the rescue boat have to travel to reach the island if it heads due north?

20.3.2 Trigonometry Word Problems

1. The legs of a right triangle are 8 and 6 inches, respectively. What is the sine of the triangle's smallest interior angle?

2. The legs of a right triangle are 8 and 6 inches, respectively. What is the cosine of the triangle's smallest interior angle?

3. One leg of a right triangle is 10 inches, and the hypotenuse is 12. What is the sine of the triangle's smallest interior angle?

4. One leg of a right triangle is 10 inches, and the hypotenuse is 12. What is the tangent of the triangle's second smallest interior angle?

5. The tangent of a right triangle's smallest angle is $\frac{6}{7}$, and its sides are all integers. What is a possible value of the length of the hypotenuse?

Math Tip

Draw It Out: If there is no triangle figure given to you, take the time to draw one. If a triangle is given in the problem, be sure to label all of the sides. In either case, make sure you write out the trigonometric formula you plan to use before you start plugging in values.

Lesson 20 – Trig Geometry

20.4.1 Set One

1. For ∠D in △DEF below, which of the following trigonometric expressions has a value of $\frac{4}{5}$?

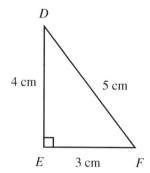

A. cos D
B. csc D
C. sec D
D. sin D
E. tan D

DO YOUR FIGURING HERE.

2. For right triangle △DEF, sin ∠E = $\frac{2}{5}$. What is cos ∠E ?

F. $-\frac{2}{5}$

G. $\frac{3}{3}$

H. $\frac{5}{2}$

J. $\frac{\sqrt{21}}{5}$

K. $\frac{\sqrt{29}}{5}$

GO ON TO THE NEXT PAGE

3. In the figure below, what is the cosine of ∠DEF ?

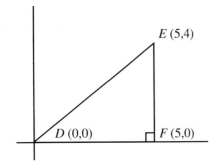

A. $\dfrac{4}{\sqrt{41}}$

B. $\dfrac{4}{5}$

C. $\dfrac{5}{\sqrt{41}}$

D. $\dfrac{3}{5}$

E. $\dfrac{5}{3}$

END OF SET ONE
STOP! DO NOT GO ON TO THE NEXT PAGE
UNTIL TOLD TO DO SO.

20.4.2 Set Two

4. Which of the following expressions is equal to tan θ for the triangle below?

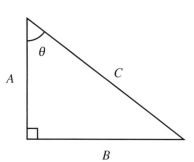

F. $\dfrac{C}{A}$

G. $\dfrac{C}{B}$

H. $\dfrac{A}{C}$

J. $\dfrac{B}{C}$

K. $\dfrac{B}{A}$

5. An angle in a right triangle has a measure θ. If $\cos\theta = \dfrac{5}{13}$ and $\tan\theta = \dfrac{12}{5}$, then $\sin\theta = ?$

A. $\dfrac{5}{12}$

B. $\dfrac{5}{13}$

C. $\dfrac{12}{13}$

D. $\dfrac{12}{\sqrt{194}}$

E. $\dfrac{12}{\sqrt{313}}$

DO YOUR FIGURING HERE.

GO ON TO THE NEXT PAGE

6. The triangle below is given with measurements in feet. Which of the following trigonometric expressions has a value of $\frac{12}{13}$?

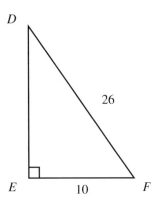

F. sin F
G. cos F
H. tan F
J. sin D
K. tan D

DO YOUR FIGURING HERE.

20.4.3 Set Three

7. A 30-meter zip line extends from a tall tree to a shorter tree at an angle of 40°, as shown in the figure below. Which of the following expressions shows the distance, in meters, between the two trees?

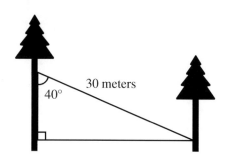

DO YOUR FIGURING HERE.

- A. $30 \cos 40°$
- B. $30 \sin 40°$
- C. $30 \tan 40°$
- D. $\dfrac{30}{\cos 40°}$
- E. $\dfrac{30}{\sin 40°}$

8. A tree casts a 30-foot shadow on the ground. The angle from the end of the shadow to the top of the tree is 30°, as shown in the figure below. What is the height of the tree, in feet?

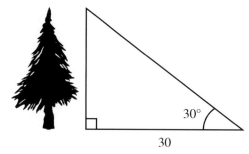

- F. $30 \cos 30°$
- G. $30 \sin 30°$
- H. $30 \tan 30°$
- J. $\dfrac{30}{\sin 30}$
- K. $\dfrac{30}{\tan 30}$

GO ON TO THE NEXT PAGE

9. In the right triangle below, if $\tan \theta = \dfrac{\sqrt{20}}{4}$, then $\cos \theta = ?$

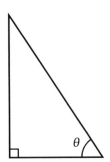

A. $\dfrac{4}{6}$

B. $\dfrac{4}{20}$

C. $\dfrac{\sqrt{20}}{6}$

D. $1 - \dfrac{2\sqrt{20}}{20}$

E. $\sqrt{1 - \left(\dfrac{2\sqrt{20}}{20}\right)^2}$

20.4.4 Set Four

10. Jason sees a tall building from across town. He turns 90° and walks 100 yards. Jason then turns to face the building, and the angle between his line of sight and his path is 35° as shown below. Which of the following is the closest to the distance from Jason's original position to the building, in yards?

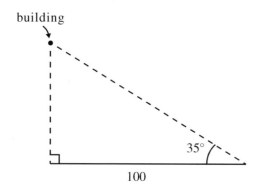

(Note: sin 35° = 0.57, cos 35° = 0.82, tan 35° = 0.70)

F. 57
G. 70
H. 82
J. 122
K. 143

DO YOUR FIGURING HERE.

GO ON TO THE NEXT PAGE

11. According to the measurements given in the figure below, what is the distance, in meters, from the car to the parking garage?

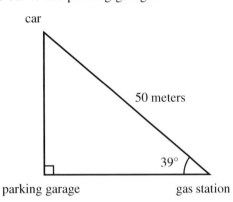

- **A.** 50 cos 39°
- **B.** 50 sin 39°
- **C.** 50 tan 39°
- **D.** $\dfrac{\sin 39°}{50}$
- **E.** $\dfrac{\tan 39°}{50}$

12. When the sun strikes the level ground at an angle of 60°, a building casts a shadow 20 meters long, as shown in the figure below. How tall is the building to the nearest meter?

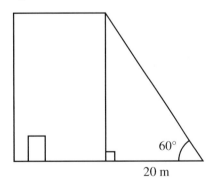

(Note: sin(60) ≈ 0.87, cos(60) ≈ 0.5, tan(60) ≈ 1.73)

- **F.** 10
- **G.** 12
- **H.** 17
- **J.** 35
- **K.** 40

END OF SET FOUR
STOP! DO NOT GO ON TO THE NEXT PAGE
UNTIL TOLD TO DO SO.

20.4.5 Set Five

13. In the right triangle $\triangle ABC$ below, $\sin B = \dfrac{7}{10}$. Which of the following expressions is equal to $\sin C$?

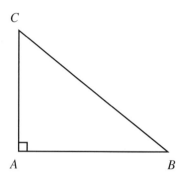

A. $\dfrac{10}{7}$

B. $\dfrac{\sqrt{149}}{7}$

C. $\dfrac{\sqrt{51}}{7}$

D. $\dfrac{\sqrt{149}}{10}$

E. $\dfrac{\sqrt{51}}{10}$

DO YOUR FIGURING HERE.

GO ON TO THE NEXT PAGE

14. Let θ be an angle in a right triangle. If $\sin \theta = \dfrac{20}{29}$, and $\tan \theta = \dfrac{20}{21}$, $\cos \theta = ?$

F. $\dfrac{20}{29}$

G. $\dfrac{20}{\sqrt{1282}}$

H. $\dfrac{21}{\sqrt{1282}}$

J. $\dfrac{21}{\sqrt{1241}}$

K. $\dfrac{21}{29}$

15. The right triangle below is given with dimensions in meters. What is $\tan \theta$?

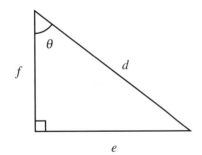

A. $\dfrac{d}{e}$

B. $\dfrac{d}{f}$

C. $\dfrac{e}{d}$

D. $\dfrac{e}{f}$

E. $\dfrac{f}{e}$

END OF SET FIVE
STOP! DO NOT GO ON TO THE NEXT PAGE
UNTIL TOLD TO DO SO.

Lesson 20 – Trig Geometry

Sum It Up

Trig Geometry

Right Triangle
A triangle in which one angle measures 90°

Vertex
The endpoint where two line segments or rays come together

Leg
Either of the sides of a right triangle that come together to form the 90° angle

Hypotenuse
The side of a right triangle that is opposite the 90° angle

Adjacent Side
In a polygon, either of the sides that come together to form a particular angle; in trigonometry, the side next to the angle that is not the hypotenuse

Opposite Side
In a triangle, the side that does not form a particular angle

Angle
The figure formed by two rays or line segments that share a common endpoint

Sine
In a right triangle, the ratio of the angle's opposite side to the hypotenuse

Cosine
In a right triangle, the ratio of the angle's adjacent side to the hypotenuse

Tangent
In a right triangle, the ratio of the angle's opposite side to the angle's adjacent side

ACT® Mastery Math

Sum It Up

Tips and Techniques

Process of Elimination: Start eliminating answer choices as soon as you figure out one side of a right triangle. For example, if a question asks for the sine of a certain angle where the hypotenuse of the triangle is $\sqrt{85}$, eliminate all answer choices without $\sqrt{85}$ in the denominator.

Draw It Out: If there is no triangle figure given to you, take the time to draw one. If a triangle is given in the problem, be sure to label all of the sides. In either case, make sure you write out the trigonometric formula you plan to use before you start plugging in values.

Lesson 21

Slope

$y = -\frac{1}{2}x + 5$

CAPTION:

ACT® Mastery Math

21.1 Entrance Ticket

Solve the questions below.

1. The points A(–5,4), B(1,5), C(3,2), and D(–2,2) are shown below in the standard (x,y) coordinate plane. What is the slope of $\overrightarrow{AC}$?

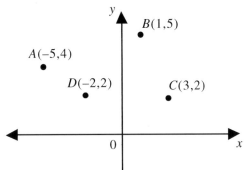

- A. –4
- B. –3
- C. $-\dfrac{1}{3}$
- D. $-\dfrac{1}{4}$
- E. 1

2. Joni and her father are reviewing the slope of lines for her homework. Joni's father has asked her to graph the population, P, of their town (which is increasing regularly) over the course of y years. Joni's father then chooses two points at random on the graph and asks Joni about the slope between two points. Joni notes that the slope between any two points on this graph is always:

- F. undefined.
- G. the same negative value.
- H. the same positive value.
- J. a positive value that decreases as y increases.
- K. a positive value that decreases as P increases.

Lesson 21 – Slope

21.1 Entrance Ticket

3. The points (–4,8) and (0,4) lie on the same straight line. What is the slope-intercept equation of the line?
   A. $y = 4x - 4$
   B. $y = x + 3$
   C. $y = x + 4$
   D. $y = -x + 4$
   E. $y = -2x + 8$

21.2 Learning Targets

1. Understand and recognize the concept of slope and determine the slope in linear equations and graphs

2. Understand and utilize the concept of slope to solve simple and complex problems

Self-Assessment

Circle the number that corresponds to your confidence level in your knowledge of this subject before beginning the lesson. A score of 1 means you are completely lost, and a score of 4 means you have mastered the skills. After you finish the lesson, return to the bottom of this page and circle your new confidence level to show your improvement.

Before Lesson

1   2   3   4

After Lesson

1   2   3   4

Lesson 21 – Slope

21.3.1 Slope in Linear Equations and Graphs

Example:
A high school is building a new ramp for wheelchair access to the gym. The law requires a grade of at most 5% (for every 100 inches long the ramp is, it can be no more than 5 inches high). The gym is set 4 feet above the place where the ramp will start, and to maximize space, the school wants the shortest ramp allowed by law. You are the school's contractor, and the principal wants to know how long the ramp will be, in feet. What will you tell him?

1. Points (0,4) and (6,2) are on a line. The slope is _____.

2. Points (−3,1) and (8,0) are on a line. The slope is _____.

21.3.1 Slope in Linear Equations and Graphs

3. Points (4,–4) and (1,2) are on a line. The slope is _____.

4. A line's slope is 3 and contains points (2,–2) and (9,y). y = _____.

5. A line's slope is $-\dfrac{1}{2}$ and contains (–6,–2). Name another point on this line: _____.

Lesson 21 – Slope

21.3.1 Slope in Linear Equations and Graphs

Example:

$4x - 2y = 8$ \qquad Slope: _____

1. $y = \dfrac{1}{4}x - 9$. \qquad What is the slope? _____

    What is the *y*-intercept? _____

2. $y = -7x + 10$. \qquad What is the slope? _____

    What is the *y*-intercept? _____

ACT® Mastery Math

21.3.1 Slope in Linear Equations and Graphs

3. $5x - y = 8$.   What is the slope? _____

   What is the y-intercept? _____

4. $\frac{1}{2}x + 8y = 24$.   What is the slope? _____

   What is the y-intercept? _____

5. $3x + y = 3x - y + 30$.   What is the slope? _____

   What is the y-intercept? _____

Math Tip

Draw It Out: Most slope questions can be solved by using a formula. However, if you find yourself struggling on one of these questions, try drawing out the points. You can then determine the direction of the slope and eliminate from there.

Entrance Ticket   Learning Targets   Slope in Linear Equations and Graphs   Slope Word Problems   ACT Practice   Sum It Up

21.3.2 Slope Word Problems

Example:
George is headed for retirement at his job within 10 years. His boss has agreed to let him reduce his schedule from the 20 days per month he works now to retirement (0 days per month) by decreasing the number of days he works per month by 2 each year.

George makes $200 per workday. How much money will George be making per month after 5 years?

1. In 1979, zoologists estimated the number of fish in a local pond to be about 540. In 1989, 10 years later, the zoologists estimated that the number of fish had increased to 990. Assuming that the fish population increased linearly, how many fish lived in the pond in 1986?
   A. 900
   B. 855
   C. 835
   D. 810
   E. 765

2. A local construction company requires all roofs that it installs to have a minimum slope of 0.20. If the roof in the figure below is 5 feet tall, what is the maximum acceptable value for *x*, in feet?

   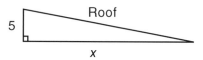

   F. 4
   G. 5
   H. $5\frac{1}{5}$
   J. 20
   K. 25

21.3.2 Slope Word Problems

3. In order to determine the slope between two stars that made up a constellation, astronomers captured an image of the night sky and superimposed an image of a standard (x,y) coordinate plane, aligning the x-axis with the horizon. The astronomers drew a line connecting the two stars, which were located at points $(-3,7)$ and $(8,-15)$. What is the slope of the line connecting these two stars?

   A. -2

   B. $-\dfrac{5}{8}$

   C. $-\dfrac{1}{2}$

   D. $\dfrac{4}{7}$

   E. 2

Lesson 21 – Slope

21.4.1 Set One

1. On a standard (x,y) coordinate plane, what is the slope of a line that passes through the points $(9,-6)$ and $(-8,7)$?

   A. $-\dfrac{17}{13}$

   B. -1

   C. $-\dfrac{13}{17}$

   D. $-\dfrac{1}{17}$

   E. 1

DO YOUR FIGURING HERE.

2. The y-intercept of the line with equation $y = bx + c$ is less than the y-intercept of the line with equation $y = bx + d$. Which of the following *must* be true regarding the relationship between c and d ?

   F. $c \geq d$
   G. $c > d$
   H. $c = d$
   J. $c \leq d$
   K. $c < d$

3. What is the slope of the line given by $8x - 24y = -48$?

   A. -24

   B. -3

   C. $-\dfrac{1}{3}$

   D. $\dfrac{1}{3}$

   E. 8

END OF SET ONE
STOP! DO NOT GO ON TO THE NEXT PAGE
UNTIL TOLD TO DO SO.

21.4.2 Set Two

4. Which of the following is an equation for the line passing through the point (−7,3) and the origin on the standard (x,y) coordinate plane?

   F. $x - y = -10$
   G. $x + y = -4$
   H. $3x + 7y = 0$
   J. $3x - 7y = 16$
   K. $7x + 3y = 16$

5. Land surveyors give the grade of hills with a rise:run ratio. A 4:3 grade is shown below. Which of the following grades would be the least steep?

   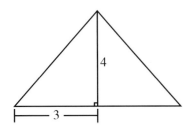

   A. 1:5
   B. 1:3
   C. 2:6
   D. 6:2
   E. 12:9

6. What is the slope of the line that passes through points (4,3) and (5,−5) in the standard (x,y) coordinate plane?

   F. 8
   G. $\frac{1}{8}$
   H. 0
   J. $-\frac{1}{8}$
   K. −8

END OF SET TWO
STOP! DO NOT GO ON TO THE NEXT PAGE
UNTIL TOLD TO DO SO.

Lesson 21 – Slope

21.4.3 Set Three

7. For all c, what is the slope of the line connecting the points (c,d) and $(c,-d)$ on the standard (x,y) coordinate plane?

   A. 0

   B. $\dfrac{c}{d}$

   C. $\dfrac{d}{c}$

   D. $-\dfrac{d}{c}$

   E. Undefined

8. What is the slope of the line parallel to $6x + 3y = 12$?

   F. -3

   G. -2

   H. $\dfrac{1}{2}$

   J. 2

   K. 12

9. What is the slope of $\overrightarrow{AB}$ in the graph below?

   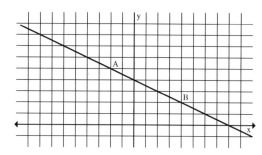

   (Note: Grid lines are spaced every 1 unit.)

   A. -2

   B. $-\dfrac{1}{2}$

   C. $\dfrac{1}{2}$

   D. 2

   E. $\sqrt{1^2 + 2^2}$

DO YOUR FIGURING HERE.

END OF SET THREE
STOP! DO NOT GO ON TO THE NEXT PAGE
UNTIL TOLD TO DO SO.

21.4.4 Set Four

10. The points $A(2,8)$ and $B(5,-1)$ lie in the standard (x,y) coordinate plane. What is the slope of the line segment, $\overline{AB}$, created by points A and B?

   F. -3
   G. -1
   H. $\dfrac{1}{3}$
   J. 1
   K. 3

11. In the standard (x,y) coordinate plane below, $\triangle OTU$ has base $\overline{OT}$, A is the midpoint of $\overline{OT}$, B is the midpoint of $\overline{TU}$, and C is the midpoint of $\overline{OU}$. Which of the following statements is *always* true?

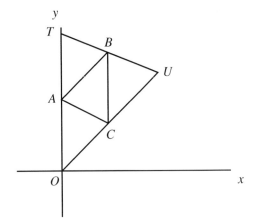

   A. $\overline{AB} \cong \overline{BC}$

   B. $\overline{OA} \cong \overline{CU}$

   C. The product of the slope of $\overline{BC}$ and the slope of $\overline{OA}$ is -1.

   D. The product of the slope of $\overline{BC}$ and the slope of $\overline{CU}$ is -1.

   E. The slope of $\overline{BC}$ and the slope of $\overline{OA}$ are both undefined.

DO YOUR FIGURING HERE.

GO ON TO THE NEXT PAGE.

12. In the standard (x,y) coordinate plane, which of the following is the slope of the line parallel to the line $y = \frac{7}{2}x - 7$?

F. -7

G. $-\frac{2}{7}$

H. $\frac{2}{7}$

J. $\frac{7}{2}$

K. 7

DO YOUR FIGURING HERE.

END OF SET FOUR
STOP! DO NOT GO ON TO THE NEXT PAGE UNTIL TOLD TO DO SO.

21.4.5 Set Five

13. The line given by the equation $9x - 3y = 12$ lies in the standard (x,y) coordinate plane. What is the slope of this line?

    A. 9
    B. 3
    C. $\frac{1}{3}$
    D. –3
    F. –9

14. What is the slope of the line given by the equation $y = 2x - 7$ lying in the standard (x,y) coordinate plane?

    F. –7
    G. –2
    H. $\frac{2}{7}$
    J. 2
    K. 7

15. Given the points $(-10,9)$ and $(4,2)$ on the standard (x,y) coordinate plane, what is the equation of the line that passes through them?

    A. $y = -10x + 9$
    B. $y = 4x + 2$
    C. $y = 2x - 6$
    D. $y = -\frac{1}{2}x + 4$
    E. $y = -2x + 10$

DO YOUR FIGURING HERE.

END OF SET FIVE
STOP! DO NOT GO ON TO THE NEXT PAGE
UNTIL TOLD TO DO SO.

Lesson 21 – Slope

Sum It Up

Slope

Slope-Intercept Form
$y = mx + b$

Standard Form
$ax + by = c$

Slope
How steep a line is

Rate of Change
Another way to say *slope*

Positive Slope
Increases from left to right

Negative Slope
Decreases from left to right

Zero Slope
Horizontal line

Undefined Slope
Vertical line

Slope Formula

$$m = \frac{rise}{run} = \frac{y_2 - y_1}{x_2 - x_1}$$

ACT® Mastery Math

Sum It Up

Tips and Techniques

Draw It Out: Most of the perimeter questions can be solved by drawing the shapes and labeling them carefully. If the ACT does not give you the figure or label all of the information, just draw it out.

Use Ratios: Ratios can be a useful tool for determining perimeter and dimensions of polygons when there are unknown sides.

Lesson 22

Function Graphs: Coordinate Plane

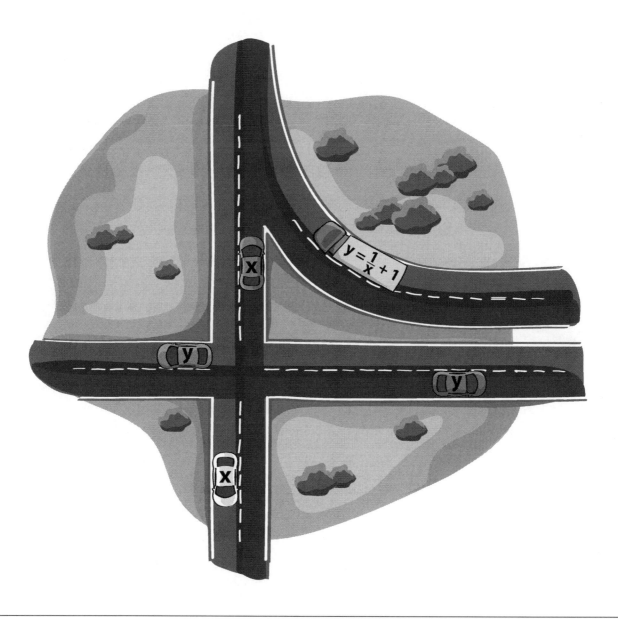

CAPTION:

ACT® Mastery Math

22.1 Entrance Ticket

Solve the questions below.

1. The line shown below in the standard (x,y) coordinate plane is represented by one of the following equations. Which one is it?

   A. $y = -\frac{3}{4}x - 4$

   B. $y = \frac{3}{4}x - 4$

   C. $y = \frac{3}{4}x + 4$

   D. $y = \frac{4}{3}x - 4$

   E. $y = \frac{4}{3}x + 4$

   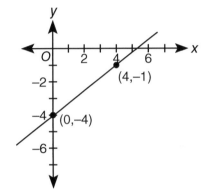

2. Cholesterol levels tend to increase linearly with age. Suppose that the average cholesterol level of 30-year-olds is 120 and the average cholesterol level of 60-year-olds is 180. Given this model, what would be the average cholesterol level of 45-year-olds?
   F. 140
   G. 145
   H. 150
   J. 155
   K. 160

Lesson 22 – Function Graphs: Coordinate Plane

22.1 Entrance Ticket

3. The graphs of the equations $y = x^3$ and $y = -x + 2$ are shown below in the standard (x,y) coordinate plane. What real values of x, if any, satisfy the equation $x^3 < -x + 2$?

   A. No real values
   B. $x < 0$
   C. $x < 1$
   D. $0 < x < 1$
   E. $x > 1$

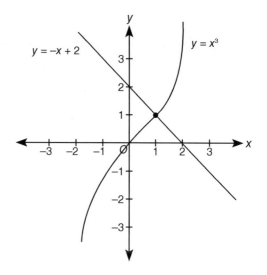

ACT® Mastery Math

22.2 Learning Targets

1. Graph linear equations in the (x,y) coordinate plane and determine slope and y-intercept

2. Graph linear and non-linear inequalities and solve related problems

Self-Evaluation

Circle the number that corresponds to your confidence level in this subject before completing the lesson. A score of 1 means you're completely lost, and a score of 4 means you've mastered it. Once you finish the lesson, come back and circle your new confidence level beneath the first one to see how you've improved.

Before Lesson

1   2   3   4

After Lesson

1   2   3   4

Entrance Ticket | Learning Targets | Graphing Lines/Linear Equations | Graphing Inequalities | ACT Practice | Sum It Up

Lesson 22 – Function Graphs: Coordinate Plane

22.3.1 Graphing Linear Equations

(3,2)
m = 5

(1,–3)
(–6,2)

1. $y = 7x + 1$ slope: _____   y-int: _____
2. $y = -\frac{1}{2}x - 8$ slope: _____   y-int: _____
3. $10x + y = 3$ slope: _____   y-int: _____   slope-intercept form: _____
4. $4x - 3y = 12$ slope: _____   y-int: _____   slope-intercept form: _____
5. The y-intercept of a line that includes the point (–3,5) and has a slope of $-\frac{1}{3}$ is _____.
6. The y-intercept of a line that includes the point (–1,–2) and has a slope of 1 is _____.
7. Both (9,0) and (–1,4) are on a line. What is the line's slope? _____
8. Both (0,3) and (–2,–2) are on a line. What is the line's slope? _____

Math Tip

Process of Elimination: When an ACT question requires you to examine a graph, you can almost always immediately eliminate a few answers that do not have the correct y-intercept or slope direction. If you cannot eliminate right away, be sure to cross off answers as you discover more features of the graph.

Entrance Ticket   Learning Targets   Graphing Lines/Linear Equations   Graphing Inequalities   ACT Practice   Sum It Up

22.3.2 Graphing Inequalities

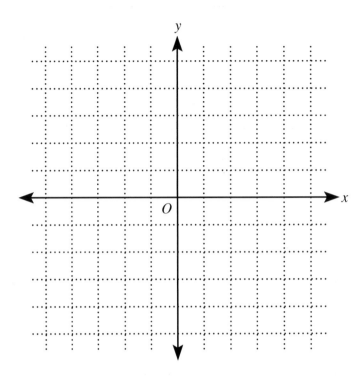

Lesson 22 – Function Graphs: Coordinate Plane

22.3.2 Graphing Inequalities

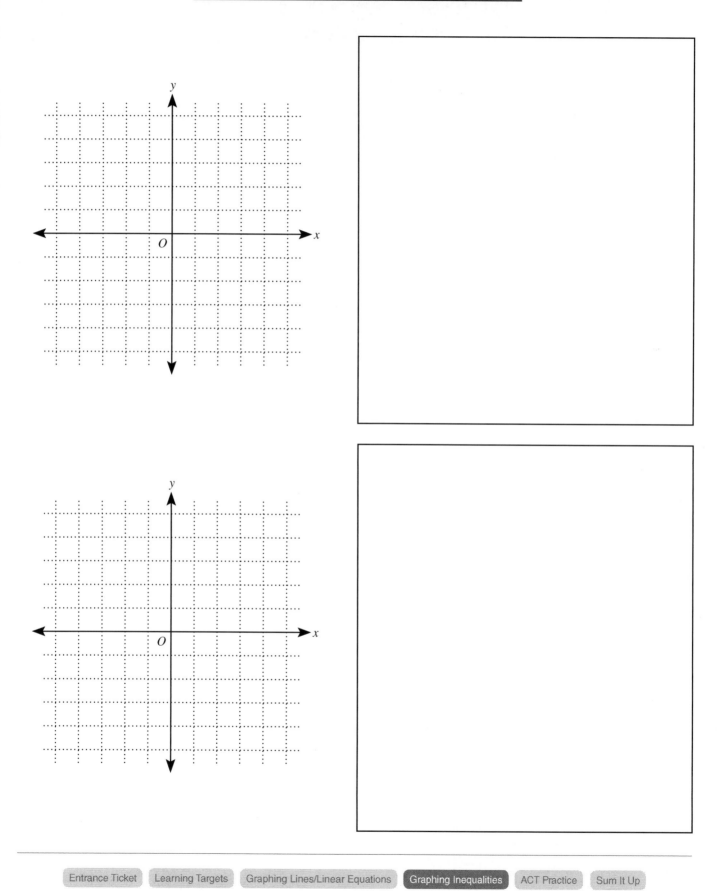

22.4.1 Set One

DO YOUR FIGURING HERE.

1. One of the following is an equation of the linear relation shown in the standard (x,y) coordinate plane below. Which one is it?

   A. $y = 7x$
   B. $y = 3x$
   C. $y = 7x + 3$
   D. $y = 3x - 7$
   E. $y = 3x + 7$

   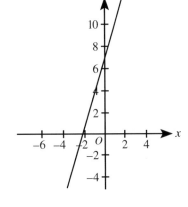

2. The point $(4,-3)$ is shown in the standard (x,y) coordinate plane below. Which of the following is another point on the line through the point $(4,-3)$ with a slope of $-\dfrac{1}{3}$?

   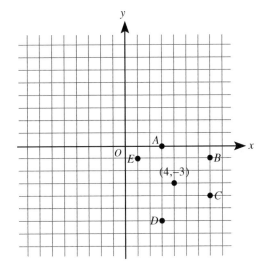

   F. $A\ (3,\ 0)$
   G. $B\ (7, -1)$
   H. $C\ (7, -4)$
   J. $D\ (3, -6)$
   K. $E\ (1, -1)$

GO ON TO THE NEXT PAGE

Lesson 22 – Function Graphs: Coordinate Plane

3. Which quadrants of the standard (x,y) coordinate plane below contain points on the graph of the equation $2y - 6x = 10$?

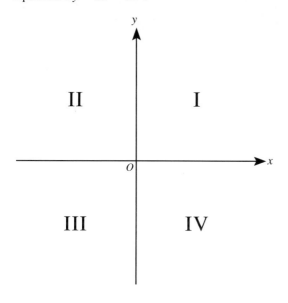

DO YOUR FIGURING HERE.

A. I and III only
B. I, II, and III only
C. I, II, and IV only
D. I, III, and IV only
E. II, III, and IV only

END OF SET ONE
STOP! DO NOT GO ON TO THE NEXT PAGE
UNTIL TOLD TO DO SO.

22.4.2 Set Two

4. Which of the following equations is graphed below?

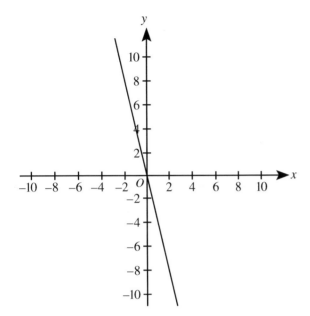

DO YOUR FIGURING HERE.

F. $y = -4x$

G. $y = -\dfrac{1}{4}x$

H. $y = \dfrac{1}{4}x$

J. $y = 4x$

K. $y = x - 4$

GO ON TO THE NEXT PAGE

5. Point E has coordinates (x,y) and lies on the standard (x,y) coordinate plane. If x and y have the same signs, then point E *must* be located in which of the 4 quadrants shown below?

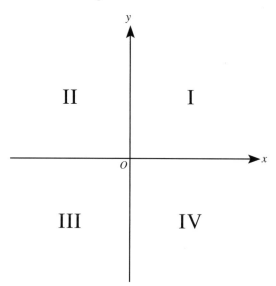

A. I only
B. III only
C. I or II only
D. I or III only
E. II or IV only

6. The graph, in the standard (x,y) coordinate plane, of which of the following lines contains the point (7,0) and makes a 45° angle with the x-axis at the x-intercept?

F. $y = x - 7$
G. $y = x + 7$
H. $y = 135x$
J. $y + 45 = x - 7$
K. $7y = x + 7$

END OF SET TWO
STOP! DO NOT GO ON TO THE NEXT PAGE
UNTIL TOLD TO DO SO.

22.4.3 Set Three

7. One of the following graphs in the standard (x,y) coordinate plane is the graph of $y \geq ax + b$ for some negative a and some positive b. Which graph?

A.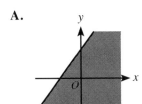

B.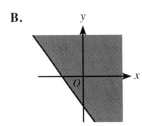

C.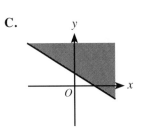

D.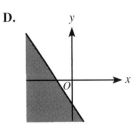

E.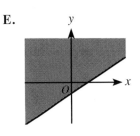

Lesson 22 – Function Graphs: Coordinate Plane

8. Which of the following systems of inequalities is represented by the shaded region of the graph below?

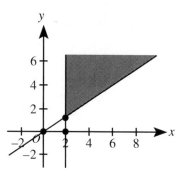

DO YOUR FIGURING HERE.

F. $y \geq -\frac{2}{3}x$ and $x \leq 2$

G. $y \geq -\frac{2}{3}x$ and $x \geq 2$

H. $y \geq \frac{2}{3}x$ or $x \leq 2$

J. $y \geq \frac{2}{3}x$ and $x \leq 2$

K. $y \geq \frac{2}{3}x$ and $x \geq 2$

GO ON TO THE NEXT PAGE

9. Consider the set of all points (x,y) that satisfy all 3 of the conditions below:

$$y \geq 0$$
$$y \leq x + 8$$
$$y \leq -2x + 8$$

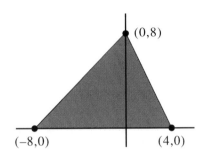

The graph of this set is ΔQRS and its interior, which is shown shaded in the standard (x,y) coordinate plane above. Let this set be the domain of the function $H(x,y) = 2x - 6y$.

What is the minimum value of $H(x,y)$ when x and y satisfy the 3 conditions given?

A. 16
B. 8
C. −8
D. −16
E. −48

END OF SET THREE
STOP! DO NOT GO ON TO THE NEXT PAGE UNTIL TOLD TO DO SO.

22.4.4 Set Four

10. In the standard (x,y) coordinate plane below, a straight line passes through the 3 indicated points. What is the value of a?

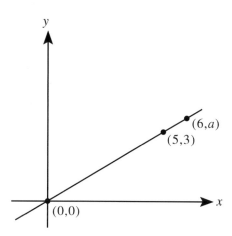

DO YOUR FIGURING HERE.

F. $-\dfrac{18}{5}$

G. $-\dfrac{5}{3}$

H. $\dfrac{5}{3}$

J. $\dfrac{18}{5}$

K. 4

GO ON TO THE NEXT PAGE

11. Which of the following is the graph of the equation $y - 2x = -8$ in the standard (x,y) coordinate plane?

DO YOUR FIGURING HERE.

A.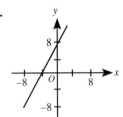

D.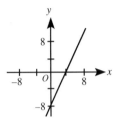

B.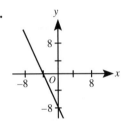

E.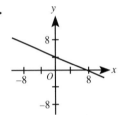

C.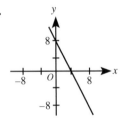

Lesson 22 – Function Graphs: Coordinate Plane

12. Which of the following graphs in the standard (x,y) coordinate plane represents the solution set of the inequality $|x + y| \leq 1$?

DO YOUR FIGURING HERE.

F.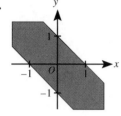

J.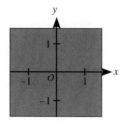

G.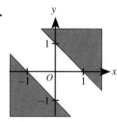

K.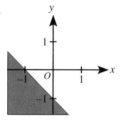

H.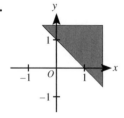

END OF SET FOUR
STOP! DO NOT GO ON TO THE NEXT PAGE
UNTIL TOLD TO DO SO.

22.4.5 Set Five

13. One of the following graphs shows only points where the *y*-coordinate is 4 greater than the *x*-coordinate. Which graph is it?

A.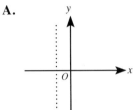

D.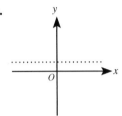

B.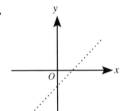

E.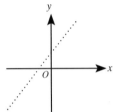

C.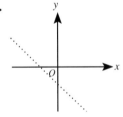

DO YOUR FIGURING HERE.

14. Point Z is to be graphed in a quadrant, not on an axis, of the standard (x,y) coordinate plane below.

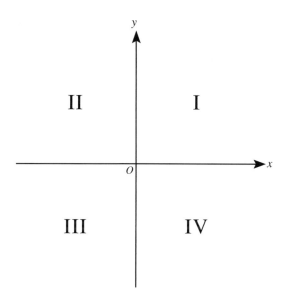

If the x-coordinate and the y-coordinate of point Z are both negative, then point Z must be located in:

F. Quadrant I only
G. Quadrant I or II only
H. Quadrant I or III only
J. Quadrant II only
K. Quadrant III only

DO YOUR FIGURING HERE.

GO ON TO THE NEXT PAGE

15. The triangle △XYZ is graphed in the standard (x,y) coordinate plane below. Which of the following is an equation of $\vec{YZ}$?

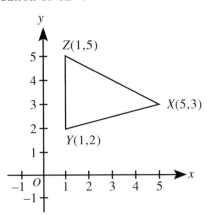

A. $y = 1$

B. $x = 1$

C. $y = -2x + 5$

D. $y = -\frac{1}{2}x + \frac{11}{2}$

E. $y = \frac{1}{4}x + \frac{7}{4}$

Lesson 22 – Function Graphs: Coordinate Plane

Sum It Up

Function Graphs: Coordinate Plane

Linear Equation
An algebraic equation in which the graphed function is a straight line; does not contain variables with exponents

Slope
The steepness of a line, represented by the rise-over-run formula:

$$m = \frac{y_2 - y_1}{x_2 - x_1}$$

Y-Intercept
The point on a graph where the function intersects with the *y*-axis

Slope-Intercept Form
$y = mx + b$

Tips and Techniques

Process of Elimination: Cross off anything that is obviously wrong based on the slope and the *y*-intercept.

Lesson 23

Circles and Parabolas

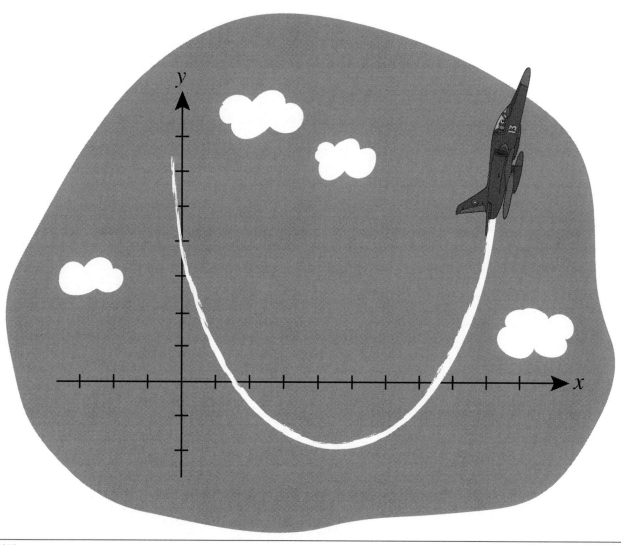

CAPTION:

ACT® Mastery Math

23.1 Entrance Ticket

Solve the questions below.

1. A circle in the standard (x,y) coordinate plane has the equation $x^2 + (y - 12)^2 = 17$. What is the radius of the circle, in coordinate units, and what are the coordinates of the center of the circle?

	radius	center
A.	$\sqrt{17}$	(0, 12)
B.	8.5	(0, 12)
C.	17	(0, 12)
D.	$\sqrt{17}$	(0,−12)
E.	8.5	(0,−12)

2. What is the area of the circle $x^2 + y^2 = 25$ in the standard (x,y) coordinate plane?

   F. 5π
   G. 10π
   H. 25π
   J. 125π
   K. 625π

3. A certain parabola in the standard (x,y) coordinate plane has the equation $y = 5(x - 7)^2 + 3$. What is the vertex of this parabola?

   A. (−7,−3)
   B. (−7, 3)
   C. (7,−3)
   D. (7, 3)
   E. (14, 3)

Lesson 23 – Circles and Parabolas

23.2 Learning Targets

1. Recognize special characteristics of parabolas and circles, such as the vertex of a parabola and the center, intercepts, or radius of a circle

2. Find the equation of a circle when given the center and a tangent

Self-Assessment

Circle the number that corresponds to your confidence level in your knowledge of this subject before beginning the lesson. A score of 1 means you are completely lost, and a score of 4 means you have mastered the skills. After you finish the lesson, return to the bottom of this page and circle your new confidence level to show your improvement.

Before Lesson

1   2   3   4

After Lesson

1   2   3   4

23.3.1 The Circle Equation

Center: _____   Radius: _____

Center: _____   Radius: _____

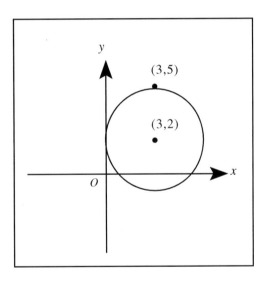

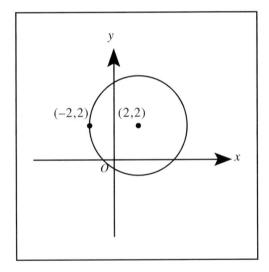

Equation: $(x-3)^2 + (y-2)^2 = $ _____

Equation: $(x-$ ____$)^2 + (y-$ ____$)^2 = $ ____

Lesson 23 – Circles and Parabolas

23.3.1 The Circle Equation

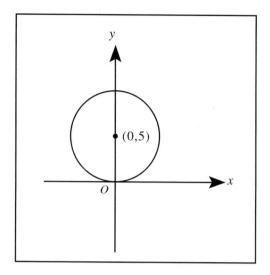

Equation: (_____)² + (_____)² = _____

Equation: $x^2 + y^2 = 81$

Center: _____ **Radius:** _____

ACT® Mastery Math

23.3.2 Parabolas, Circles, and Tangents

Parabolas:

1. _____

2. _____

3. _____

If *a* is positive _____

If *a* is negative _____

Lesson 23 – Circles and Parabolas

23.3.2 Parabolas, Circles, and Tangents

1. Equation: $y = -2(x + 7)^2 + 1$

Vertex: _____   Opens: _____

2. Equation: $y = -(x - 5)^2 - 3$

Vertex: _____   Opens: _____

3. Equation: $y = -3(x - 2)^2 - 1$

Vertex: _____   Opens: _____

4. Equation: $y = 7(x + 7)^2 + 4$

Vertex: _____   Opens: _____

5. Equation: $y = -2x^2 + 3$

Vertex: _____   Opens: _____

Math Tip

Negative Paranoia: Whenever an ACT question asks about the equation of a parabola or the equation of a circle, look carefully at the negative signs. A common mistake is to confuse negative values with negative coordinate points.

Entrance Ticket   Learning Targets   The Circle Equation   Parabolas, Circles, and Tangents   ACT Practice   Sum It Up

23.3.2 Parabolas, Circles, and Tangents

Center: _____

Tangent Line: _____

Point of Tangent: _____

Radius: _____

Equation of Circle: _____

Center: (3,0)   **Tangent line:** $y = 1$

Center: _____

Tangent Line: _____

Point of Tangent: _____

Radius: _____

Equation of Circle: _____

Lesson 23 – Circles and Parabolas

23.4.1 Set One

1. In the standard (x,y) coordinate plane, a circle has center $(-7,13)$ and radius 9 coordinate units. Which of the following equations describes this circle?

   A. $(x + 7)^2 + (y - 13)^2 = 9$
   B. $(x - 7)^2 + (y + 13)^2 = 9$
   C. $(x - 7)^2 - (y + 13)^2 = 9$
   D. $(x - 7)^2 - (y + 13)^2 = 81$
   E. $(x + 7)^2 + (y - 13)^2 = 81$

DO YOUR FIGURING HERE.

2. What are the coordinates of the center of the circle with a radius of 1 and whose equation is $x^2 + 10x + y^2 - 8y + 40 = 0$ in the standard (x,y) coordinate plane?

   F. $(-5,-4)$
   G. $(-5, 4)$
   H. $(4,-5)$
   J. $(5,-4)$
   K. $(5, 4)$

3. Which of the following equations represents a circle in the standard (x,y) coordinate plane with its center at $(-5,6)$ and a radius of 3 units?

   A. $(x - 5)^2 + (y - 6)^2 = 9$
   B. $(x - 5)^2 + (y + 6)^2 = 9$
   C. $(x + 5)^2 + (y - 6)^2 = 9$
   D. $(x - 5)^2 + (y + 6)^2 = 3$
   E. $(x + 5)^2 + (y - 6)^2 = 3$

END OF SET ONE
STOP! DO NOT GO ON TO THE NEXT PAGE
UNTIL TOLD TO DO SO.

23.4.2 Set Two

4. What are the coordinates of the center of a particular circle which has the equation $x^2 + (y - 7)^2 = 13$, and what is its radius, in coordinate units?

	center	radius
F.	(0,−7)	$\sqrt{13}$
G.	(0,−7)	6.5
H.	(0, 7)	$\sqrt{13}$
J.	(0, 7)	6.5
K.	(0, 7)	13

DO YOUR FIGURING HERE.

5. A particular circle has a center of (−4,9) and a radius 7 coordinate units in the standard (x,y) coordinate plane. Which of the following equations describes this circle?

   A. $(x - 4)^2 - (y + 9)^2 = 49$
   B. $(x - 4)^2 - (y + 9)^2 = 7$
   C. $(x - 4)^2 + (y + 9)^2 = 7$
   D. $(x + 4)^2 + (y - 9)^2 = 49$
   E. $(x + 4)^2 + (y - 9)^2 = 7$

6. A particular circle in the standard (x,y) coordinate plane intersects the y-axis at (0,2) and (0,−14). The radius of the circle is 10 coordinate units. Which of the following could be the center of the circle?

   I. (6,−6)
   II. (0,−6)
   II. (−6,−6)

   F. I only
   G. II only
   H. III only
   J. I and III only
   K. I, II, and III

END OF SET TWO
STOP! DO NOT GO ON TO THE NEXT PAGE
UNTIL TOLD TO DO SO.

Lesson 23 – Circles and Parabolas

23.4.3 Set Three

7. What value of k gives the minimum value for p in the equation $p = -5k + k^2$?

   A. 2
   B. $\dfrac{5}{2}$
   C. $\dfrac{15}{4}$
   D. 5
   E. $\dfrac{15}{2}$

DO YOUR FIGURING HERE.

8. In the standard (x,y) coordinate plane, a particular circle has center $(9,4)$ and is tangent to the y-axis. The point (x,y) lies on the circle if and only if x and y satisfy which of the equations below?

   F. $(x + 9)^2 + (y + 4)^2 = 81$
   G. $(x + 9)^2 + (y + 4)^2 = 16$
   H. $(x + 9)^2 + (y + 4)^2 = 9$
   J. $(x - 9)^2 + (y - 4)^2 = 81$
   K. $(x - 9)^2 + (y - 4)^2 = 16$

9. A particular circle in the standard (x,y) coordinate plane is centered at the origin and lies tangent to the line $x = -5$. What is the radius of this circle?

   A. 5
   B. 10
   C. $\sqrt{5}$
   D. $5\sqrt{2}$
   E. $5\sqrt{3}$

END OF SET THREE
STOP! DO NOT GO ON TO THE NEXT PAGE
UNTIL TOLD TO DO SO.

23.4.4 Set Four

10. Which of the following equations does NOT represent a line in the standard (x,y) coordinate plane?

    F. $4x = 24$

    G. $y = -2$

    H. $x + y = 3$

    J. $y = \dfrac{2}{3}x + 6$

    K. $2y = x^3 - 25$

DO YOUR FIGURING HERE.

11. The graph of the equation $\dfrac{x^2}{25} + \dfrac{y^2}{49} = 1$ has a y-intercept at which of the following points?

    A. $(0, 49)$
    B. $(0, 25)$
    C. $(0, 10)$
    D. $(0, 7)$
    E. $(0, 5)$

12. The equation $(x - 3)^2 + (y - 5)^2 = 29$ describes a circle which intersects the x-axis at two points, one of which is $(1,0)$. What is the other point at which this circle intersects the x-axis?

    F. $(-5, 0)$
    G. $(-1, 0)$
    H. $(0, 1)$
    J. $(1, 0)$
    K. $(5, 0)$

END OF SET FOUR
STOP! DO NOT GO ON TO THE NEXT PAGE
UNTIL TOLD TO DO SO.

Lesson 23 – Circles and Parabolas

23.4.5 Set Five

13. Each of the graphs below has equal scales on its axes. Which of the graphs only shows points for which the y-coordinate is 1 more than the square of the x-coordinate?

DO YOUR FIGURING HERE.

A.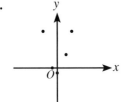

B.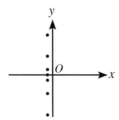

C.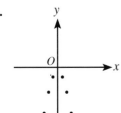

D.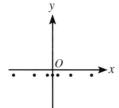

E.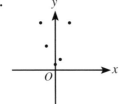

GO ON TO THE NEXT PAGE

14. Each of the following graphs shows a quadratic function in the standard (x,y) coordinate plane. Only one of the functions has two real zeros. Which one?

F.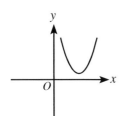

G.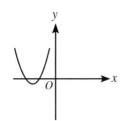

H.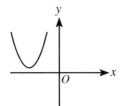

J.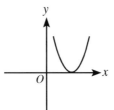

K.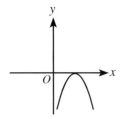

15. Which of the following equations describes a circle in the standard (x,y) coordinate plane with center $(4,-1)$ and a radius of 7 coordinate units?

    A. $x^2 + y^2 - 8x + 2y = 7$
    B. $x^2 + y^2 - 8x + 2y = 32$
    C. $x^2 + y^2 - 8x + 2y = 49$
    D. $x^2 + y^2 + 8x - 2y = 32$
    E. $x^2 + y^2 + 8x - 2y = 49$

END OF SET FIVE
STOP! DO NOT GO ON TO THE NEXT PAGE
UNTIL TOLD TO DO SO.

Lesson 23 – Circles and Parabolas

Sum It Up

Circles and Parabolas

Circle in Standard Form:

$(x - h)^2 + (y - k)^2 = r^2$

(h,k) is the center

r is the radius

Parabola in Vertex Form:

$y = a(x - h)^2 + k$

(h,k) is the vertex

a is a constant that determines the narrowness and direction of the parabola

If a is positive, the parabola opens upward

If a is negative, the parabola opens downward

Tangent
A line that touches a circle at exactly one point

Tips and Techniques

Negative Paranoia: Whenever an ACT question asks about the equation of a parabola or the equation of a circle, look carefully at the negative signs. A common mistake is to confuse negative values with negative coordinate points.

Lesson 24

Factors

CAPTION:

ACT® Mastery Math

24.1 Entrance Ticket

Solve the questions below.

1. What are all the positive factors of 9 ?
   A. 3
   B. 1, 9
   C. 1, 3, 9
   D. 9, 18, 27
   E. 1, 3, 5, 7, 9

2. An equal amount of nickels, dimes, and quarters have a total value of S cents. Which of the following is NOT necessarily a divisor of S ?
   F. 4
   G. 8
   H. 10
   J. 20
   K. 50

3. Find the least common multiple of 80, 130, and 90.
   A. 100
   B. 300
   C. 936
   D. 9,360
   E. 936,000

Lesson 24 – Factors

24.2 Learning Targets

1. Determine single and multiple factors of a number or set of numbers

2. Determine the least common multiple of multiple numbers and use this skill to solve problems

Self-Assessment

Circle the number that corresponds to your confidence level in your knowledge of this subject before beginning the lesson. A score of 1 means you are completely lost, and a score of 4 means you have mastered the skills. After you finish the lesson, return to the bottom of this page and circle your new confidence level to show your improvement.

Before Lesson

1   2   3   4

After Lesson

1   2   3   4

24.3.1 Determining Factors and Multiples

7	12

16	21

39	48

55	59

66	100

24.3.1 Determining Factors and Multiples

	2
	3
	4
	5
	6
	7
	8
	9
	10

Math Tip

Process of Elimination: If a question asks for factors or divisors of a number, eliminate answer choices that are **larger** than the original number because factors and divisors are always less than or equal to their multiple. If the question asks for numbers that are multiples of a certain number or divisible by another number, eliminate answer choices that are **smaller** than the numbers the question gives.

24.3.2 Prime Factorization and Least Common Multiple

60

Round 1

_____

Round 2

_____

Round 3

_____

Round 4

_____

Round 5

_____

24.3.2 Prime Factorization and Least Common Multiple

Traffic light #1 on Nashville Avenue turns green every 2 minutes and remains green for 45 seconds. Traffic light #2 on Nashville Avenue turns green every 3 minutes and remains green for 1 minute (there is a turning arrow at this intersection). If both lights turn green at noon, what time will it be when both traffic lights turn green at the exact same time again?

Math Tip

Plug In: If you have to find the least common multiple of a set of numbers, plug in the answers to find the solution more quickly. Start with the smallest answer choice and divide by the largest factor given in the question. Repeat until you find an answer that works with every factor or until you eliminate four answer choices.

24.4.1 Set One

1. Which of the following numbers is NOT a factor of 156 ?

    A. 3
    B. 4
    C. 8
    D. 12
    E. 13

DO YOUR FIGURING HERE.

2. What is the greatest 2-digit integer that is a multiple of 7 and is divisible by 4 ?

    F. 28
    G. 56
    H. 84
    J. 98
    K. 112

3. How many positive integers are factors of 45?

    A. 4
    B. 5
    C. 6
    D. 7
    E. 10

END OF SET ONE
STOP! DO NOT GO ON TO THE NEXT PAGE
UNTIL TOLD TO DO SO.

24.4.2 Set Two

4. All of the following answer choices are factors of 777 EXCEPT:
   - F. 1
   - G. 3
   - H. 7
   - J. 17
   - K. 21

DO YOUR FIGURING HERE.

5. In a lab, a scientist is running an experiment on a sample of radioactive particles. She observes that each day, half of the current number of particles disappears. If she wants to have 2 particles of the original sample left on the 5th day, what is the minimum number of particles she should start with?
   - A. 8
   - B. 10
   - C. 12
   - D. 16
   - E. 32

6. Banana Inc. is producing 25 batches of smartphones. The company's quality control department randomly picks a sample phone from each batch for testing. Which of the following percentages is possible as the percentage of the samples that pass?
   - F. 75%
   - G. 77%
   - H. 88%
   - J. 98%
   - K. 99%

END OF SET TWO
STOP! DO NOT GO ON TO THE NEXT PAGE
UNTIL TOLD TO DO SO.

24.4.3 Set Three

7. What is the greatest prime factor of 132 ?
   A. 3
   B. 5
   C. 7
   D. 11
   E. 13

   DO YOUR FIGURING HERE.

8. Which of the following is the greatest common divisor of 42, 45, and 66 ?
   F. 3
   G. 6
   H. 9
   J. 18
   K. 66

9. What are the three largest prime numbers that are less than 58 ?
   A. 2, 3, and 5
   B. 3, 5, and 7
   C. 31, 43, and 53
   D. 43, 45, and 51
   E. 43, 47, and 53

END OF SET THREE
STOP! DO NOT GO ON TO THE NEXT PAGE
UNTIL TOLD TO DO SO.

24.4.4 Set Four

10. Find the least common multiple of 2, 3, 4, 5, 6, and 7.

- F. 1
- G. 42
- H. 420
- J. 1008
- K. 5040

DO YOUR FIGURING HERE.

11. The number 35 has how many prime factors?

- A. 1
- B. 2
- C. 4
- D. 5
- E. 6

12. A faucet drips every 9 seconds. Another faucet drips every 6 seconds. If the two faucets drip at the same time, how many seconds do you need to wait until they drip together again?

- F. 3
- G. 15
- H. 18
- J. 36
- K. 54

END OF SET FOUR
STOP! DO NOT GO ON TO THE NEXT PAGE
UNTIL TOLD TO DO SO.

24.4.5 Set Five

13. If positive integer p is divisible by 9, 15, and 18, what is the smallest possible value of p ?

    A. 45
    B. 54
    C. 72
    D. 90
    E. 162

    DO YOUR FIGURING HERE.

14. What is the least common multiple of 70, 30, and 20 ?

    F. 42
    G. 50
    H. 120
    J. 420
    K. 42,000

15. What is the least common denominator for adding $\frac{1}{4}$, $\frac{3}{14}$, and $\frac{4}{7}$?

    A. 14
    B. 28
    C. 56
    D. 196
    E. 392

END OF SET FIVE
STOP! DO NOT GO ON TO THE NEXT PAGE
UNTIL TOLD TO DO SO.

Lesson 24 – Factors

Sum It Up

Factors

Factor
A whole number that can be multiplied with another whole number to produce a given number

Divisor
A synonym for *factor*

Multiple
A number that can be divided by another without a remainder

Remainder
The number left over when one number is divided into another

Integer
A whole number with no fraction or decimal

Prime Number
A number that is only divisible by itself and 1

ACT® Mastery Math

Sum It Up

Tips and Techniques

Process of Elimination: If a question asks for factors or divisors of a number, eliminate answer choices that are **larger** than the original number because factors and divisors are always less than or equal to their multiple.

Process of Elimination: If the question asks for numbers that are multiples of a certain number or divisible by another number, eliminate answer choices that are **smaller** than the numbers the question gives.

Plug In: If you have to find the least common multiple of a set of numbers, plug in the answers to find the solution more quickly. Start with the smallest answer choice and divide by the largest factor given in the question. Repeat until you find a choice that works with every factor or until you eliminate four answer choices.

Lesson 25

Quadratic Equations

CAPTION:

ACT® Mastery Math

25.1 Entrance Ticket

Solve the questions below.

1. What values of x are solutions for $x^2 + 3x = 10$?
   A. −5 and −2
   B. −5 and 2
   C. 5 and 2
   D. 5 and 7
   E. 7 and 3

2. Which of the following is a factor of the polynomial $x^2 - 5x - 36$?
   F. $x - 9$
   G. $x - 6$
   H. $x - 3$
   J. $x + 9$
   K. $x + 12$

3. What is the product of the 2 solutions of the equation $x^2 + 2x - 15 = 0$?
   A. −30
   B. −15
   C. −8
   D. 5
   E. 15

Lesson 25 – Quadratic Equations

25.2 Learning Targets

1. Factor a quadratic equation

2. Solve quadratic equations

Self-Assessment

Circle the number that corresponds to your confidence level in your knowledge of this subject before beginning the lesson. A score of 1 means you are completely lost, and a score of 4 means you have mastered the skills. After you finish the lesson, return to the bottom of this page and circle your new confidence level to show your improvement.

Before Lesson

1   2   3   4

After Lesson

1   2   3   4

25.3.1 Working With Quadratic Equations

Factor the expression: $x^2 + 7x + 12$

Expand the polynomial expression: $(x + 3)(x + 4)$

Lesson 25 – Quadratic Equations

25.3.1 Working With Quadratic Equations

Factor the expression: $x^2 - 4x - 12$

Expand the polynomial expression: $(x + 2)(x - 6)$

25.3.1 Working With Quadratic Equations

If $x^2 - 2x = 15$, what are the possible values of x?

If $x(3x - 11) = 42$, what are the possible values of x?

Math Tip

Check Answers with FOIL: If you are feeling unsure after factoring an equation, use the FOIL method to check your answer. Just as "reverse FOIL" gives you the factored form of the expression, FOIL will give you the expanded quadratic form of the expression. If you get the same expression that you started with, you know you have the correct answer.

25.3.2 Quadratic Equation Challenge

Round 1: Through the Forest

1. What values of x are solutions for the equation $x^2 + 7x = -12$?
    - A. -4 and -3
    - B. -4 and 0
    - C. -3 and 0
    - D. -3 and 4
    - E. 3 and 4

Round 2: Up the Mountain

2. What values of x are solutions for the equation $x^2 + 8x = 33$?
    - A. -11 and -6
    - B. -11 and -3
    - C. -11 and 3
    - D. -3 and 6
    - E. 3 and 11

25.3.2 Quadratic Equation Challenge

Round 3: Into the Caves

3. Which of the following values is a zero of the function $f(x) = 2x^3 - 7x^2 - 15x$?

    A. -5
    B. $-\dfrac{3}{2}$
    C. 3
    D. 6
    E. 10

Round 4: Save the Princess

4. Which of the following values is a zero of the function $f(x) = 3x^3 - 17x^2 - 6x$?

    A. -6
    B. -3
    C. $-\dfrac{1}{3}$
    D. $\dfrac{1}{3}$
    E. 3

Lesson 25 – Quadratic Equations

25.3.2 Quadratic Equation Challenge

Round 5: Collect the Gold

5. Which of the following values of x is in the solution set of the equation $x^2 + 3x - 10 = 30$?

   A. -10
   B. -8
   C. -5
   D. 0
   E. 8

Round 6: Slay the Dragon

6. Which of the following values of x is in the solution set of the equation $x^2 - 3x - 16 = 12$?

   A. -16
   B. -12
   C. -4
   D. -3
   E. 3

Entrance Ticket | Learning Targets | Working With Quadratic Equations | Quadratic Equation Challenge | ACT Practice | Sum It Up

25.4.1 Set One

1. Which of the following expressions is a factored form of $x^2 + 6x + 8$?

   A. $(x - 1)(x - 8)$
   B. $(x - 2)(x - 4)$
   C. $(x + 2)(x - 4)$
   D. $(x + 4)(x + 2)$
   E. $(x + 6)(x + 2)$

   DO YOUR FIGURING HERE.

2. What is the sum of the solutions of the equation $x^2 - 8x + 12 = 0$?

   F. -8
   G. -4
   H. 4
   J. 7
   K. 8

3. Which of the following values of x is a solution to the equation $x^2 - 8x + 3 = -4$?

   A. -7
   B. -3
   C. 1
   D. 3
   E. 4

END OF SET ONE
STOP! DO NOT GO ON TO THE NEXT PAGE
UNTIL TOLD TO DO SO.

Lesson 25 – Quadratic Equations

25.4.2 Set Two

4. Which of the following expressions is a factor of the expression $x^2 + 2x - 24$?

    F. $x - 6$
    G. $x - 2$
    H. $x + 2$
    J. $x + 4$
    K. $x + 6$

DO YOUR FIGURING HERE.

5. What are the solutions to the equation $x^2 - 4x = 32$?

    A. −16 or 2
    B. −8 or 4
    C. −4 or 8
    D. −2 or 16
    E. 4 or 16

6. What is the sum of the 2 solutions to the equation $x^2 + 4x - 21 = 0$?

    F. −21
    G. −7
    H. −4
    J. 0
    K. 3

END OF SET TWO
STOP! DO NOT GO ON TO THE NEXT PAGE
UNTIL TOLD TO DO SO.

25.4.3 Set Three

7. Which of the following expressions is a factored form of the expression $3x^2 - 10x - 8$?

    A. $(3x - 4)(x + 2)$
    B. $(3x - 2)(x - 4)$
    C. $(3x - 2)(x + 4)$
    D. $(3x + 2)(x - 4)$
    E. $(3x + 4)(x + 2)$

DO YOUR FIGURING HERE.

8. The equation $9x^2 = 12x$ can be factorized. Which of the following are the solutions to the equation?

    F. $x = 0$ or $x = 1$

    G. $x = 0$ or $x = \dfrac{4}{3}$

    H. $x = 1$ or $x = 1$

    J. $x = 2$ or $x = \dfrac{4}{3}$

    K. $x = \dfrac{4}{3}$ or $x = \dfrac{4}{3}$

9. Which of the following expressions is equivalent to the expression $-2x^2 - x$?

    A. $-x(2x + 1)$
    B. $-x(2x - 1)$
    C. $-x(1 - 2x)$
    D. $x(2x - 1)$
    E. $x(x + 1)$

END OF SET THREE
STOP! DO NOT GO ON TO THE NEXT PAGE
UNTIL TOLD TO DO SO.

25.4.4 Set Four

10. Which of the following expressions is equivalent to the expression $x^2 - 6x + 9$?

F. $(x - 4.5)(x - 2)$
G. $(x - 4.5)(x + 2)$
H. $(x - 3)^2$
J. $(x + 3)(x - 3)$
K. $(x + 3)^2$

DO YOUR FIGURING HERE.

11. Which of the following is a zero of the function $f(x) = 3x^3 - 5x^2 - 2x$?

A. -3
B. -2
C. $-\frac{1}{3}$
D. $\frac{1}{3}$
E. $\frac{2}{5}$

12. What is the value of x, if $(x - 2)(x + 5) + 3x - 2 = -21$?

F. -6
G. -5
H. -3
J. 2
K. 4

END OF SET FOUR
STOP! DO NOT GO ON TO THE NEXT PAGE UNTIL TOLD TO DO SO.

25.4.5 Set Five

13. Let P be the profits of a hotel in dollars, and x be the number of guests at the hotel in a season. The profits of the hotel for the season are modeled by $P = x^2 + 100x - 120,000$. What is the smallest number of guests that the hotel needs in a season in order to not lose money?

    A. 200
    B. 300
    C. 400
    D. 600
    E. 1200

DO YOUR FIGURING HERE.

14. What are the possible values of x for $\frac{x-3}{2} = \frac{5}{x}$?

    F. −5 and −2
    G. −5 and 2
    H. −3 and 5
    J. 5 and −2
    K. 5 and 2

15. The trinomial $x^2 - 4x - 12 = 0$ can be solved by factoring the left hand side of the equation into 2 binomials in the form $(x + a)(x + b)$. What is the polynomial sum of these 2 binomials?

    A. $2x - 12$
    B. $2x - 4$
    C. $2x - 1$
    D. $2x + 1$
    E. $2x + 4$

END OF SET FIVE
STOP! DO NOT GO ON TO THE NEXT PAGE
UNTIL TOLD TO DO SO.

Lesson 25 – Quadratic Equations

Sum It Up

Quadratic Equations

Quadratic Equation
An equation whose highest term is raised to a power of 2

Polynomial
An expression consisting of two or more terms

Binomial
A polynomial that contains two terms

Equation
States that two expressions or terms are equal

Expression
Consists of terms including both numbers and variables

Factor
For a given number or expression, any number/expression that divides evenly into the original

Tips and Techniques

Check Answers with FOIL: When you have finished the problem and arrived at a solution, use the FOIL method to check your answer. Just as "reverse FOIL" gives you the factored form of the expression, FOIL will give you the expanded quadratic form of the expression. If you get the same expression that you started with, you know you have the correct answer!

Lesson 26

Probability

CAPTION:

ACT® Mastery Math

26.1 Entrance Ticket

Solve the questions below.

1. The 15-member quiz bowl team needs to choose a secretary for their executive board. They decide that the secretary, who will be chosen at random, CANNOT be the president or the vice president of the team. What is the probability that Conor, who is a member of the team but not the president or vice president, will be chosen?

   A. 0
   B. $\dfrac{1}{15}$
   C. $\dfrac{1}{13}$
   D. $\dfrac{2}{13}$
   E. $\dfrac{1}{3}$

2. Lorenzo is rolling a pair of regular, 6-sided dice numbered 1 to 6. What is the probability that the sum of the values of the two dice is equal to 10 ?

   F. $\dfrac{1}{18}$
   G. $\dfrac{1}{12}$
   H. $\dfrac{4}{5}$
   J. $\dfrac{5}{36}$
   K. $\dfrac{5}{18}$

3. A bowl contains 60 marbles, all either red, yellow, or orange. A marble is randomly removed from the bowl and then returned to the bowl. The probability that this marble is red is $\dfrac{1}{6}$. The probablility that this same marble is yellow is $\dfrac{3}{5}$. How many orange marbles are in the bag?

   A. 6
   B. 12
   C. 14
   D. 20
   E. 46

Entrance Ticket | Learning Targets | Probability of Single Event | Probability of Multiple Events | ACT Practice | Sum It Up

Lesson 26 – Probability

26.2 Learning Targets

1. Solve problems by calculating simple probability of single and multiple events

2. Recognize different types of probability and apply basic probability rules

3. Apply one or more math operations in solving probability problems

Self-Assessment

Circle the number that corresponds to your confidence level in your knowledge of this subject before beginning the lesson. A score of 1 means you are completely lost, and a score of 4 means you have mastered the skills. After you finish the lesson, return to the bottom of this page and circle your new confidence level to show your improvement.

Before Lesson

1   2   3   4

After Lesson

1   2   3   4

ACT® Mastery Math

26.3.1 Probability of Single Event

Desired Result	Number of Desired Outcomes	Number of Possible Outcomes	Probability

Lesson 26 – Probability

26.3.1 Probability of Single Event

1. Probability of picking numbers 2 through 10: _____

2. Probability of picking a joker: _____

3. Probability of picking a multiple of 2: _____

4. Probability of not picking hearts: _____

Math Tip

Process of Elimination: Figure out the number of chances that make up the "whole," which will either be the denominator of the fraction or share a common factor with the whole. Eliminate any answer choice with a denominator larger than the whole and any answer choice that does not share a common factor with the whole.

Entrance Ticket | Learning Targets | Probability of Single Event | Probability of Multiple Events | ACT Practice | Sum It Up

26.3.2 Probability of Multiple Events

1. The probability of picking a 2, 3, or 4 twice: _____

2. The probability of picking 2 or 3 on the first draw and 4 or 5 on the second draw: _____

3. The probability of NOT picking a 4 or 6 on the first draw and picking a 5 on the second draw: _____

4. The probability of picking double sixes on the very next draw after picking double sixes on the previous draw: _____

26.4.1 Set One

1. A bowl contains 7 chocolates, 3 salt-water taffies, and 9 peppermint candies. If an item is selected at random from the bowl, what is the probability that a salt-water taffy will be selected?

   A. $\dfrac{1}{19}$

   B. $\dfrac{1}{16}$

   C. $\dfrac{3}{19}$

   D. $\dfrac{3}{16}$

   E. $\dfrac{1}{3}$

DO YOUR FIGURING HERE.

2. The circular face of a spinner at the state fair has 5 equal sections: red, orange, yellow, green, and blue, as shown in the figure below. After being spun, the arrow of the spinner is equally likely to point to any of the 5 sections. What is the probability that, after the arrow has been spun, the section the arrow is pointing to is blue?

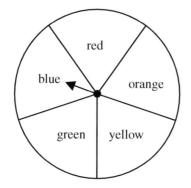

   F. $\dfrac{1}{20}$

   G. $\dfrac{1}{9}$

   H. $\dfrac{1}{5}$

   J. $\dfrac{1}{4}$

   K. $\dfrac{4}{5}$

GO ON TO THE NEXT PAGE

3. In a bag of 300 pieces of candy, 30% of the pieces are chocolate. If a piece of candy is randomly selected from the bag, what is the probability that the candy picked is NOT chocolate?

A. $\dfrac{1}{10}$

B. $\dfrac{3}{10}$

C. $\dfrac{1}{2}$

D. $\dfrac{7}{10}$

E. $\dfrac{9}{10}$

DO YOUR FIGURING HERE.

END OF SET ONE
STOP! DO NOT GO ON TO THE NEXT PAGE
UNTIL TOLD TO DO SO.

26.4.2 Set Two

4. A spinner for a board game has 8 numbered sections, each with equal central angles, as shown in the figure below. If the arrow on the spinner is spun randomly, what is the probability that the arrow will point to a sector whose number is a prime number?

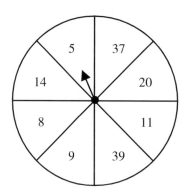

F. $\frac{1}{8}$

G. $\frac{1}{4}$

H. $\frac{3}{8}$

J. $\frac{1}{2}$

K. $\frac{5}{8}$

DO YOUR FIGURING HERE.

5. The stem-and-leaf plot below shows the number of points a basketball player on the New Orleans Krewe scored in each of 15 games.

Stem	Leaf
0	8
1	0 4 7 7 7 8 9
2	3 5 5 6 8
3	1 2

(Note: For example, 20 points would have a stem value of 2 and a leaf value of 0.)

If a game represented in the stem-and-leaf plot is randomly chosen, what is the probability that the basketball player scored exactly 17 points in that game?

A. $\dfrac{1}{5}$

B. $\dfrac{3}{5}$

C. $\dfrac{3}{19}$

D. $\dfrac{17}{294}$

E. $\dfrac{51}{294}$

DO YOUR FIGURING HERE.

6. If a number is chosen at random from the set {1, 2, 3, 4, ..., 18}, what is the probability that the number chosen is a factor of 17 ?

F. 0

G. $\dfrac{1}{18}$

H. $\dfrac{1}{9}$

J. $\dfrac{2}{9}$

K. $\dfrac{17}{18}$

END OF SET TWO
STOP! DO NOT GO ON TO THE NEXT PAGE
UNTIL TOLD TO DO SO.

26.4.3 Set Three

7. A jar contains 16 marbles, each of which is a solid color. There are 9 red marbles and 7 white marbles. Colby will draw one marble at random and then, without replacing it, will draw another marble from the jar at random. Which of the following expressions shows the probability of Colby drawing 2 white marbles?

   A. $\dfrac{7}{16} + \dfrac{3}{16}$

   B. $\dfrac{7}{16} \cdot \dfrac{3}{16}$

   C. $\dfrac{7}{16} \cdot \dfrac{6}{15}$

   D. $\dfrac{9}{16} + \dfrac{8}{15}$

   E. $\dfrac{9}{16} \cdot \dfrac{8}{15}$

8. A standard deck of cards has 4 suits (spades, hearts, clubs, and diamonds), each containing 13 cards. The players take turns, each drawing a card at random from the deck and placing the card face up on the table. When it is the fifth player's turn, there are 2 diamonds, 1 heart, and 1 club on the table. What is the probability that the fifth player will draw a diamond?

   F. $\dfrac{1}{52}$

   G. $\dfrac{11}{48}$

   H. $\dfrac{1}{4}$

   J. $\dfrac{9}{11}$

   K. $\dfrac{11}{13}$

9. You rolled a standard 6-sided die numbered from 1 to 6 ten times, recording the numbers that you rolled each time. You recorded: 4, 2, 5, 5, 5, 1, 6, 1, 2, 6. What is the probability that your next roll will be a 3 ?

A. $\left(\dfrac{1}{6}\right)^{11}$

B. $\left(\dfrac{1}{6}\right)^{10}$

C. $\dfrac{1}{6}$

D. $\dfrac{5}{6}$

E. 1

DO YOUR FIGURING HERE.

END OF SET THREE
STOP! DO NOT GO ON TO THE NEXT PAGE
UNTIL TOLD TO DO SO.

26.4.4 Set Four

10. "Rolling doubles" occurs when you roll the same number on each of two dice. What is the probability of rolling doubles with a pair of regular, 6-sided dice numbered from 1 to 6 ?

F. $\frac{1}{36}$

G. $\frac{1}{18}$

H. $\frac{1}{12}$

J. $\frac{1}{9}$

K. $\frac{1}{6}$

DO YOUR FIGURING HERE.

11. A fair coin and a 6-sided die numbered from 1 to 6 are tossed at the same time. What is the probability they will land so that the side facing up on the coin is heads and the side facing up on the die is an odd number?

A. $\frac{1}{12}$

B. $\frac{1}{6}$

C. $\frac{1}{4}$

D. $\frac{1}{2}$

E. $\frac{2}{3}$

12. The probability of rolling a 6 on a regular 6-sided die numbered 1 to 6 is $\frac{1}{6}$. What is the probability of rolling a 6 five times in a row?

F. $\frac{1}{6}$

G. $\frac{1}{36}$

H. $\frac{1}{216}$

J. $\frac{1}{1,296}$

K. $\frac{1}{7,776}$

DO YOUR FIGURING HERE.

END OF SET FOUR
STOP! DO NOT GO ON TO THE NEXT PAGE
UNTIL TOLD TO DO SO.

26.4.5 Set Five

13. Which of the following is NOT a possible value for a probability?

    A. 0.0704

    B. 0.33

    C. $\dfrac{1}{2}$

    D. $\dfrac{100}{100}$

    E. $\dfrac{9}{8}$

14. A 40-employee paper company needs to choose someone to speak at a press conference. They decide that the speaker, who will be chosen at random, CANNOT be any of the 5 executive officers of the company. What is the probability that Astrid, who is an employee of the company but NOT an executive officer, will be chosen?

    F. $\dfrac{1}{40}$

    G. $\dfrac{1}{35}$

    H. $\dfrac{1}{8}$

    J. $\dfrac{3}{20}$

    K. $\dfrac{1}{5}$

15. A bowl contains 21 pieces of candy: 3 cherry, 10 lemon, and 8 apple. How many additional cherry pieces must be added to the bowl so that the probability of randomly selecting a cherry piece is $\dfrac{2}{5}$?

    A. 4
    B. 9
    C. 10
    D. 19
    E. 21

DO YOUR FIGURING HERE.

END OF SET FIVE
STOP! DO NOT GO ON TO THE NEXT PAGE
UNTIL TOLD TO DO SO.

ACT® Mastery Math

Sum It Up

Probability

Probability
The chance or likelihood that an event will occur

Outcome
A possible result of a probability experiment

Desired Outcome
A result that someone wants from a probability experiment

Possible Outcome
Any possible result from a probability experiment

Odds
An expression of probability that uses a ratio to compare the number of things you are looking for to the number of things you are *not* looking for

Conditional
The probability of an event happening, given that another event has already occurred; also considered dependent probability

Independence
An event that is not affected by previous events.

Joint Probability
Measuring the probability of two events occurring together and at the same point in time

Tips and Techniques

Process of Elimination: Figure out the number of chances that make up the "whole," which will either be the denominator of the fraction or share a common factor with the whole. Eliminate any answer choice with a denominator larger than the whole and any answer choice that doesn't share a common factor with the whole.

Lesson 27

Patterns and Sequences

CAPTION:

ACT® Mastery Math

27.1 Entrance Ticket

Solve the questions below.

1. The third term of an arithmetic sequence is –8, and the fourth term is –20. What is the second term? (Note: In an arithmetic sequence, consecutive terms differ by the same amount.)
   A. –32
   B. –14
   C. 4
   D. 12
   E. 20

2. The first 5 terms of a geometric sequence are 0.778, –2.33, 7, –21, and 63. What is the 6th term?
   F. –189
   G. –84
   H. 42
   J. 84
   K. 189

3. Dalton is saving up money to buy a car. He deposits $10 in his savings account the 1st month. Each month after that, he deposits $5 more than the amount he deposited the previous month. Thus, Dalton's deposit is $15 the 2nd month, $20 the 3rd month, and so on. He makes his final deposit of $95 the 18th month. How much money does Dalton have in his account after these 18 deposits?
   A. $475
   B. $850
   C. $900
   D. $945
   E. $950

Entrance Ticket | Learning Targets | Arithmetic Sequences and Sums | Geometric Sequences and Other Patterns | ACT Practice | Sum It Up

Lesson 27 – Patterns and Sequences

27.2 Learning Targets

1. Recognize arithmetic sequences of numbers and their patterns, calculate sums of numbers in these sequences, and solve related problems

2. Recognize geometric sequences of numbers and their patterns, recognize non-arithmetic and non-geometric sequences and patterns, and solve related problems

Self-Assessment

Circle the number that corresponds to your confidence level in your knowledge of this subject before beginning the lesson. A score of 1 means you are completely lost, and a score of 4 means you have mastered the skills. After you finish the lesson, return to the bottom of this page and circle your new confidence level to show your improvement.

Before Lesson

1   2   3   4

After Lesson

1   2   3   4

ACT® Mastery Math

27.3.1 Arithmetic Sequences and Sums

1. ____, 36, 27, 18; Common difference: _____

2. –4, ____, 3, 6.5; Common difference: _____

3. 5, 11, 17, ____; Common difference: _____

4. Find the fifth term in a sequence starting at 7 with a common difference of –3.5.

5. Find the first term in a sequence whose third term is –5 with a common difference of –4.

Lesson 27 – Patterns and Sequences

27.3.1 Arithmetic Sequences and Sums

1. In the arithmetic sequence 1, 5, 9 … , what is the common difference, and what is the sum of the first 10 items?

2. If Jordan deposits $20 in the bank the first month, then increases that deposit amount by $5 each month, how much will Jordan have deposited after one year?

3. Kordayshia stacks cans of chili at the grocery store in a pyramid-shaped display. She places 24 cans on the base level, with 4 fewer cans in each successive level for a total of 6 levels. What is the common difference between these levels, and how many total cans did she use?

27.3.1 Arithmetic Sequences and Sums

1. The difference between consecutive numbers below is the same. What are the 2 missing numbers?

   21, ___, ___, 48

   A. 27, 34
   B. 28, 32
   C. 29, 37
   D. 30, 39
   E. 31, 38

2. The first few terms of an arithmetic sequence are $1\frac{3}{8}$, $3\frac{1}{2}$, and $5\frac{5}{8}$, in that order. What is the next term in the sequence?

   F. $6\frac{7}{8}$

   G. $7\frac{1}{4}$

   H. $7\frac{1}{2}$

   J. $7\frac{3}{4}$

   K. 8

27.3.1 Arithmetic Sequences and Sums

3. Antonio is creating a sculpture for art class. He arranges stacks of cans so that each successive level of cans has 2 fewer cans than the level below it, and the top level has 3 cans. Such a stack with 2 levels is shown below. Antonio wants to make a similar stack with 10 levels. How many cans would Antonio use to build this stack?

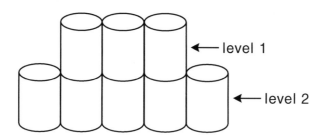

A. 90
B. 100
C. 110
D. 120
E. 130

Math Tip

Plug In: When you are working with sequence questions, oftentimes the best strategy is to plug in the answer choices. If you struggle to find the correct pattern, try the answers.

27.3.2 Geometric Sequences and Other Patterns

1. How do you know that a sequence is geometric and not arithmetic?

   _____

   _____

   _____

2. How do you find the common ratio?

   _____

   _____

   _____

Lesson 27 – Patterns and Sequences

27.3.2 Geometric Sequences and Other Patterns

1. ____ , 36 , 18 , 9 ; Common ratio: _____

2. −4 , ____ , −36 , 108 ; Common ratio: _____

3. 5 , 20 , 80 , ____ ; Common ratio: _____

4. Find the fifth term in a sequence starting at 7 with a common ratio of −2.

5. Find the first term in a sequence whose third term is 5 with a common ratio of $\frac{1}{4}$.

27.3.2 Geometric Sequences and Other Patterns

1. What is the 5th term in this sequence of "square" numbers, defined by the figures below: 1, 4, 9,...?

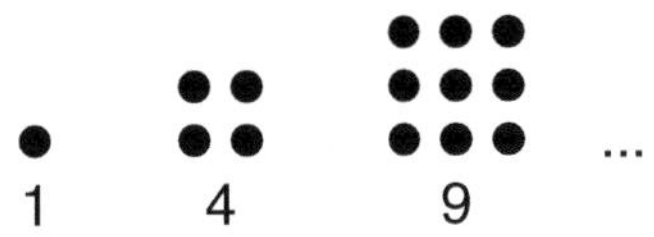

   A. 8
   B. 21
   C. 23
   D. 25
   E. 27

2. There is a pattern when adding together the first n of what are called the triangle numbers, as illustrated below.

   $$1 + 3 = 4 = \frac{2(2+1)(2+2)}{6}$$

   $$1 + 3 + 6 = 10 = \frac{3(3+1)(3+2)}{6}$$

   $$1 + 3 + 6 + 10 = 20 = \frac{4(4+1)(4+2)}{6}$$

   Which of the following is an expression for the sum of the first n triangle numbers?

   F. $\dfrac{n(n+1)}{2n}$

   G. $\dfrac{n(n+1)(n+2)}{2n}$

   H. $\dfrac{n(n+1)}{6}$

   J. $\dfrac{n(n+n-1)(n+n)}{6}$

   K. $\dfrac{n(n+1)(n+2)}{6}$

27.3.2 Geometric Sequences and Other Patterns

3. The sum of a sequence of consecutive even numbers, in which the smallest number is 2, divided by the number of terms in the sequence plus 1, is always equal to the number of terms in the sequence. For example $\frac{2+4}{2+1} = 2$, and $\frac{2+4+6}{3+1} = 3$. One of the sequences that follows this pattern equals 8. What is the largest number in this sequence?

   A. 8
   B. 10
   C. 12
   D. 14
   E. 16

4. One can build a chain of equilateral triangles out of matchsticks as shown below. How many matchsticks are needed to construct a chain of 30 triangles?

   F. 33
   G. 60
   H. 61
   J. 75
   K. 90

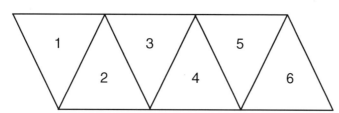

Math Tip

Start Small: When you have to solve a difficult pattern or one that is not arithmetic or geometric, draw a smaller example to understand the pattern. Once you have an idea, scale it up to answer the question. If all else fails, mark and move.

27.4.1 Set One

1. Which of the following statements is NOT true about the arithmetic sequence shown below?

    19, 15, 11, 7, 3, ... ?

    A. The sixth term is –1.
    B. The sum of the first 4 terms is 52.
    C. The seventh term is –5.
    D. The common difference of consecutive terms is –4.
    E. The common ratio of consecutive terms is –4.

DO YOUR FIGURING HERE.

2. The third term of an arithmetic sequence is 18, and the fourth term is 9. What is the second term?

    (Note: In an arithmetic sequence, consecutive terms differ by the same amount.)

    F. –9
    G. 0
    H. $\frac{9}{2}$
    J. 27
    K. 36

3. In the arithmetic sequence below, how many terms are there between 17 and 41, not including 17 and 41?

    9, 13, 17, 21, ... , 41

    A. 4
    B. 5
    C. 6
    D. 12
    E. 24

END OF SET ONE
STOP! DO NOT GO ON TO THE NEXT PAGE
UNTIL TOLD TO DO SO.

Lesson 27 – Patterns and Sequences

27.4.2 Set Two

4. The second term of an arithmetic sequence is –11, and the third term is –30. What is the first term?

   (Note: In an arithmetic sequence, consecutive terms differ by the same amount.)

   F. –49
   G. –21
   H. 8
   J. 11
   K. 30

DO YOUR FIGURING HERE.

5. Which of the following statements describes the total number of dots in the first n rows of the right triangular arrangement illustrated below?

   ●   1st Row

   ● ●   2nd Row

   ● ● ●   3rd Row

   ● ● ● ●   4th Row

   ● ● ● ● ●   5th Row

   A. The total is always equal to 15 regardless of the number of rows.
   B. The total is equal to 2 times the number of rows, plus 1.
   C. The total is equal to 3 times the number of rows.
   D. The total is equal to the number of rows plus the square of the number of rows all divided by 2.
   E. There is no consistent relationship between this total and the number of rows.

6. The terms of an arithmetic series are such that the difference between consecutive terms is constant. For example, in 2 + 5 + 8 + 11 + 14, the difference between consecutive terms is 3. If the first term in an arithmetic series is 4, the last term is 144, and the sum is 592, what are the first 3 terms?

   F. 4, 16, 28
   G. 4, 24, 44
   H. 4, $48\frac{1}{2}$, 93
   J. 4, 66, 128
   K. 4, 128, 1,188

END OF SET TWO
STOP! DO NOT GO ON TO THE NEXT PAGE
UNTIL TOLD TO DO SO.

27.4.3 Set Three

7. What is the 7th term of the geometric sequence $\frac{1}{16}, -\frac{1}{4}, 1, -4, \ldots$?

- A. −256
- B. −64
- C. 16
- D. 64
- E. 256

8. What is the 6th term of the geometric sequence $1, -3, 9, -27, \ldots$?

- F. −243
- G. −81
- H. 81
- J. 243
- K. 729

9. If 2 is the first term and 1,250 is the 5th term of a geometric sequence, which of the following is the second term?

- A. 5
- B. 10
- C. 25
- D. 50
- E. 100

DO YOUR FIGURING HERE.

END OF SET THREE
STOP! DO NOT GO ON TO THE NEXT PAGE
UNTIL TOLD TO DO SO.

27.4.4 Set Four

10. At a local farmers market, a display of honey jars has been arranged into a pyramid with 4 levels. The figure below shows an overhead view of the top level of the honey jars (circles shaded) and the level of jars below it (circles unshaded). In the display, each level is a square with sides 1 jar longer than the level above it. How many jars of honey are there in the display?

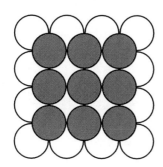

F. 18
G. 36
H. 64
J. 82
K. 86

11. In the geometric sequence below, the 1st term is 2. If it can be determined, what is the 7th term?

$$2, -6, 18, -54, 162, \ldots ?$$

A. −1,458
B. −486
C. 486
D. 1,458
E. Cannot be determined from the given information.

12. Let q, r, s, and t be distinct, positive integers. What is the 4th term of the geometric sequence below?

$$qrs,\ q^2rst,\ q^3rst^2,\ \ldots$$

F. $q^3r^2st^2$
G. q^4rst^3
H. $q^4r^2st^3$
J. q^5rst^3
K. q^5rst^4

END OF SET FOUR
STOP! DO NOT GO ON TO THE NEXT PAGE
UNTIL TOLD TO DO SO.

27.4.5 Set Five

13. What is the fourth term of the geometric sequence 54, –18, 6, … ?

    A. –12
    B. –2
    C. –1
    D. 1
    E. 2

14. When written in decimal form, the fraction $\frac{1}{13}$ repeats: 0.076923076923… In this decimal form, what is the 100th digit to the right of the decimal point?

    F. 0
    G. 2
    H. 6
    J. 7
    K. 9

15. The population of a particular bacteria is directly proportional to its population the day before. If there are 180 bacteria on day one, there will be 240 bacteria on day two. If a sequence is constructed from the number of bacteria counted each day, which of the following options would best describe that sequence?

    A. Arithmetic with common difference –60

    B. Arithmetic with common difference 60

    C. Geometric with common ratio $\frac{3}{4}$

    D. Geometric with common ratio $\frac{4}{3}$

    E. Neither arithmetic nor geometric

DO YOUR FIGURING HERE.

END OF SET FIVE
STOP! DO NOT GO ON TO THE NEXT PAGE
UNTIL TOLD TO DO SO.

Lesson 27 – Patterns and Sequences

Sum It Up

Patterns and Sequences

Arithmetic Sequence
A sequence made by *adding* the same value each time

Common Difference
The difference between each number in an arithmetic sequence

Geometric Sequence
A sequence made by *multiplying* by the same value each time

Common Ratio
The ratio of one term to the previous term; any term divided by the common ratio equals the term right before it

Tips and Techniques

Plug In: When you are working with sequence questions, it is often the best strategy to plug in the answer choices. If you struggle to find the correct pattern, try plugging in the answers.

Start Small: Whenever you have to solve a difficult pattern or one that is not arithmetic or geometric, draw a smaller example to understand the pattern. Once you have an idea, scale it up to answer the question. If all else fails, mark and move.

Lesson 28

Counting

CAPTION:

ACT® Mastery Math

28.1 Entrance Ticket

Solve the questions below.

1. Westpond High School took its senior class of 50 students on a whitewater rafting field trip. The school rented 10 rafts. Each of the rafts contained at least 1 person but no more than 6 people. At most, how many rafts contained exactly 3 people?
   A. 3
   B. 4
   C. 5
   D. 6
   E. 7

2. An ice cream cone at Mike's Dairy Shoppe consists of exactly 1 type of cone, 1 ice cream flavor, and 1 choice of topping. How many different ice cream cone combinations are possible when choosing from 3 types of cones, 10 ice cream flavors, and 6 toppings?
   F. 19
   G. 48
   H. 60
   J. 148
   K. 180

3. Five classmates are making up a game on the playground. The players stand evenly spaced around a circle. The player with the ball (the thrower) bounces it to another player (the catcher). The catcher cannot be the player to the thrower's immediate left or right and cannot be the player who last bounced the ball. A player bounces the ball as the first thrower. Which number pass will be that player's first catch?
   A. 5th
   B. 6th
   C. 7th
   D. 8th
   E. 9th

Entrance Ticket | Learning Targets | Combinations | Permutations | ACT Practice | Sum It Up

448

Lesson 28 – Counting

28.2 Learning Targets

1. Calculate large sums using counting shortcuts

2. Recognize patterns, combinations, diagrams, etc. used to quickly calculate sums

Self-Assessment

Circle the number that corresponds to your confidence level in your knowledge of this subject before beginning the lesson. A score of 1 means you are completely lost, and a score of 4 means you have mastered the skills. After you finish the lesson, return to the bottom of this page and circle your new confidence level to show your improvement.

Before Lesson

1   2   3   4

After Lesson

1   2   3   4

ACT® Mastery Math

28.3.1 Combinations

1. Elizabeth has 2 hats, 7 shirts, and 3 pairs of shoes. How many distinct outfits, each consisting of a hat, a shirt, and a pair of shoes, can Elizabeth wear?

2. If a particular shop offers 6 different types of bread, 5 different types of meat, and 5 different types of cheese, and if each sandwich can only contain one type of bread, one type of meat, and one type of cheese, how many possible sandwiches can be made?

Lesson 28 – Counting

28.3.1 Combinations

1. What is the maximum number of distinct diagonals that can be drawn in the heptagon shown below?

   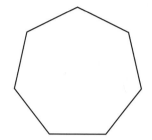

   A. 6
   B. 7
   C. 13
   D. 14
   E. 15

2. Hexagons have 9 diagonals, as illustrated below.

   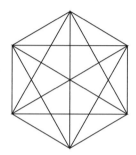

   How many diagonals does the nonagon below have?

   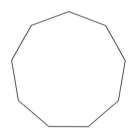

   F. 24
   G. 27
   H. 31
   J. 35
   K. 40

Math Tip

Find the Pattern: If one method is taking too long, try something different. Draw out the question and try to identify a pattern. Sometimes, your own drawing may be easier to understand than a mathematical formula.

ACT® Mastery Math

28.3.2 Permutations

1. A student is working on her new schedule for her junior year of college. She needs to schedule 4 classes for the first semester and has 10 classes to choose from. How many combinations of class schedules can the student have?

2. A pizza chain offers a delivery deal of 2 medium 3-topping pizzas for $10. The pizza chain offers 13 different toppings. You want to order a delivery, but you don't want any toppings ordered twice. How many possible topping combinations do you have to choose from?

Lesson 28 – Counting

28.3.2 Permutations

3. A roller coaster has 10 carts that will seat up to 3 people each. If 24 people are seated in the carts and NO carts are empty, what is the greatest possible number of carts that could be filled with 3 people?
   A. 4
   B. 5
   C. 6
   D. 7
   E. 8

Math Tip

Draw It Out: If you're unsure of how to approach a problem, or if it seems especially complicated, draw out the scenario. This is often a quick and simple way to find the solution. **Remember that the test is timed**, so don't get bogged down by trying to draw the shapes perfectly.

28.4.1 Set One

1. Lisa is sewing a regular hexagonal button into a shirt, as shown in the figure below. The button has one hole in each of its vertices. How many different stitches would Lisa need to make in order to stitch her thread through each possible pair of holes?

   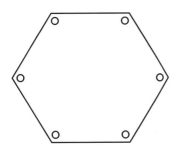

   A. 15
   B. 14
   C. 12
   D. 9
   E. 6

2. At a school prom, 1 boy and 1 girl will be chosen as prom king and queen. If there are 225 boys and 250 girls attending the prom, how many different boy-girl combinations for prom king and queen are possible?

   F. 25
   G. 225
   H. 250
   J. 475
   K. 56,250

3. What is the maximum number of distinct diagonals that can be drawn in the pentagon shown below?

   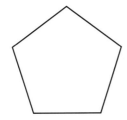

   A. 5
   B. 6
   C. 7
   D. 8
   E. 9

DO YOUR FIGURING HERE.

END OF SET ONE
STOP! DO NOT GO ON TO THE NEXT PAGE
UNTIL TOLD TO DO SO.

28.4.2 Set Two

4. Nemo has 5 swimsuits, 2 pairs of flippers, and 3 pairs of goggles, which can be worn in any combination. He needs to choose a combination of swimwear to wear to a family pool party. How many different combinations consisting of 1 swimsuit, 1 pair of flippers, and 1 pair of goggles are possible for Nemo to wear to the pool party?

   F. 30
   G. 25
   H. 20
   J. 15
   K. 10

5. June owns a small deli. They offer lunch combos every day in which a customer can get a sandwich, chips, and a drink for $5. Their deli offers 8 types of sandwiches, 4 types of chips, and 5 types of drinks. How many distinct lunch combos can be made at June's deli?

   A. 17
   B. 32
   C. 60
   D. 160
   E. 800

6. The points $V(1,4)$, $W(3,6)$, $X(7,5)$, $Y(5,1)$, and $Z(2,2)$ are shown in the standard (x,y) coordinate plane below.

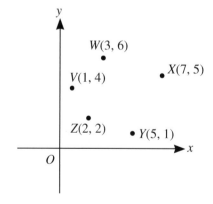

   How many distinct lines are there that each contains at least 2 of the 5 given points?

   F. 5
   G. 7
   H. 9
   J. 10
   K. 25

DO YOUR FIGURING HERE.

END OF SET TWO
STOP! DO NOT GO ON TO THE NEXT PAGE
UNTIL TOLD TO DO SO.

28.4.3 Set Three

7. Alex and 4 friends are playing baseball on the same team. Each time they play a game, they switch the batting order to a sequence that has not yet been used. What is the maximum number of games they can play before they have to repeat a batting order they have already used?

    A. 240
    B. 120
    C. 24
    D. 15
    E. 5

8. How many 3-letter orderings, where no letter is repeated, can be made using the letters of the word TRUCK ?

    F. 125
    G. 60
    H. 30
    J. 15
    K. 12

9. Edwin is setting up cones for the boundaries of an ultimate Frisbee field. The field will be 50 yards long and 20 yards wide. Edwin places a cone on every corner, every 10 yards on the long sides of the field, and every 5 yards on the short sides of the field. How many cones does Edwin need to use for the field?

    A. 14
    B. 16
    C. 18
    D. 20
    E. 22

DO YOUR FIGURING HERE.

END OF SET THREE
STOP! DO NOT GO ON TO THE NEXT PAGE
UNTIL TOLD TO DO SO.

28.4.4 Set Four

10. Flash cards are available in 20 different colors, and markers are available in 10 different colors. You are required to write 3 capitalized letters from the standard 26-letter alphabet on a flashcard, using any color flash card and marker. Letters may be repeated, but the first letter CANNOT be A or B. How many different 3-letter flash cards can be made?

    F. $20 \times 10 \times 26 \times 3$
    G. $20 \times 10 \times 26 \times 25 \times 24$
    H. $20 \times 10 \times 26^2 \times 24$
    J. $20 \times 10 \times 26^3$
    K. $20^3 \times 10^3 \times 26^2 \times 24$

DO YOUR FIGURING HERE.

11. Surfer Joe has 7 beach towels of different colors that he uses for the 7 days of the week. He hangs them on a laundry line when he is not using them. In how many different orders can the 7 towels be hung from the laundry line?

    A. 7
    B. 24
    C. 120
    D. 720
    E. 5,040

12. Bruce works at a local general store. If Bruce uses only pennies, nickels, dimes, and quarters when making change, what is the least number of coins needed to make change totaling 68¢ ?

    F. 6
    G. 7
    H. 8
    J. 9
    K. 10

END OF SET FOUR
STOP! DO NOT GO ON TO THE NEXT PAGE
UNTIL TOLD TO DO SO.

28.4.5 Set Five

13. The first 2 questions on a test are multiple choice, each with 6 possible answers. The next 4 questions on the test are True/False, with only 2 possible answer choices. If Charley answers the 6-question test randomly, how many different combinations of answer choices could he make?

    A. 1,152
    B.   576
    C.   278
    D.   20
    E.   14

14. A T-shirt company stamps a unique product code on every T-shirt it produces. The code consists of 2 uppercase letters from the 26-letter standard alphabet followed by 2 digits ranging from 0 to 9. How many T-shirts can the company make before it is forced to repeat a product code?

    F. $2(26) \times 2(10)$
    G. 26×10
    H. $26^2 \times 10$
    J. $26^2 \times 10^2$
    K. $26^4 \times 10^2$

15. A plane contains 9 distinct horizontal lines and 9 distinct vertical lines. These lines divide the plane into separate regions. How many of these separate regions have a finite, nonzero area?

    A. 64
    B. 72
    C. 81
    D. 90
    E. 100

DO YOUR FIGURING HERE.

END OF SET FIVE
STOP! DO NOT GO ON TO THE NEXT PAGE
UNTIL TOLD TO DO SO.

Lesson 28 – Counting

Sum It Up

Counting

Combination
A way of selecting things from a collection such that the order does not matter

Permutation
A way of selecting things from a collection in which the order chosen is important

Diagonal
A straight line across the inside of a shape that extends from one vertex to another vertex

Tips and Techniques

Draw It Out: If you're unsure of how to approach a problem, or if it seems especially complicated, draw out the scenario. This is often a quick and simple way to find the solution. **Remember that the test is timed,** so don't get bogged down by trying to draw the shapes perfectly.

Find the Pattern: If one method is taking too long, try something different. Draw out the question and try to identify a pattern. Sometimes, you can draw an easier example and figure it out from there.

Lesson 29

Ratios and Proportions

I think someone got the house-to-dog ratio wrong.

CAPTION:

29.1 Entrance Ticket

Solve the questions below.

1. The recipe for lemonade calls for 2 cups of lemon juice and 5 cups of water. If you follow the recipe, how many cups of lemon juice will be needed to make 70 cups of lemonade?
   A. 20
   B. 22
   C. 35
   D. 42
   E. 50

2. Adam cut a piece of string 42 inches long into 2 pieces. The ratio of the lengths of the 2 pieces is 3:4. What is the length, to the nearest inch, of the shorter piece?
   F. 7
   G. 12
   H. 18
   J. 21
   K. 24

3. On a map, $\frac{1}{3}$ inch represents 25 miles. How many inches on this map represent 325 miles?

   A. $1\frac{1}{3}$

   B. $4\frac{1}{3}$

   C. 13

   D. 75

   E. $108\frac{1}{3}$

Lesson 29 – Ratios and Proportions

29.2 Learning Targets

1. Determine the value of ratios

2. Use ratios to determine other values

3. Use proportions to solve for other values

Self-Assessment

Circle the number that corresponds to your confidence level in your knowledge of this subject before beginning the lesson. A score of 1 means you are completely lost, and a score of 4 means you have mastered the skills. After you finish the lesson, return to the bottom of this page and circle your new confidence level to show your improvement.

Before Lesson

1   2   3   4

After Lesson

1   2   3   4

ACT® Mastery Math

29.3.1 Using Ratios to Determine Values

1. Adam cut a 36-inch long piece of wood into 2 pieces. The ratio of the lengths of the 2 pieces is 2:7. What is the length, to the nearest inch, of the shorter piece?

2. At a picnic, a 16-foot long sandwich is cut into 2 pieces. The ratio of the lengths of the 2 pieces is 3:1. What is the length, to the nearest foot, of the longer piece?

3. A 100-yard field is divided into 2 sections. The ratio of the two sections is 2:5. What is the length, to the nearest yard, of the shorter section?

4. A 180-second song is divided into 2 sections. The ratio of the two sections is 3:4. What is the length, to the nearest second, of the longer section?

Lesson 29 – Ratios and Proportions

29.3.1 Using Ratios to Determine Values

5. The lengths of the 3 sides of a triangle are in the ratio 4:5:6. The perimeter of the triangle is 90 centimeters. What is the length, in centimeters, of the longest side of the triangle?

6. A new 75-mile road is divided into 3 sections. The ratio of the 3 sections is 1:2:3. What is length, to the nearest half mile, of the shortest section?

When solving proportions _____

_____

_____

Math Tip

Draw It Out: Ratio questions can involve many different facts and quantities. Before you start the problem, write down all the key information you have for each piece of the ratio. This will help you keep the information straight as you do the calculations.

29.3.2 Solve Using Proportions

1. A recipe for 100 cookies requires 2.5 sticks of butter. About how many sticks of butter are required for 90 cookies?

2. Harvey is reading a map of the Rocky Mountains. The map is drawn to scale so that 1.1 inches represents 88 miles. How many miles does 1.3 inches represent?

3. A soccer team requires 2 water coolers per 12 players. How many water coolers need to be brought for a team of 18 players?

4. A bakery orders 30 tubs of frosting for every 143 bags of flour. How many tubs of frosting would it order with a purchase of 312 bags of flour, to the nearest tub?

Lesson 29 – Ratios and Proportions

29.3.2 Solve Using Proportions

5. A zoo usually earns $4 from concessions for every $11 of tickets that it sells. If it earned $345 in concessions one afternoon, approximately how much money did it make selling tickets, to the nearest dollar?

Math Tip

Show Your Work: The key to successfully answering proportion questions is to show your work. Make sure you set up the fractions, pay attention to the units, label everything correctly, and show your work on every step. If you do this, you will avoid the ACT trap answers choices.

29.4.1 Set One

1. There are 45 boys and 54 girls in your school's senior class. What is the ratio of boys to girls?
    A. 1:5
    B. 1:6
    C. 5:6
    D. 5:11
    E. 6:5

DO YOUR FIGURING HERE.

2. Tommy, Joel, and Garrett shared a supreme pizza from Pizza Kingdom. Tommy ate $\frac{3}{8}$ of the pizza, Joel ate $\frac{1}{2}$ of the pizza, and Garrett ate the rest. What is the ratio of Tommy's share to Joel's share to Garrett's share?
    F. 3:2:8
    G. 3:4:1
    H. 3:8:2
    J. 8:2:1
    K. 8:4:1

GO ON TO THE NEXT PAGE

3. Anna conducted a survey for a school project to determine which of the 7 colors of the rainbow were most popular. Each student who responded to the survey selected 1 color as his or her favorite. The pie chart below shows the number of students who selected each of the 7 colors. A total of 50 students responded to the survey.

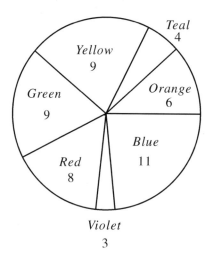

In this survey, what is the ratio of the number of students who selected *Red* to the number of students who selected *Violet*?

A. 3:8
B. 3:11
C. 4:25
D. 8:3
E. 8:11

29.4.2 Set Two

4. Oscar's traveling swim team consists of freshmen, sophomores, and juniors only. The ratio of freshmen to sophomores to juniors is 2:4:3. There are exactly 8 freshmen on the swim team. How many people are on the entire swimming team?

   F. 18
   G. 28
   H. 36
   J. 54
   K. 72

5. Which of the following ratios is equivalent to the ratio of 2^4 to 4^2 ?

   A. 1 to 1
   B. 1 to 2
   C. 1 to 4
   D. 1 to 8
   E. 1 to 16

6. The pie graph below shows the distribution of registered runners, by age group, for a community 5K run. Runners from each age group are randomly selected to win door prizes after the race. What are the odds (in age group : not in age group) that the first person called for a door prize is in the age group of 30–39 years?

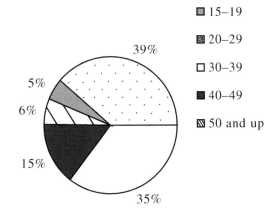

■ 15–19
▩ 20–29
□ 30–39
■ 40–49
▨ 50 and up

   F. 3:17
   G. 3:7
   H. 7:13
   J. 35:30
   K. 39:61

DO YOUR FIGURING HERE.

END OF SET TWO
STOP! DO NOT GO ON TO THE NEXT PAGE
UNTIL TOLD TO DO SO.

29.4.3 Set Three

7. The corner convenience store sells candy bars at 4 for $2.91. At this price, how much would the store charge for 3 candy bars?
   A. $0.73
   B. $1.11
   C. $1.46
   D. $1.99
   E. $2.18

DO YOUR FIGURING HERE.

8. Dorothy is an architect, and she is building a scale model of a house that is 40 feet high, 56 feet long, and 88 feet wide. What should be the dimensions, in feet, of the model Dorothy is building if the ratio of the scale model to the house is 1:8 ?

	Height	Length	Width
F.	$\frac{5}{8}$	$\frac{7}{8}$	$\frac{11}{8}$
G.	5	7	11
H.	40	7	11
J.	320	56	88
K.	320	448	704

GO ON TO THE NEXT PAGE

9. A student is working on an art assignment with a partner. They are drawing a section of their city from a bird's-eye view using a coordinate plane, as shown below, to ensure the distance between buildings is as realistic as possible. The space between adjacent grid lines is 1 inch, and each space represents 2 miles.

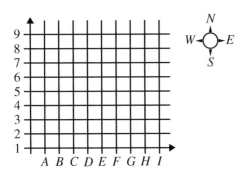

The teacher tells the students that the school should be $3\frac{1}{2}$ inches from the town hall in the drawing. About how many miles apart are these two buildings?

A. 9
B. 7
C. 6
D. 5
E. 3

29.4.4 Set Four

10. The shadows of a basketball goal and a nearby light pole (both vertical and on level ground) were measured at the same time. The basketball goal's shadow was 4 feet long, and the light pole's shadow was 6 feet long. If the basketball goal is 10 feet tall, about how many feet tall is the light pole?

    F. 7
    G. 15
    H. 20
    J. 24
    K. 40

DO YOUR FIGURING HERE.

11. A recipe for 1 tub of ice cream calls for $2\frac{1}{4}$ cups of milk. What is the maximum number of these tubs of ice cream that can be made with $11\frac{5}{8}$ cups of milk?

    A. 5
    B. 6
    C. 9
    D. 13
    E. 14

12. The ratio of x to y is 3 to 2, and the ratio of z to y is 5 to 1. What is the ratio of x to z?

    F. 1:5
    G. 2:5
    H. 3:1
    J. 3:5
    K. 3:10

END OF SET FOUR
STOP! DO NOT GO ON TO THE NEXT PAGE
UNTIL TOLD TO DO SO.

29.4.5 Set Five

13. Tony is making a scale drawing of his rectangular backyard. The yard is 20 feet wide by 36 feet long. Every $\frac{1}{8}$ inch on the scaled drawing represents 1 foot of the yard. What will be the dimensions, in inches, of Tony's backyard in the scale drawing?

    A. $2\frac{1}{2}$ by $4\frac{1}{2}$
    B. 3 by $5\frac{1}{4}$
    C. 10 by 18
    D. 80 by 144
    E. 160 by 288

DO YOUR FIGURING HERE.

14. A biology class at East River High School is composed of both boys and girls. The teacher is conducting a study to find the average height of the students in the class. The average height for the boys is 68 inches, and the average height for the girls is 62 inches. If the ratio of boys to girls is 4:7, what is the average height per student? Round your answer to the nearest inch.

    F. 63
    G. 64
    H. 65
    J. 66
    K. 67

GO ON TO THE NEXT PAGE

Lesson 29 – Ratios and Proportions

15. Mariah, a fifth grade school teacher, asked each of her 30 students which 1 of the 4 seasons he or she preferred. The numbers of students who preferred each season is given in the table below.

Season	Number of Students
Spring	3
Summer	11
Fall	6
Winter	10
Total	30

If Mariah's class is representative of the fifth grade as a whole, how many students out of the 240-person fifth grade class can she predict will prefer the winter?

A. 24
B. 33
C. 75
D. 80
E. 90

DO YOUR FIGURING HERE.

END OF SET FIVE
STOP! DO NOT GO ON TO THE NEXT PAGE
UNTIL TOLD TO DO SO.

ACT® Mastery Math

Sum It Up

Ratios and Proportions

Ratio
A comparison between two numbers that shows a relationship

Proportion
Two ratios that have been set equal to one another

Cross-Multiplying
When $\dfrac{a}{b} = \dfrac{c}{d}$, $ad = bc$.

Tips and Techniques

Draw It Out: If you are dealing with a complex ratio question, be sure to draw out everything to understand how all of the parts relate to each other.

Show Your Work: Show your work when setting up proportions and pay special attention to the units to avoid making careless errors.

Lesson 30

Number Concepts and Properties

CAPTION:

ACT® Mastery Math

30.1 Entrance Ticket

Solve the questions below.

1. Among the following arithmetic operations, which could the symbol □ represent, given that the equation $(3 \square 1)^3 + (7 \square 2)^2 = 33$ is true?

   I. Addition
   II. Subtraction
   III. Division

   A. I only
   B. II only
   C. III only
   D. I and II only
   E. I, II, and III

2. If c is any positive integer, which of the following expressions *must* be an odd integer?

   F. $\dfrac{c}{7}$
   G. $c + 7$
   H. $7c$
   J. c^7
   K. 7^c

3. What are the possible values of g such that $fg^2 = 32$, $f < 20$, $g < 20$, and f and g are integers?

   A. −2, 2
   B. −4, 4
   C. −1, 1, −2, 2
   D. −1, 1, −4, 4
   E. −2, 2, −4, 4

Lesson 30 – Number Concepts and Properties

30.2 Learning Targets

1. Recognize and perform basic operations, including inequalities, involving multiple number types

2. Recognize and perform operations, including inequalities, using square roots, absolute value, exponents, and fractions

Self-Assessment

Circle the number that corresponds to your confidence level in your knowledge of this subject before beginning the lesson. A score of 1 means you are completely lost, and a score of 4 means you have mastered the skills. After you finish the lesson, return to the bottom of this page and circle your new confidence level to show your improvement.

Before Lesson

1   2   3   4

After Lesson

1   2   3   4

ACT® Mastery Math

30.2 Quick Check

Vocabulary Word
1. Square Root ____
2. Perfect Square ____
3. Sum ____
4. Difference ____
5. Product ____
6. Quotient ____
7. Rational Number ____
8. Irrational Number ____
9. Odd Number ____
10. Even Number ____
11. Negative Number ____
12. Absolute Value ____
13. Multiple ____
14. Factor ____
15. Integer ____
16. Reciprocal ____

Definition

A. The result of adding two numbers together

B. Any integer that can be evenly divided by two

C. The number or expression that, when multiplied by a given number, yields a product of 1 (Ex: $\frac{1}{5}$ is the ____ of 5)

D. Any number (– or +) that can be written without fractions/decimals (Ex: –3, –1, 4, 1,383, etc.)

E. The result of dividing one number into another

F. A number's distance from 0

G. A whole number that can be multiplied with another whole number to produce a given number (Ex: 1, 2, 4, and 16 are ____s of 16)

H. Any real number that can be represented as the fraction $\frac{p}{q}$, where $q \neq 0$

I. The result of multiplying two numbers together

J. A number that is the product of any integer and the original (Ex: 16, 32, 48, etc. are ____s of 16)

K. Any real number that cannot be represented as the fraction $\frac{p}{q}$ (Ex: $\sqrt{2}$, π, etc.)

L. The product of an integer and itself

M. Any integer that cannot be divided by 2 evenly

N. For any number b, the number a, such that $a^2 = b$. For example, 3 and –3 are the ____s of 9. *Note that a is only rational if b is a perfect square.

O. Any number less than 0

P. The result of subtracting one number from another

Lesson 30 – Number Concepts and Properties

30.3.1 Basic Number Concepts

100-point questions	200-point questions	300-point questions	400-point questions
1.	1.	1.	1.
2.	2.	2.	2.
3.	3.	3.	3.
4.	4.	4.	4.
5.	5.	Notes:	
6.	6.		
7.	7.		
8.	8.		

Entrance Ticket | Learning Targets | Quick Check | Basic Number Concepts | Number Concept Proficiency | ACT Practice | Sum It Up

30.3.2 Number Concept Proficiency

1. $-7x^2(9y^3)$

2. $|-8|(5x)|4|$

3. $-|12x|(7y)$

4. If $|-5x| \leq 15$, then ___ $\leq x \leq$ ___.

5. $\dfrac{1}{2} \div \dfrac{1}{6} =$ ___

6. State all of the prime numbers between 10 and 30. ___

7. State all of the perfect squares less than 50. ___

8. $\sqrt{3}\,(\sqrt{12}) =$ ___

9. $(-4x)^3 =$ ___

10. What is the sum of the units digits of all even perfect squares less than 150? ___

Math Tip

Mark and Move: Move as quickly as possible on the math test, spending the majority of your time on questions you understand and are confident you can get right. If you do not know the needed rules and definitions for a question, do not allow yourself to get stuck. Time is of the essence! Give it your best guess and move on.

30.4.1 Set One

1. Justine starts with a long list of numbers, each of which she must multiply by $\frac{3}{4}$ and then divide by $\frac{1}{8}$. She could get the same results by multiplying each number on her list by which of the following numbers?

   A. $\frac{3}{32}$
   B. $\frac{1}{3}$
   C. $\frac{3}{2}$
   D. 6
   E. 24

DO YOUR FIGURING HERE.

2. How many prime numbers are there between 20 and 40 ?
   F. 4
   G. 5
   H. 6
   J. 7
   K. 8

3. If a and b are positive integers, such that the greatest common factor of ab^4 and a^3b^2 is 98, then b could equal which of the following?
   A. 98
   B. 49
   C. 14
   D. 7
   E. 2

END OF SET ONE
STOP! DO NOT GO ON TO THE NEXT PAGE
UNTIL TOLD TO DO SO.

30.4.2 Set Two

4. If the product of two numbers is equal to 1, the numbers are *reciprocals*. If a and b are reciprocals and $a > 1$, then b must be:

    F. greater than 1
    G. between 0 and 1
    H. equal to 0
    J. between 0 and -1
    K. less than -1

DO YOUR FIGURING HERE.

5. Which of the following is true for all consecutive integers a and b such that $a < b$?

    A. $a < 0$
    B. $b > 0$
    C. $a + b$ is even
    D. $a^2 - b^2$ is odd
    E. $a^2 + b^2$ is even

6. What are the possible values of b, such that $ab^2 = 36$, $a < 30$, $b < 30$, and a and b are integers?

    F. $-2, 2$
    G. $-3, 3$
    H. $-1, 1, -2, 2$
    J. $-1, 1, -3, 3$
    K. $-2, 2, -3, 3$

END OF SET TWO
STOP! DO NOT GO ON TO THE NEXT PAGE
UNTIL TOLD TO DO SO.

30.4.3 Set Three

7. If the product of 7 integers is positive, at least how many of these 7 integers *must* be positive?
   - A. 1
   - B. 2
   - C. 3
   - D. 4
   - E. 5

DO YOUR FIGURING HERE.

8. A certain perfect square has exactly 5 digits (that is, it is an integer between 10,000 and 99,999). The positive square root of the perfect square must have how many digits?
   - F. 1
   - G. 2
   - H. 3
   - J. 4
   - K. Cannot be determined from the given information

9. What is the least common multiple of 4, $2x$, $8y$, and $5xy$?
   - A. $8xy$
   - B. $16xy$
   - C. $32xy$
   - D. $40xy$
   - E. $320x^2y^2$

END OF SET THREE
STOP! DO NOT GO ON TO THE NEXT PAGE
UNTIL TOLD TO DO SO.

30.4.4 Set Four

10. Suppose that a, b, and c each stand for a digit from 0 through 9 and

$$\begin{array}{r} a84 \\ +5b7 \\ \hline 1{,}19c \end{array}$$

What is the value of the product of $a \cdot b \cdot c$?

F. 0
G. 8
H. 48
J. 61
K. 601

DO YOUR FIGURING HERE.

11. If f and g are real numbers such that $f < -1$ and $g > 1$, then which of the following inequalities *must* be true?

A. $f^{-2} > g^{-2}$

B. $\dfrac{f}{g} > 1$

C. $|g|^2 > |f|$

D. $f^2 + 1 < g^2 + 1$

E. $\dfrac{g}{2} - 3 > \dfrac{f}{2} - 3$

12. If the inequality $|f| > |g|$ is true, then which of the following *must* be true?

F. $f < 0$
G. $f < g$
H. $f > g$
J. $g = f$
K. $g \neq f$

END OF SET FOUR
STOP! DO NOT GO ON TO THE NEXT PAGE
UNTIL TOLD TO DO SO.

30.4.5 Set Five

13. If $4 \leq a \leq 9$ and $-8 \leq b \leq -7$, what is the maximum value of $|2b - a|$?

- A. 25
- B. 23
- C. 20
- D. 18
- E. 15

14. When x, y, and z are real numbers and $x^2 y^6 z > 0$, which of the following must be greater than 0?

- F. xy
- G. xz
- H. zy
- J. xyz
- K. $x^2 z$

15. On the real number line, -0.621 is between $\dfrac{x}{100}$ and $\dfrac{(x+1)}{100}$ for some integer x. What is the value of x?

- A. -621
- B. -63
- C. -62
- D. -7
- E. -6

DO YOUR FIGURING HERE.

END OF SET FIVE
STOP! DO NOT GO ON TO THE NEXT PAGE
UNTIL TOLD TO DO SO.

ACT® Mastery Math

Sum It Up

Number Concepts and Properties

Perfect Square
The product of an integer and itself

Rational Number
Any real number that can be represented as the fraction $\frac{p}{q}$, where $q \neq 0$

Irrational Number
Any real number that cannot be represented as the fraction $\frac{p}{q}$ (e.g. $\sqrt{2}$, π, etc.)

Integer
Any number, negative or positive, that can be written without fractions/decimals (e.g. –3, –1, 4, 1,383, etc.)

Reciprocal
The number or expression that, when multiplied by a given number, yields a product of 1 (e.g. $\frac{1}{5}$ is the reciprocal of 5)

Tips and Techniques

Mark and Move: Time is of the essence! Spend most of your time on questions you understand. Make quick educated guesses on problems that you do not understand. Mark an answer and move on to the next question.

Lesson 31

Math Strategy

CAPTION:

ACT® Mastery Math

31.1 Entrance Ticket

Solve the questions below.

1. The expression $\dfrac{4 + \dfrac{5}{6}}{2 + \dfrac{2}{12}}$ is equal to:

   A. $\dfrac{13}{29}$

   B. $1\dfrac{3}{26}$

   C. $2\dfrac{3}{13}$

   D. $4\dfrac{1}{2}$

   E. 7

2. A bag has 4 green cards, 9 blue cards, 3 purple cards, and x pink card(s). Each card is a solid color. What is the probability that a card randomly chosen from the bag is purple?

   F. $\dfrac{1}{16}$

   G. $\dfrac{3}{16}$

   H. $\dfrac{1}{3}$

   J. $\dfrac{3 + x}{16 + x}$

   K. $\dfrac{3}{16 + x}$

3. The local community decides to install a pool beside the park. The pool area will be a rectangular region of 100 yards by 150 yards with an area of 15,000 square yards. The pool itself will take up an area of 25 yards by 50 yards with an area of 1,250 square yards. The community will put up a fence so that only paying members can enter. What is the perimeter of the pool area, in yards, that the fence will cover?

   A. 150
   B. 250
   C. 450
   D. 500
   E. 650

Lesson 31 – Math Strategy

31.2 Learning Targets

1. Recognize when to use appropriate strategies to answer standard ACT questions

2. Develop a method to address difficult questions during the test

Self-Assessment

Circle the number that corresponds to your confidence level in your knowledge of this subject before beginning the lesson. A score of 1 means you are completely lost, and a score of 4 means you have mastered the skills. After you finish the lesson, return to the bottom of this page and circle your new confidence level to show your improvement.

Before Lesson

1   2   3   4

After Lesson

1   2   3   4

ACT® Mastery Math

31.3.1 Show Your Work

1. The ratio of x to y is 5 to 7, and the ratio of z to y is 6 to 14. What is the ratio of x to z ?
   A. 5 to 3
   B. 5 to 6
   C. 5 to 12
   D. 10 to 7
   E. 10 to 13

2. If $f(x) = x^3 + 5x$ and $g(x) = \sqrt[3]{x}$, then what is the value of $\dfrac{f(4)}{g(8)}$?
   F. $\dfrac{1}{21}$
   G. 24
   H. 42
   J. 64
   K. 84

Math Tip

Show Your Work: It is easy to make a mistake on an ACT problem. Each problem takes multiple steps, and many incorrect answer choices are designed to match your errors.

Lesson 31 – Math Strategy

31.3.1 Show Your Work

3. The expression $\dfrac{7 + \dfrac{1}{2}}{3 + \dfrac{3}{8}}$ is equal to:

   A. 2

   B. $2\dfrac{2}{9}$

   C. 3

   D. $7\dfrac{7}{8}$

   E. $10\dfrac{7}{8}$

4. What is $\dfrac{1}{5}$ of 37% of $4,300 ?

   F. $ 18.20
   G. $ 31.82
   H. $ 182.00
   J. $ 318.20
   K. $1,820.00

31.3.2 Process of Elimination

1. $7x^3 \cdot 2x^8$ is equivalent to:
   - A. $9x^5$
   - B. $9x^{11}$
   - C. $14x^{11}$
   - D. $9x^{24}$
   - E. $14x^{24}$

2. A certain perfect square has exactly 3 digits (that is, it is an integer between 100 and 999). The positive square root of the perfect square must have how many digits?
   - F. 1
   - G. 2
   - H. 3
   - J. 4
   - K. Cannot be determined from the given information

Math Tip

Process of Elimination: The most useful strategy you can use on a multiple-choice test is to eliminate any wrong answers you can identify, even if you don't know how to find the correct one. Look for any choice that might seem too small, too large, or otherwise contradictory to the information in the question. Eliminate those choices first.

Lesson 31 – Math Strategy

31.3.2 Process of Elimination

3. Which of the following inequalities represents the graph shown below on the real number line?

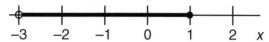

   A. $-3 \le x \le 1$
   B. $-3 < x \le 1$
   C. $-3 \le x < 1$
   D. $1 < x \le -3$
   E. $1 \le x < -3$

4. Carl bought a dress for his girlfriend. The dress cost $83.00, and the tax on the dress was 7%. How much did Carl spend on the dress with tax?

   F. $ 83.07
   G. $ 83.58
   H. $ 88.81
   J. $ 89.39
   K. $141.10

ACT® Mastery Math

31.3.3 Plug In

1. If x is an odd integer, which of the following expressions must be an even integer?

   A. $9 + x$

   B. x^9

   C. 9^x

   D. $\dfrac{x}{9}$

   E. $9x$

2. A 56-foot rope is cut into 2 pieces whose lengths are in the ratio 3:5. What is the length of the longer piece, in feet?

   F. 7

   G. 13

   H. $13\dfrac{1}{3}$

   J. 21

   K. 35

Math Tip

Plug In: Quite a few questions can be solved by plugging in test values or even the answer choices. This strategy is best reserved for when you get stuck, but it can sometimes be the fastest and easiest way to solve a complicated question.

Lesson 31 – Math Strategy

31.3.3 Plug In

3. Jeffrey has been putting money in his savings account for the past 4 weeks, with weekly deposits of $135, $236, $583, and $318. How much money must Jeffrey deposit next week in order to maintain this exact deposit average for these weeks?

   A. $236
   B. $254
   C. $272
   D. $318
   E. $583

4. John, Carl, and Toby are all employees of a laundromat. John earns three times as much as Carl, and Carl earns $4,000 more than Toby. If x represents the amount that Toby earns, which of the following expressions represents the total amount earned by all 3 employees, in dollars?

   F. $5x + 16,000$
   G. $5x + 12,000$
   H. $4x + 16,000$
   J. $4x + 12,000$
   K. $3x + 16,000$

31.3.4 Draw It Out

1. William is stacking boxes on top of each other in a step shape. William plans on stacking 15 rows high, with each row containing 1 fewer box than the row below it. The bottom row consists of 30 boxes. Part of the first 4 rows is shown below. How many boxes will be on the 14th row?

   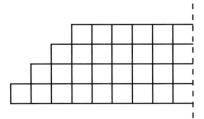

   A. 14
   B. 15
   C. 16
   D. 17
   E. 18

2. An 8-inch-by-14-inch rectangle is cut along its diagonal to form 2 triangles. What is the area of each of the triangles, in square inches?

   F. 11
   G. 16.12
   H. 22
   J. 56
   K. 112

Math Tip

Draw It Out: There are many questions on the ACT that don't give you the whole picture. It could be a geometry question that is missing a figure or a word problem with many moving parts. Fortunately, you have space in your booklet, so draw it out.

Lesson 31 – Math Strategy

31.3.4 Draw It Out

3. In a local town election, every member of the town voted. The results were as follows: 25% for Carly, 35% for Jeb, 14% for Carlos, 16% for Kim, and x for other candidates. If the results were to be graphed on a circle graph, what would be the degree measure of the other section?
   A. 72
   B. 36
   C. 20
   D. 18
   E. 10

4. On the standard (x,y) coordinate plane, what is the midpoint of the line segment with endpoints (2,11) and (–4,5) ?
   F. (–2,16)
   G. (–1, 7)
   H. (–1, 8)
   J. (0, 7)
   K. (2, 9)

31.3.5 Objects in the Mirror Are Exactly as They Appear

1. In the figure below, the measures of 4 angles of pentagon *DEFGH* are given. What is the measure of ∠*E* ?

   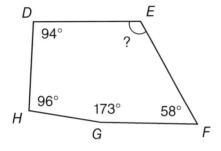

   A. 94°
   B. 96°
   C. 105°
   D. 119°
   E. 129°

2. The figure below shows a side view of a cylindrical tank partially filled with water. The tank has a radius of 5 meters. The tank is filled with water to a point where the maximum depth of the water in the tank is 3 meters.

   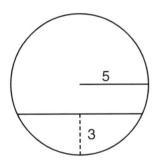

   What is the length of the chord created by the surface of the water?
   F. $\sqrt{21}$
   G. $2\sqrt{21}$
   H. 10
   J. 15
   K. $4\sqrt{21}$

Math Tip

Objects in the Mirror Are Exactly as They Appear: One of the most helpful things about ACT geometry questions is that the images are almost perfectly drawn to scale, even if the question says they are not. If you get stuck on a really complex geometry question, try to eliminate a few answers just by looking at the figures.

31.3.5 Objects in the Mirror Are Exactly as They Appear

3. The figure below is composed of square *ABCD* and equilateral triangle △*ABE*. The length of $\overline{BC}$ is 8 inches. What is the perimeter of pentagon *AEBCD*, in inches?

A. 24
B. 32
C. 40
D. 48
E. 56

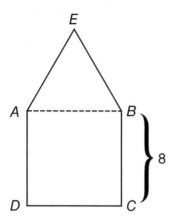

4. The measure of each interior angle of a regular *x*-sided polygon is $\frac{(x-2)180}{x}$. A regular hexagon is shown below. What is the measure of the designated angle, in degrees?

F. 60
G. 108
H. 120
J. 240
K. 252

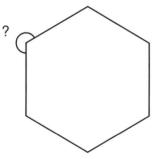

31.4.1 Set One

1. On level ground, a 60-foot-tall vertical building casts a 10-foot shadow. At the same time, another vertical building casts a 25-foot shadow. How many feet tall is the second building?
   A. 10
   B. 25
   C. 60
   D. 120
   E. 150

DO YOUR FIGURING HERE.

2. Given $f(x) = 2x^2 + 3x + 4$, what is $f(x + h)$?
   F. $2x^2 + 3x + h + 4$
   G. $2x^2 + h^2 + 3x + h + 4$
   H. $2(x^2 + h^2) + 3(x + h) + 4$
   J. $2(x + h)^2 + 3(x + h) + 4$
   K. $2(x + h)^2 + 3(x + h) + 4(x + h)$

3. Which of the following graphs represents the solution set of the inequality $|x| > 3$ on a real number line?

   A.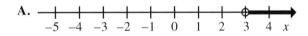

   B.

   C.

   D.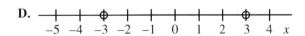

   E.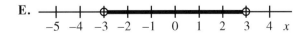

END OF SET ONE
STOP! DO NOT GO ON TO THE NEXT PAGE
UNTIL TOLD TO DO SO.

31.4.2 Set Two

4. If 30% of a given number is 3, then what is 25% of the given number?

    F. 0.75
    G. 1
    H. 2.25
    J. 2.5
    K. 4

DO YOUR FIGURING HERE.

5. Points A, B, C, and D lie on a line in the order given. Point B is the midpoint of $\overline{AC}$, $\overline{BD}$ is 6 inches long, and $\overline{AD}$ is 10 inches long. How long is $\overline{CD}$, in inches?

    A. 2
    B. 3
    C. 4
    D. 5
    E. 6

6. Mountville High won a lacrosse game by 4 points on Tuesday. On Thursday, they scored 6 more goals than on Tuesday and again won by 4. The sum of the opponents' scores for the 2 games was 14. How many goals did Mountville score on Tuesday?

    F. 4
    G. 6
    H. 8
    J. 10
    K. 12

END OF SET TWO
STOP! DO NOT GO ON TO THE NEXT PAGE
UNTIL TOLD TO DO SO.

31.4.3 Set Three

7. What is the circumference, in centimeters, of a circle with a radius of 2.5 centimeters?

    A. $\dfrac{2.5}{\pi}$

    B. 1.25π

    C. 3.75π

    D. 5π

    E. 10π

DO YOUR FIGURING HERE.

8. Jill has been traveling at n miles per hour for 4 hours. How many miles has Jill traveled in terms of n?

    F. $\dfrac{4}{n}$

    G. $\dfrac{n}{4}$

    H. $4n$

    J. $4 + n$

    K. n^4

9. The equation shown below is true for which value of x?

    $$5(x + 2) - 3(x - 6) = 7x$$

    A. $-\dfrac{8}{5}$

    B. $-\dfrac{5}{8}$

    C. $\dfrac{5}{28}$

    D. $\dfrac{8}{5}$

    E. $\dfrac{28}{5}$

END OF SET THREE
STOP! DO NOT GO ON TO THE NEXT PAGE
UNTIL TOLD TO DO SO.

31.4.4 Set Four

10. A map is drawn to scale so that 1.2 cm represents 30 miles. How many miles does 1.4 cm represent?

- F. 32.5
- G. 35
- H. 37.5
- J. 40
- K. 42.5

DO YOUR FIGURING HERE.

11. In a regular hexagon, all 6 interior angles are congruent. What is the measure of each interior angle of a regular hexagon?

- A. 72°
- B. 108°
- C. 120°
- D. 135°
- E. 140°

12. The formula for the volume, V, of a right circular cylinder in terms of its radius, r, and its height, h, is $V = \pi r^2 h$. What is the radius, in inches, of a right circular cylinder that has a volume of $2,028\pi$ cubic inches and a height of 12 inches?

- F. 12
- G. 13
- H. 144
- J. 156
- K. 169

END OF SET FOUR
STOP! DO NOT GO ON TO THE NEXT PAGE
UNTIL TOLD TO DO SO.

31.4.5 Set Five

13. The operation € is defined as follows:

$x \mathbin{\text{€}} y = \dfrac{x^3 - y^2}{y^3 - x^2}$, where x and y are real numbers.

What is the value of $(3) \mathbin{\text{€}} (4)$?

A. -5

B. $-\dfrac{1}{5}$

C. $\dfrac{1}{5}$

D. 5

E. 55

DO YOUR FIGURING HERE.

14. Which polynomial must be added to $x^3 + 2x + 15$ so that the sum is $5x^3 + 6x + 6$?

F. $6x^3 + 8x + 21$
G. $5x^3 + 4x + 21$
H. $5x^3 + 4x - 9$
J. $4x^3 + 4x - 9$
K. $4x^3 + 8x - 9$

15. What is the volume, in cubic inches, of a cube if the area of 1 square face is 121 square inches?

A. 11
B. 121
C. 968
D. 1,331
E. 14,641

END OF SET FIVE
STOP! DO NOT GO ON TO THE NEXT PAGE
UNTIL TOLD TO DO SO.

Lesson 31 – Math Strategy

Sum It Up

Tips and Techniques

Show Your Work: It is easy to make a mistake on an ACT problem. Each problem takes multiple steps, and many incorrect answer choices are designed to match your errors.

Process of Elimination: The most useful strategy you can use on a multiple-choice test is to eliminate any wrong answers you can identify, even if you don't know how to find the correct one. Look for any choice that might seem too small, too large, or otherwise contradictory to the information in the question. Eliminate those choices first.

Plug In: Quite a few questions can be solved by plugging in test values or even the answer choices. This strategy is best reserved for when you get stuck, but it can sometimes be the fastest and easiest way to solve a complicated question.

Draw It Out: There are many questions on the ACT that don't give you the whole picture. It could be a geometry question that is missing a figure or a word problem with many moving parts. Fortunately, you have space in your booklet, so draw it out.

Objects in the Mirror Are Exactly as They Appear: One of the most helpful things about ACT geometry questions is that the images are almost perfectly drawn to scale, even if the question says they are not. If you get stuck on a really complex geometry question, try to eliminate a few answers just by looking at the figures.

Lesson 32

Math Pacing

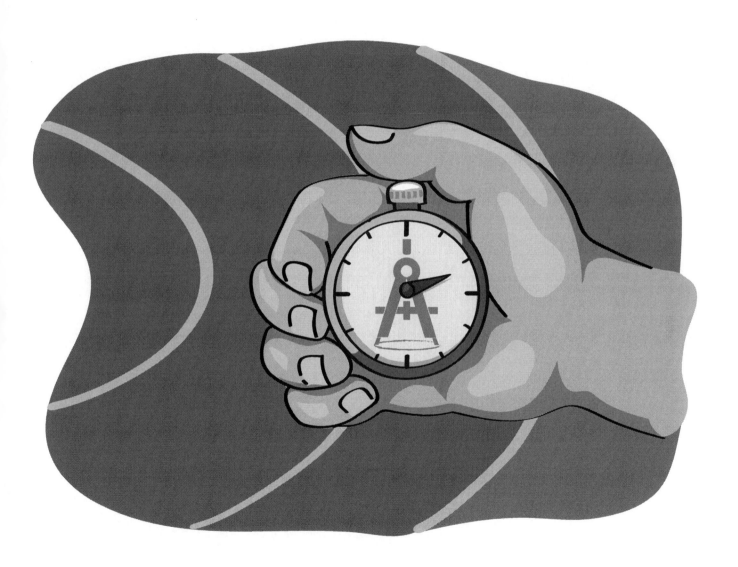

CAPTION:

ACT® Mastery Math

32.1 Entrance Ticket

What are your goals for the math test on the ACT? How do you plan to achieve them? What could stand in your way? Answer these questions in complete sentences.

Lesson 32 – Math Pacing

32.2 Learning Targets

1. Set a personalized pacing goal for the math test based on ACT scoring tables

2. Follow a personalized pacing plan for the math test

Self-Assessment

Circle the number that corresponds to your confidence level in your knowledge of this subject before beginning the lesson. A score of 1 means you are completely lost, and a score of 4 means you have mastered the skills. After you finish the lesson, return to the bottom of this page and circle your new confidence level to show your improvement.

Before Lesson

1   2   3   4

After Lesson

1   2   3   4

ACT® Mastery Math

32.3 Setting a Pacing Plan

Scale Score	Raw Score (Correct answers)	Scale Score	Raw Score (Correct answers)
36	60	18	28
35	59	17	25
34	58	16	20
33	58	15	17
32	57	14	14
31	55	13	12
30	53	12	9
29	52	11	7
28	50	10	6
27	47	9	5
26	45	8	4
25	42	7	3
24	40	6	3
23	37	5	2
22	36	4	1
21	34	3	1
20	32	2	1
19	30	1	0

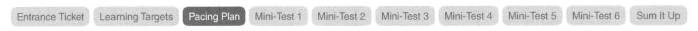

Lesson 32 – Math Pacing

32.3 Setting a Pacing Plan

Math Blitz

The math blitz pacing strategy should be used if your goal score is _____.

You want to spend _____ minutes to answer the first 20 questions.

Allow _____ minutes for the middle 20 questions.

Then you'll have _____ minutes for the final 20 questions.

Cherry Picking

The cherry picking pacing strategy should be used if your goal score is _____.

If you know how to solve a question, _____.

If you are unable to answer a question, _____.

32.3 Setting a Pacing Plan

Goal Scale Score: _____   Pacing Strategy Chosen: _____

Overal Goal Raw Score: _____

Target Raw Score (1–10): _____
Actual Raw Score (1–10): _____

Target Raw Score (11–20): _____
Actual Raw Score (11–20): _____

Target Raw Score (21–30): _____
Actual Raw Score (21–30): _____

Target Raw Score (31–40): _____
Actual Raw Score (31–40): _____

Target Raw Score (41–50): _____
Actual Raw Score (41–50): _____

Target Raw Score (51–60): _____
Actual Raw Score (51–60): _____

Math Tip

Mark and Move: Since difficult questions are mixed throughout the test, you should be prepared to use the mark and move technique quite often. As soon as you get stuck on a question, eliminate what you can, mark your best guess, and move on. You probably won't have time to revisit these questions, but if you have extra time, go back and check your work.

32.4.1 Mini Test 1

Attempts: _____ Correct: _____

DO YOUR FIGURING HERE.

1. If $5x + 2 = 7x - 7$, then $x = ?$
   A. $\frac{2}{9}$
   B. $\frac{1}{3}$
   C. $\frac{2}{3}$
   D. $\frac{3}{2}$
   E. $\frac{9}{2}$

2. The expression $x[(y - w) + z]$ is equivalent to:
   F. $xy - xw + xz$
   G. $xy - w + z$
   H. $xy + xw + xz$
   J. $xy - xw - xz$
   K. $xy - w + xz$

3. The toxicity level of a lake is found by dividing the amount of dissolved toxins the lake water currently has per liter by the maximum safe amount of dissolved toxins that the water can hold per liter and then converting it to a percentage. If the river currently has 0.86 milligrams of dissolved toxins per liter of water and the maximum safe amount of dissolved toxins is 1.04 milligrams per liter, what is the toxicity level of the lake water, to the nearest percentage?
   A. 86%
   B. 84%
   C. 83%
   D. 80%
   E. 79%

GO ON TO THE NEXT PAGE

4. A rectangular pasture that measures 250 meters by 300 meters is completely fenced around its borders. What is the approximate length, in meters, of the surrounding fence?

   F. 75,000
   G. 1,100
   H. 750
   J. 600
   K. 550

5. So far, Michael has earned the following scores on five 100-point tests this semester: 72, 94, 85, 83, 97. What score must he earn on the sixth 100-point test of the semester if he wants to make an 88-point average for the six tests?

   A. 100
   B. 97
   C. 88
   D. 85
   E. He cannot make an average of 88.

6. Which two numbers should be placed in the blanks below so that the difference between consecutive numbers is the same?

   19, __, __, 55

   F. 20, 53
   G. 27, 50
   H. 30, 48
   J. 31, 43
   K. 34, 42

7. Mrs. Cook is a teacher whose salary is $23,125 for a 185-day school year. In Mrs. Cook's school district, substitute teachers are paid at a rate of $90 per day. If a substitute is paid to teach Mrs. Cook's class in her absence one day, how much less does the school district pay in salary by paying a substitute teacher instead of paying Mrs. Cook for that day?

   A. $215
   B. $125
   C. $ 90
   D. $ 45
   E. $ 35

DO YOUR FIGURING HERE.

GO ON TO THE NEXT PAGE

8. If a marble is randomly chosen from a bag that contains exactly 6 purple marbles, 4 blue marbles, and 10 green marbles, what is the probability that the marble will NOT be green?

   F. $\frac{1}{5}$

   G. $\frac{3}{10}$

   H. $\frac{1}{3}$

   J. $\frac{1}{2}$

   K. $\frac{3}{5}$

DO YOUR FIGURING HERE.

9. Zach has 3 pairs of shoes, 8 shirts, and 5 pairs of jeans. How many distinct outfits—each consisting of a pair of shoes, a shirt, and a pair of jeans—can Zach select?

   A. 240
   B. 120
   C. 40
   D. 16
   E. 8

10. $4x^2y \cdot 2x^3y \cdot 3xy^2$ is equivalent to:

    F. $9x^6y^2$
    G. $9x^6y^4$
    H. $12xy^{10}$
    J. $24x^6y^2$
    K. $24x^6y^4$

END OF MINI TEST ONE
STOP! DO NOT GO ON TO THE NEXT PAGE
UNTIL TOLD TO DO SO.

32.4.2 Mini Test 2

Attempts: _____ Correct: _____

DO YOUR FIGURING HERE.

11. Which of the following is a solution to the equation $x^2 - 25x = 0$?

    A. −25
    B. −5
    C. 5
    D. 25
    E. 125

12. Craig ran $2\frac{3}{3}$ miles on Wednesday and $3\frac{1}{4}$ miles on Thursday. What was the total distance Craig ran during those two days, in miles?

    F. $5\frac{3}{12}$
    G. $5\frac{2}{7}$
    H. $5\frac{3}{7}$
    J. $5\frac{9}{12}$
    K. $5\frac{11}{12}$

13. The ratio of the side lengths for a triangle is exactly 9:12:15. In another triangle, which is similar to the first, the shortest side is 18 inches long. To the nearest hundredth of an inch, what is the length of the longest side of the other triangle?

    A. 18.25
    B. 24.00
    C. 25.50
    D. 30.00
    E. Cannot be determined from the given information

GO ON TO THE NEXT PAGE

Lesson 32 – Math Pacing

14. The formula for the volume V of a sphere with radius r is $V = \frac{4}{3}\pi r^3$. If the radius of a spherical rubber ball is $2\frac{3}{4}$ inches, what is its volume, to the nearest cubic inch?

   F. 8
   G. 11
   H. 56
   J. 77
   K. 87

DO YOUR FIGURING HERE.

15. For the triangle $\triangle PQR$ shown below, what is $\sin R$?

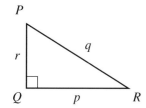

   A. $\frac{r}{q}$
   B. $\frac{r}{p}$
   C. $\frac{p}{r}$
   D. $\frac{q}{r}$
   E. $\frac{p}{q}$

16. If x and y are positive integers such that the greatest common factor of x^2y^2 and xy^3 is 50, then which of the following could equal y?

   F. 50
   G. 25
   H. 10
   J. 5
   K. 2

GO ON TO THE NEXT PAGE

17. If x is a real number such that $x^3 = 729$, then $x^2 + \sqrt{x} = ?$

   A. 738
   B. 732
   C. 90
   D. 84
   E. 12

DO YOUR FIGURING HERE.

18. A circle in the standard (x,y) coordinate plane is tangent to the x-axis at 4 and tangent to the y-axis at 4. Which of the following is an equation of the circle?

   F. $(x - 4)^2 + (y - 4)^2 = 16$
   G. $(x + 4)^2 + (y + 4)^2 = 16$
   H. $(x - 4)^2 + (y - 4)^2 = 4$
   J. $x^2 + y^2 = 16$
   K. $x^2 + y^2 = 4$

19. What expression must the center cell of the table below contain so that the sums of each row and each column are equivalent?

$4x$	$4x$	$2x$
x	?	$6x$
$5x$	$3x$	$2x$

   A. $2x$
   B. $3x$
   C. $4x$
   D. $5x$
   E. $6x$

20. At a plant, 160,000 tons of petrochemicals are required to produce 100,000 tons of plastic. How many tons of petrochemicals are required to produce 5,000 tons of plastic?

   F. 8,000
   G. 10,000
   H. 16,000
   J. 80,000
   K. 100,000

END OF MINI TEST TWO
STOP! DO NOT GO ON TO THE NEXT PAGE
UNTIL TOLD TO DO SO.

32.4.3 Mini Test 3

Attempts: _____ Correct: _____

DO YOUR FIGURING HERE.

21. A chord 20 inches long is 4 inches from the center of a circle, as shown below. What is the radius of the circle, to the nearest tenth of an inch?

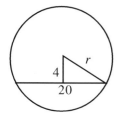

- A. 4.0
- B. 10.7
- C. 10.8
- D. 11.0
- E. 21.6

22. Workers for a roofing company lean a 20-foot ladder against a building. The side of the building is perpendicular to the level ground so that the base of the ladder is 5 feet away from the base of the building. To the nearest foot, how far up the building does the ladder reach?

- F. 5
- G. 10
- H. 18
- J. 19
- K. 20

23. Point C is to be graphed in a quadrant of the standard (x,y) coordinate plane below.

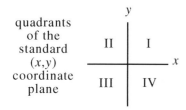

If the x-coordinate and the y-coordinate of point C are to have the same signs, then point C must be located in:

- A. Quadrant I or II.
- B. Quadrant I or III.
- C. Quadrant I or IV.
- D. Quadrant II or IV.
- E. Quadrant III or IV.

GO ON TO THE NEXT PAGE

24. What is the x-coordinate of the point in the standard (x,y) coordinate plane at which the two lines $y = 2x - 1$ and $y = x + 2$ intersect?

   F. -2
   G. 0
   H. 1
   J. 3
   K. 4

25. A square is circumscribed about a circle with a 6 foot radius, as shown below. What is the area of the square, in square feet?

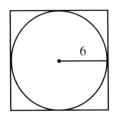

   A. 12
   B. 36
   C. 72
   D. 144
   E. 288

26. If a rectangle measures 12 meters by 16 meters, what is the length, in meters, of the diagonal of the rectangle?

   F. 14
   G. 18
   H. 20
   J. 22
   K. 28

27. Which of the following is a set of all real numbers x, such that $x + 1 > x + 8$?

   A. The set containing zero
   B. The set containing all real numbers
   C. The set containing all positive numbers
   D. The set containing all negative numbers
   E. The empty set

DO YOUR FIGURING HERE.

GO ON TO THE NEXT PAGE

28. For all pairs of real numbers P and Q where $P = 2Q + 9$, $Q = ?$

   F. $2P - 9$

   G. $\dfrac{P + 9}{2}$

   H. $\dfrac{P}{2} + 9$

   J. $\dfrac{P}{2} - 9$

   K. $\dfrac{P - 9}{2}$

29. The ratio of the radii of two circles is 5:12. What is the ratio of their circumferences?

   A. 5:12
   B. 5:12π
   C. 10:12π
   D. 10:24
   E. 25:144

30. Of the 777 graduating seniors in a certain high school, approximately $\dfrac{1}{3}$ are going to a trade school, and approximately $\dfrac{2}{7}$ of those going to a trade school are going to an art or design institute. Which of the following is the closest estimate for the number of graduating seniors going to an art or design institute?

   F. 74
   G. 75
   H. 110
   J. 219
   K. 256

END OF MINI TEST THREE
STOP! DO NOT GO ON TO THE NEXT PAGE UNTIL TOLD TO DO SO.

32.4.4 Mini Test 4

Attempts: _____ **Correct:** _____

DO YOUR FIGURING HERE.

31. What is the slope-intercept form of $4x - y + 7 = 0$?

    A. $y = -4x - 7$
    B. $y = -4x + 7$
    C. $y = x + \frac{4}{7}$
    D. $y = 4x - 7$
    E. $y = 4x + 7$

32. Parallelogram *PQRS*, with dimensions in feet, is shown in the diagram below. What is the area of the parallelogram, in square feet?

    F. 48
    G. 96
    H. 120
    J. 144
    K. 180

33. The distance *D*, in feet, that a ball can be catapulted is given by the equation $D = \frac{2}{3}T + 10$, where *T* is the applied torque in newtons. What amount of torque, in newtons, must be applied for the ball's distance to be 170 meters?

    A. 160
    B. 200
    C. 240
    D. 320
    E. 480

34. If $a = b - 3$, then $(b - a)^3 = $?

    F. −81
    G. −27
    H. −9
    J. 9
    K. 27

GO ON TO THE NEXT PAGE

35. Points B and C lie on line segment $\overline{AD}$, as shown below. Line segment $\overline{AD}$ is 40 units long, line segment $\overline{AC}$ is 15 units long, and line segment $\overline{BD}$ is 30 units long. How many units long, if it can be determined, is line segment $\overline{BC}$?

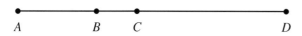

A. 20
B. 15
C. 10
D. 5
E. Cannot be determined from the given information

Use the following information to answer questions 36–37.

English Enrollment

Course	Section	Period	Enrollment
Composition	A	1	12
English I	A	1	21
	B	4	19
	C	5	20
English II	A	2	15
	B	3	16
English III	A	2	14
English IV	A	3	19

36. What is the average number of students enrolled per section in English I ?

F. 17
G. 18
H. 19
J. 20
K. 21

37. The school owns 35 anthologies, which students are required to have during their English classes. There are 4 anthologies currently being re-covered, and 1 anthology is currently missing. For which of the following class periods, if any, are there NOT enough anthologies available for each student to have his or her own anthology?

   A. Period 1
   B. Period 1 & 2
   C. Period 1 & 3
   D. Period 2 & 3
   E. There are enough anthologies for each class period.

38. After polling a class of 30 science students by a show of hands, you find that 12 students enjoy chemistry while 17 students enjoy biology. Given that information, what is the maximum number of students in this class who enjoy both chemistry and biology?

   F. 0
   G. 5
   H. 12
   J. 17
   K. 29

39. For all positive integers X, Y, and Z, which of the following expressions is equivalent to $\frac{Y}{Z}$?

   A. $\frac{Y}{Z} + \frac{X}{Y}$
   B. $\frac{Y \cdot Z}{Z \cdot Y}$
   C. $\frac{Y + X}{Z + X}$
   D. $\frac{Y \cdot X}{Z \cdot X}$
   E. $\frac{Y \cdot Y}{Z \cdot Z}$

40. If 120% of a number is 360, what is 50% of the number?

   F. 120
   G. 150
   H. 260
   J. 300
   K. 480

END OF MINI TEST FOUR
STOP! DO NOT GO ON TO THE NEXT PAGE
UNTIL TOLD TO DO SO.

32.4.5 Mini Test 5

Attempts: _____ Correct: _____

DO YOUR FIGURING HERE.

41. The hypotenuse of the right triangle $\triangle LMN$ shown below is 18 feet long. The sine of angle L is $\frac{5}{6}$. About how many feet long is line segment $\overline{MN}$?

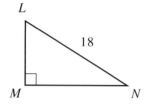

- A. 11
- B. 12
- C. 15
- D. 18
- E. Cannot be determined from the given information

42. If $x = 3t - 8$ and $y = 4 + t$, which of the following equations expresses y in terms of x?

- F. $y = 4x - 4$
- G. $y = \frac{x - 20}{3}$
- H. $y = \frac{x + 3}{20}$
- J. $y = \frac{x}{3 - 4}$
- K. $y = \frac{x + 20}{3}$

43. Hexagons have 9 diagonals, as illustrated below. How many diagonals do octagons have?

Hexagon   Octagon

- A. 8
- B. 16
- C. 20
- D. 32
- E. 40

GO ON TO THE NEXT PAGE

44. Jennifer wants to draw a circle graph showing the favorite candies of her friends. When she polled her friends, asking each his or her favorite candy, 30% of her friends said chocolate, 25% of her friends said peppermint, 15% of her friends said licorice, 15% of her friends said gum, and the remaining friends said some other type of candy. If she groups the other candies chosen by the remaining friends in the same sector, what will the degree measure of this sector be?

F. 12°
G. 24°
H. 26°
J. 48°
K. 54°

45. The number of students participating in afterschool programs at a certain high school can be shown by the following matrix.

Quizbowl	Band	Chorus	Debate
[30	60	40	30]

The principal estimates the ratio of the number of program awards that will be earned to the number of students participating with the following matrix.

$$\begin{bmatrix} \text{Quizbowl} : 0.2 \\ \text{Band} : 0.3 \\ \text{Chorus} : 0.5 \\ \text{Debate} : 0.4 \end{bmatrix}$$

Given this data, what is the principal's estimate of the number of programs awards that will be earned for these afterschool programs?

A. 60
B. 56
C. 52
D. 48
E. 36

46. After a hurricane, coastal workers removed an estimated 8,000 cubic yards of sand from the downtown area. If this sand was spread in an even layer over a rectangular segment of beach, as shown below, about how many yards deep would the new layer of sand be?

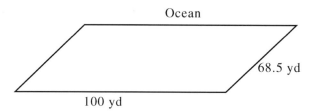

F. Less than 1
G. Between 1 and 2
H. Between 2 and 3
J. Between 3 and 4
K. More than 4

47. What is the distance in the standard (x,y) coordinate plane between points $(1,2)$ and $(4,6)$?

A. 4
B. 5
C. 7
D. 10
E. 13

48. In the figure below, *VWXY* is a trapezoid, *Z* lies on line $\overrightarrow{VY}$, and angle measures are as marked. What is the measure of $\angle WYX$?

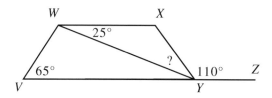

F. 25°
G. 30°
H. 45°
J. 55°
K. 65°

GO ON TO THE NEXT PAGE

49. In the set of complex numbers, where $i^2 = -1$,

$$\frac{i}{i-1} \cdot \frac{i+1}{i+1} = ?$$

A. $-i$

B. $\dfrac{i}{-2}$

C. $\dfrac{i-1}{-2}$

D. $\dfrac{1}{-2}$

E. $\dfrac{i^2 + i}{i^2 - 2i - 1}$

50. If $f(x) = x^2 + x + 4$, then $f(x + h) =$

F. $x^2 + x + h^2 + h + 4$
G. $x^2 + x + 2h + 4$
H. $x^2 + 2xh + x + h^2 + h + 4$
J. $x^2 + x + h + 4$
K. $h^2 + h + 2x + 4$

END OF MINI TEST FIVE
STOP! DO NOT GO ON TO THE NEXT PAGE
UNTIL TOLD TO DO SO.

32.4.6 Mini Test 6

DO YOUR FIGURING HERE.

51. An abandoned area of town has the shape and dimensions of the blocks given below. All borders run either north-south or east-west. A surveyor has set up his equipment halfway between point *M* and point *O*. Which of the following is the location of the surveyor from point *L* ?

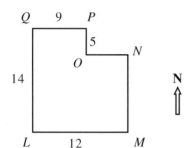

A. $9\frac{1}{2}$ blocks east and $4\frac{1}{2}$ blocks north

B. 9 blocks east and 5 blocks north

C. $10\frac{1}{2}$ blocks east and $4\frac{1}{2}$ blocks north

D. $10\frac{1}{2}$ blocks east and $5\frac{1}{2}$ blocks north

E. 12 blocks east and 9 blocks north

52. Which of the following systems of inequalities is represented by the shaded region of the graph below?

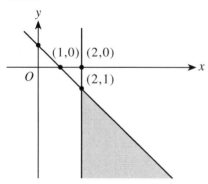

F. $y \leq x$ and $x \geq 1$
G. $y \leq -x + 1$ and $x \geq 2$
H. $y \leq -x + 1$ and $x \geq 1$
J. $y \leq x - 1$ and $x \geq 2$
K. $y \leq x + 1$ and $x \geq -2$

GO ON TO THE NEXT PAGE

53. If $\sin\theta = \frac{4}{5}$ and $\frac{\pi}{2} < \theta < \pi$, then $\cos\theta = ?$

  A. $-\frac{4}{5}$

  B. $-\frac{3}{4}$

  C. $-\frac{3}{5}$

  D. $\frac{3}{5}$

  E. $\frac{5}{3}$

DO YOUR FIGURING HERE.

54. A triangle, ΔPQR, is reflected across the x-axis to have the image $\Delta P'Q'R'$ in the standard (x,y) coordinate plane; thus, P reflects to P'. The coordinates of point P are (a,b). Which of the following coordinates best describes the location of point P'?

  F. (a,b)
  G. $(a,-b)$
  H. $(-a,b)$
  J. $(-a,-b)$
  K. Cannot be determined from the given information

GO ON TO THE NEXT PAGE

Lesson 32 – Math Pacing

55. What is $\cos \frac{\pi}{12}$, given that $\frac{\pi}{12} = \frac{\pi}{3} - \frac{\pi}{4}$ and $\cos(\alpha - \beta) = (\cos \alpha)(\cos \beta) - (\sin \alpha)(\sin \beta)$?

(Note: You may use the following table of values.)

θ	$\sin \theta$	$\cos \theta$
$\frac{\pi}{6}$	$\frac{1}{2}$	$\frac{\sqrt{3}}{2}$
$\frac{\pi}{4}$	$\frac{\sqrt{2}}{2}$	$\frac{\sqrt{2}}{2}$
$\frac{\pi}{3}$	$\sqrt{\frac{3}{2}}$	$\frac{1}{2}$

A. $-\frac{1}{2}$

B. $\frac{1}{2}$

C. $\frac{\sqrt{2}}{2}$

D. $\frac{\sqrt{2} - \sqrt{6}}{4}$

E. $\frac{\sqrt{2} + \sqrt{6}}{4}$

DO YOUR FIGURING HERE.

56. The larger of two numbers exceeds twice the smaller number by 6. The sum of twice the larger number and 4 times the smaller number is 70. If x is the smaller number, which equation below determines the correct value of x ?

F. $2(2x - 4) + 6x = 70$
G. $2(2x + 6) + 4x = 70$
H. $2(2x - 6) + 4x = 70$
J. $4(2x + 6) + 2x = 70$
K. $4(2x - 6) + 2x = 70$

GO ON TO THE NEXT PAGE

57. In the figure shown below, each pair of intersecting line segments meets at a right angle, and all the lengths given are in inches. What is the perimeter, in inches, of the figure?

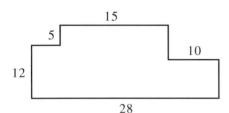

A. 70
B. 75
C. 80
D. 90
E. 95

DO YOUR FIGURING HERE.

58. Which of the following statements describes the total number of dots in the first n rows of the triangular arrangement illustrated below?

F. The total is equal to $2n$, where n is the number of rows.
G. The total is equal to n^2, where n is the number of rows.
H. The total is equal to $n!$, where n is the number of rows.
J. The total is equal to 2^n, where n is the number of rows.
K. The total is equal to $2^n - n!$, where n is the number of rows.

GO ON TO THE NEXT PAGE

59. A certain parabola in the standard (x,y) coordinate plane opens downwards and has a vertex NOT at the origin $(0,0)$. Which of the following equations could describe the parabola?

A. $x = 5y^2$
B. $y = 2(x + 3)^2 + 5$
C. $x = -2(y + 2)^2 + 4$
D. $y = -3x^2$
E. $y = -4(x + 1)^2 - 3$

DO YOUR FIGURING HERE.

60. The graph below shows the 2012 estimate of the five largest cities in the United States, to the nearest 1 million. According to the graph, the population of Houston makes up what fraction of the total population living in all five cities? Key: ☺ = 1 million people.

City	Population
New York	☺☺☺☺☺☺☺☺
Los Angeles	☺☺☺☺
Chicago	☺☺☺
Houston	☺☺
Philadelphia	☺☺

F. $\dfrac{1}{11}$

G. $\dfrac{1}{10}$

H. $\dfrac{2}{19}$

J. $\dfrac{3}{19}$

K. $\dfrac{4}{19}$

END OF MINI TEST SIX
STOP! DO NOT GO ON TO THE NEXT PAGE
UNTIL TOLD TO DO SO.

ACT® Mastery Math

Sum It Up

Tips and Techniques

Goal Score: Remember to have your goal raw score in mind on the day of the test. You should know exactly how many questions you need to get correct.

Pacing Plan: Have your plan in place before you take the ACT math test. Know how many minutes you should spend on each set of questions and how many questions you need to attempt in order to get to your goal score.

Notes

Math Glossary

<
: less than

>
: greater than

≤
: less than or equal to

≥
: greater than or equal to

=
: equal to

Acute angle
an angle that is less than 90°

Angle
a figure formed by two rays that connect at the vertex; usually measured in degrees

Area of a circle
area = πr^2

Area of a parallelogram
area = base · height

Area of a rectangle
area = length · width

Area of a trapezoid
area = $\dfrac{\text{base}_1 + \text{base}_2}{2}$ · height

Area of a triangle
area = $\dfrac{\text{base} \cdot \text{height}}{2}$

Math Glossary

Average (or mean)
a calculation of the center of a set of data
$$\frac{sum\ of\ all\ data\ items\ in\ a\ set}{total\ number\ of\ data\ items}$$

Base
bottommost line, usually of a triangle **OR** the number or variable at the "bottom" of an exponent, which is multiplied by itself the number of times indicated by the exponent

Circumference of a circle
circumference = $2\pi r$

Coefficient
the number before the base and exponent

Complementary angles
two angles whose measures add up to 90°

Congruent
equal in length or measure

Corresponding angles
angles in the same position when a transversal cuts across parallel lines; always equal

Cross-multiplication
when $\frac{a}{b} = \frac{c}{d}$, $ad = bc$.

Cubed
a term that is raised to the third power

Data
pieces of information that can be used for research or analysis; often numbers

Degrees
the measurement of an angle; denoted by the ° symbol

Denominator
the bottom number of a fraction

Depth
　the measurement of how deep something is (how far down or back it goes)

Diagonal
　the line joining two opposite corners of a straight-sided shape

Diameter
　any straight line segment that passes through the center of a circle and whose endpoints lie on the circle

Dimensions
　measurements

Equality
　the state of being the same or equal; having the same value

Equation
　a written statement showing that two expressions are equal

Equilateral
　meaning equal sides; all sides of the object are the same length

Exponent
　the power to which a number or term is raised

Expression
　a group of numbers, symbols, and operations that indicate a value

Extends
　stretches across a distance

Fraction
　a number that represents a part of a whole

Given
　stated in the word problem or labelled on the diagram

Greatest common factor (GCF)
　for any two numbers, the largest number that is divisible into both

Math Glossary

Height
the measurement from top to bottom of a figure or shape

Hypotenuse
the side opposite the right angle in a right triangle; the longest side of a right triangle

Integer
any number, negative or positive, that can be written without fractions or decimals

Irrational number
any real number that cannot be represented as the fraction $\frac{p}{q}$

Least common denominator (LCD)
the smallest denominator two fractions can share

Least common multiple (LCM)
for any given two numbers, the lowest number that has both as factors

Leg
a side of the right triangle that is not the longest side

Length
the measurement of a side of a figure or shape

Line segment
a portion of a line with fixed endpoints

Median
the middle data item in a set when all items are in numerical order

Midpoint
the point that divides a line segment exactly in half

Mixed number
a number consisting of a whole number and a fraction

Mode
the number that appears most often in a data set

Negative exponent
an expression with an exponent that is negative

Negative slope
when a line or line segment decreases from left to right

Notation
a writing system used to convey a mathematical idea

Numerator
the top number of a fraction

Obtuse angle
an angle greater than 90° but less than 180°

Parallel
two lines in a plane that are equidistant at every point; lines that never intersect or touch

Percent
parts per 100

Percent decrease
initial value − (initial value)(percent decrease) = value after decrease

Percent increase
initial value + (initial value)(percent increase) = value after increase

Percentage
a ratio expressing parts per 100

Perfect square
the product of an integer and itself

Perimeter
the sum of the measures of all the sides of a geometric object

Perpendicular
at right angles

Math Glossary

Perpendicular lines
two lines in a plane that intersect at a 90° angle

Polygon
a shape composed of straight lines, such as a triangle, square, or hexagon

Positive slope
when a line or line segment increases from left to right

Proportion
two ratios that have been set equal to one another

Pythagorean theorem
in a right triangle, the square of the hypotenuse is equal to the sum of the squares of the legs $a^2 + b^2 = c^2$

Quadrilateral
any polygon with exactly four sides, such as a square or rectangle

Radius
the length of a line segment from a circle's center to its perimeter

Range
the difference between the largest number and the smallest number in a data set

Rate of change
another way to say slope

Ratio
a comparison between two numbers that shows a relationship

Rational number
any real number that can be represented as the fraction $\frac{p}{q}$, where $q \neq 0$

Reciprocal
a number that is related to another number so that their product is equal to 1

Right angle
90° angle

Right triangle
a triangle that has a 90° angle

Slope
how steep a line is

Slope formula

$$m = \frac{\text{rise}}{\text{run}} = \frac{y_2 - y_1}{x_2 - x_1}$$

Slope-intercept form
$y = mx + b$

Square (operation)
to multiply a number by itself

Squared
a term that is raised to the second power

Standard line form
$ax + by = c$

Supplementary angles
two angles whose measures add up to 180°

Transversal line
a line that passes through two lines in a plane

Undefined slope
vertical line

Unknown number
number that is not known

Value
a number or measurement; an object's numerical worth

Vertical/opposite angles
the angles opposite one another when two lines in a plane cross; always equal

Math Glossary

Weight (average)
the value given to each item in a group when solving an average

width
the measurement from side to side of a figure or shape

Zero slope
horizontal line

ACT® Mastery Math

Contributors

Chief Academic Officer
Oliver Pope

Lead Content Editor
Lisa Primeaux-Redmond

Assistant Content Editor
Eric Manuel

Layout
Jeff Garrett, Elaine Broussard, Shannon Rawson, Lisa Primeaux-Redmond, Eric Manuel

Lesson Writers
Lisa Primeaux-Redmond, Kevin McCabe, Stephanie Bucklin, Nick Sweeney, Chad Sziszak, Elizabeth Aroh

Question Editors
Michael Laird, Irit Maor, Eric Manuel

Question Writers
Alex Levy, April Chow, Chad Sziszak, Chris Husson, Colin Takita, Dan Marchese, Eric Manuel, Tyler Munson, Wendy Seidl, Sam Knight, Sean Neuerburg, Lisa Primeaux-Redmond

Art
Nicole St. Pierre, Eliza Todorova, Roland Parker, Kayla Manuel, Anne Lipscomb

Proofreaders
Kristen Cockrell, Chrissy Vincent, Dan Marchese, Jordan Sermon, Megan Reitzell, Eric Manuel, Marcia Willis, Diana Pietrogallo, Michael Laird

Interns
Kaitlyn Mattox, Rashaud Red, Jamaica Rhoden, Chelsey Smith

ACT® Mastery created by Craig Gehring

Made in the USA
Columbia, SC
13 January 2022